# THE HISTORY OF NORTH AMERICAN RAILROADS

# THE HISTORY OF
# NORTH AMERICAN
# RAILROADS

## GENERAL EDITOR: BILL YENNE

Bison Books

First Published in 1986 by
Bison Books Ltd
176 Old Brompton Road
London SW5
England

ISBN 0 86124 272 6

Printed in Hong Kong

## Picture Credits

*Page 1:* **Canadian Pacific Railroad's** *The Canadian* in 1977, eastbound on Stoney Creek Bridge, two hundred miles from Calgary. Prior to turning passenger service over to VIA, CPR passenger service crossed the continent from Montreal to Vancouver, a total of 3045 miles.

*Page 2-3:* Great machines made this country great. Tracks spanned the nation carrying men and material through rugged countryside, mountain pass and open prairie. The railroads were the realization of the dreams of some and the vehicle for the dreams of others. They transported us into a new age of prosperity and opportunity. Pictured here is a Mount Rainier Scenic RR train running near New Reliance, Washington with Mt Rainier in the distance, recalling the days of continental expansion and the promise of the frontier.

*Below:* Southern Pacific *Pacific Fruit Express* eastbound from Araz Junction, Arizona in 1938. With refrigerated cars to cool the fruit, this freight service played a key part in the expansion of California agriculture.

# CONTENTS

# ALL ABOARD:
# AN INTRODUCTION TO NORTH AMERICAN RAILROAD HISTORY

## Bill Yenne

The history of North America's railroads is, to a certain extent, the history of North America's people and their desire to bind their continent with bands of steel for the purpose of advancing their civilization and their standard of living. In his essay on Canada's railways contained herein, Oscar Skelton compares the building of North America's rail network to the building of Europe's great cathedrals half a millenium before. In both cases it is hard to imagine the energy of the people who undertook such tasks with the limited technology available to them. In both cases it took the energy and commitment of thousands of people over many years to complete these monumental tasks, and it took the exceptional vision of a few to conceive and organize these projects. In the case of the great cathedrals, the names of the visionaries are lost, but in the case of the railroads the names of the empire builders are an indelible part of North America's history.

Today, as we enjoy the fruits of these dreams, some would accuse these great men of greed and exploitation. Perhaps this is because in today's world, when even the most ordinary of engineering projects is scrutinized by unions and conservationists, it is hard to imagine that men like Stanford and Van Horne organized programs that saw man-made rail pierce a hostile wilderness and unite the Atlantic and Pacific halves of two great nations. It is certainly true that the rail barons of the nineteenth century accumulated great empires and fantastic wealth. However, it is also true that these men started with little, risked

Images of striking contrast; diesel and steam; east and west: Modern Chessie diesels (*opposite*), and a vintage 1930s steam locomotive (*above*). The steam locomotive, formerly Southern Pacific Railroad's No 4449, is the only one of the *Coast Daylights* still in existence. Although no longer in operation for Southern Pacific, the 4449 has been restored to its original paint scheme and run by a railroad hobbyist.

everything and in the end bequeathed to the rest of us the rail network that made such a vast contribution to North American civilization and economic growth.

North America's first railroads sprang up in the heavily populated northeastern United States, and upon these early lines the first important railroad empires developed. The big railroads of the northeast corridor, known as the trunk lines, came to possess the same relationship to North America that the spinal cord has to the human body. Railroads ran to the continent's extremities with single and occasionally double-tracked lines. From Philadelphia and New York to Boston, Washington and Chicago the great trunk lines were quadruple tracked. In some places the quadruple tracks were quadrupled again. The two largest lines, the Pennsylvania Railroad and the New York Central, each had more than 25,000 miles of track.

The greatest of the trunk lines was the Pennsylvania Railroad. Founded in 1846, the Pennsylvania became the largest railroad in the world. For more than a century its lines served more of North America's industry than any other railroad. The Pennsylvania became so important that for most of the early twentieth century, it was known as the 'standard railroad of the world.'

Second only to the Pennsylvania among the trunk lines was the New York Central. It began in 1831 as the Mohawk & Hudson and grew into a rail empire of immense proportions after 1860 under the guidance of Cornelius Vanderbilt and his successors. The other great trunk lines included the Baltimore & Ohio, the Chesapeake & Ohio and the Erie Railroad (also controlled by Cornelius Vanderbilt).

Next in importance to the trunk lines were the railroads that grew up in the rich industrial heartland of the northeast. Their lifeblood was the transportation of coal, which was itself the lifeblood of the American economy from the middle of the nineteenth century until the middle of the twentieth. These roads were by no measure small, and many of them, such as the Philadelphia & Reading and the Delaware, Lackawanna & Western, reached trunk line proportions at one time or another.

Below the region of the trunk lines, in the middle Atlantic states, was the great Norfolk & Western; below it the Southern Railway spanned the entire South. In the Midwest the great railroads were those such as the Illinois Central, the Rock Island and the Wabash. Farther west, of course, was the Union Pacific, the railroad upon which the eastern United States had pinned its dreams for a transcontinental railroad at the time of the Civil War.

Any discussion of great railroads of the West begins with mention of four Sacramento, California shopkeepers. These men, Charles Crocker, Collis Huntington, Mark Hopkins and Leland Stanford, chartered the Central Pacific Railroad in 1861 to build the western half of North America's first transcontinental railroad. After they met the Union Pacific at Promontory, Utah, in 1869 to complete the historic link, the 'Big Four' spread their empire throughout the literally golden state of California. In 1868 they bought the Southern Pacific with its hub in San Francisco and in 1870 consolidated all of their spreading empire under its umbrella. By the turn of the century the Southern Pacific spanned a vast crescent in the West stretching from Louisiana to Texas, to Arizona, to California and north across Oregon. This vast railroad, stretching from the mouth of the Mississippi to the mouth of the Columbia,

The evolution of steam power convincingly portrayed in this photo of the old *CP Huntington,* built in the 1860s, sitting alongside a huge and powerful cab ahead, built in the 1920s. The CP Huntington was previously Central Pacific's #3 but became locomotive #1 when the Big Four (of which Huntington himself was one) consolidated all their holdings under the Southern Pacific.

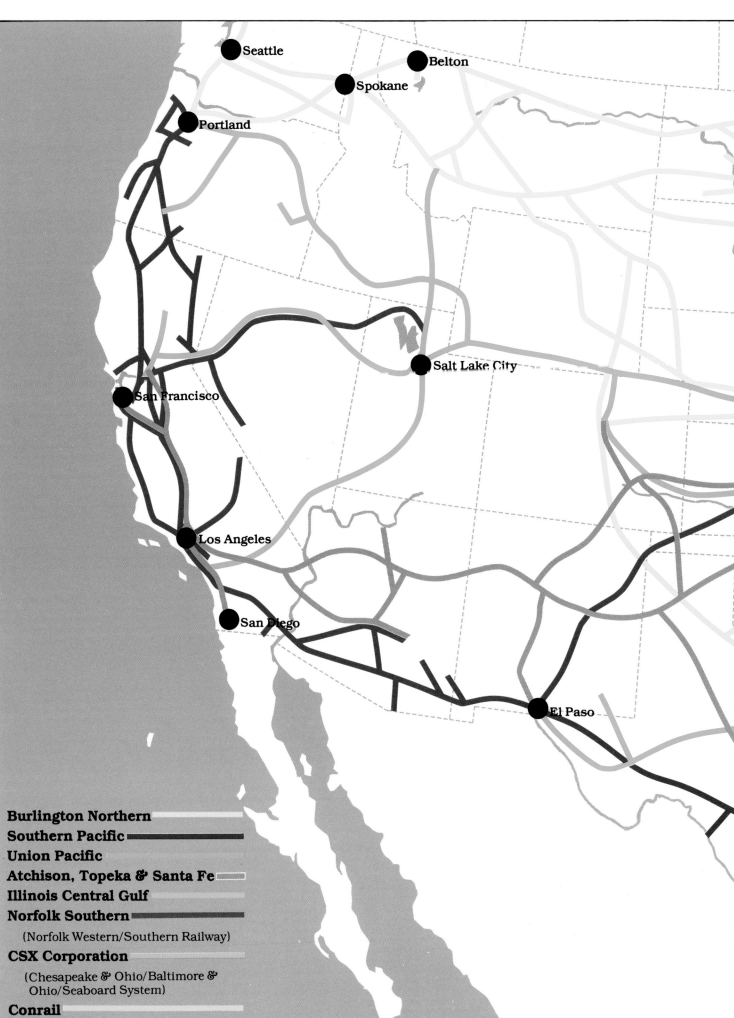

Burlington Northern
Southern Pacific
Union Pacific
Atchison, Topeka & Santa Fe
Illinois Central Gulf
Norfolk Southern
(Norfolk Western/Southern Railway)
CSX Corporation
(Chesapeake & Ohio/Baltimore &
Ohio/Seaboard System)
Conrail

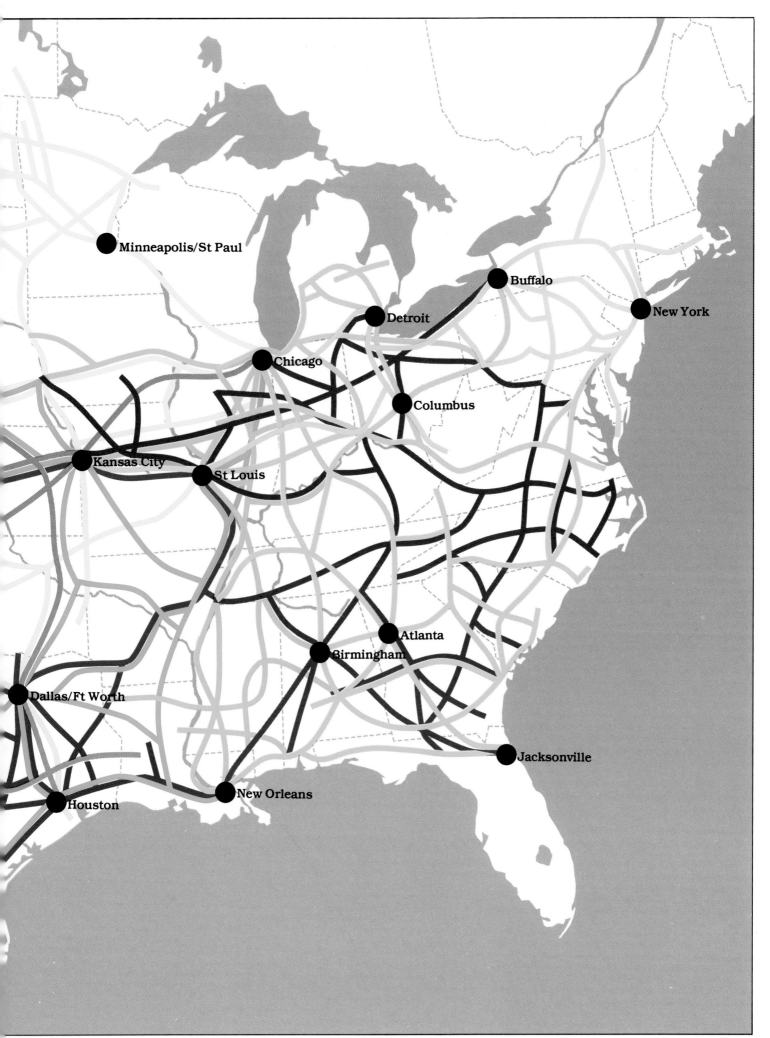

covered a larger territory than any other American railroad.

The Southern Pacific's only real competition was the Atchison, Topeka & Santa Fe, a rail line that started in Kansas and followed the Old Santa Fe Trail through the Southwest to California. On the northern tier of the United States James J Hill built the two great railroads, the Northern Pacific and the Great Northern, that linked the rail hub of Chicago with the Pacific Coast.

In Canada, the first great line was the Grand Trunk Railway, which was followed by the Canadian Northern and the Canadian Pacific. Largely the work of William Cornelius Van Horne, the Canadian Pacific completed Canada's first transcontinental railroad in 1885. The Grand Trunk followed suit and soon its Grand Trunk Pacific subsidiary linked British Columbia's Pacific ports with the St Lawrence ports of Ontario and Quebec.

The golden age of North American railroads was surely the half-century between 1880 and 1930 when railroads dominated the economic life of the continent. The great

empires had been carved out, and they all reached the apex of their glory during that era. After the end of the 1920s, the dual blights of government overregulation and worldwide depression began to take their toll. By the 1950s passenger service was gone. Few of the old names survived the recessions and changing times of the 1960s and 1970s.

Mergers and takeovers had been common for smaller railroads since the beginning of the nineteenth century; the great roads were products of such financial maneuvers. In Canada, the Grand Trunk and Canadian Northern had merged in the 1920s while the government owned Canadian National, but it was not until the 1960s that the great railroads of the United States began to crumble. Two by two they fell, leaning upon one another for support. The Erie and the Lackawanna merged. The Chesapeake & Ohio and the Baltimore & Ohio became CSX. The Norfolk & Western merged with the Southern Railway to become the Norfolk Southern.

In the Northeast, the two greatest trunk lines in history fell upon hard times themselves. By the mid-1960s, the

*Above:* **A Santa Fe freight train photographed near Flagstaff, Arizona typifies modern diesel power. Diesel engines began replacing steam engines in the late 1930s and were found to be particularly advantageous through desert areas where water was scarce.**

Pennsylvania and New York Central were shadows of their former selves. Like two aging prize-fighters staggering through their twilight years, the old trunks were forced to cling to one another to remain standing. In 1968, they merged to form the Penn Central. Two years later the new firm filed for bankruptcy.

After six years of haggling, the bankrupt Penn Central, along with several other insolvent eastern roads including the Erie Lackawanna, were funneled into the government-owned Consolidated Rail Corporation (Conrail) in 1976.

The government's action in the creation of Conrail was ironic. A merger of those same railroads at the peak of their powers would have created an entity so awesome as to have rivaled the power of the federal government itself. In 1976 Conrail struggled for life. Ten years later, however, it had recovered, thanks in part to government deregulation and to the inherent importance of the physical plant owned by Conrail's components and the region they served.

In the West and North, the old Jim Hill roads, Great Northern and Northern Pacific, merged with the Chicago,

Burlington & Quincy to form Burlington Northern in 1970. This left only Southern Pacific and the Atchison, Topeka & Santa Fe as independent roads among the one-time great powers. In 1983, however, these two merged as the Santa Fe Southern Pacific Corporation, subject to ICC approval in 1986.

The chart on the next page gives a concise overview of the evolution of America's railroads in the twentieth century. The text and pictures that follow tell some of North America's railroad history. To tell the whole story in full detail would require a series of volumes far larger than the present work, which intends to provide an overall look at the evolution of the major railroads and the major events that affected their development. The essays collected here present a journey over the main lines of this continent's rail history.

# The Largest US Railroads: 1906

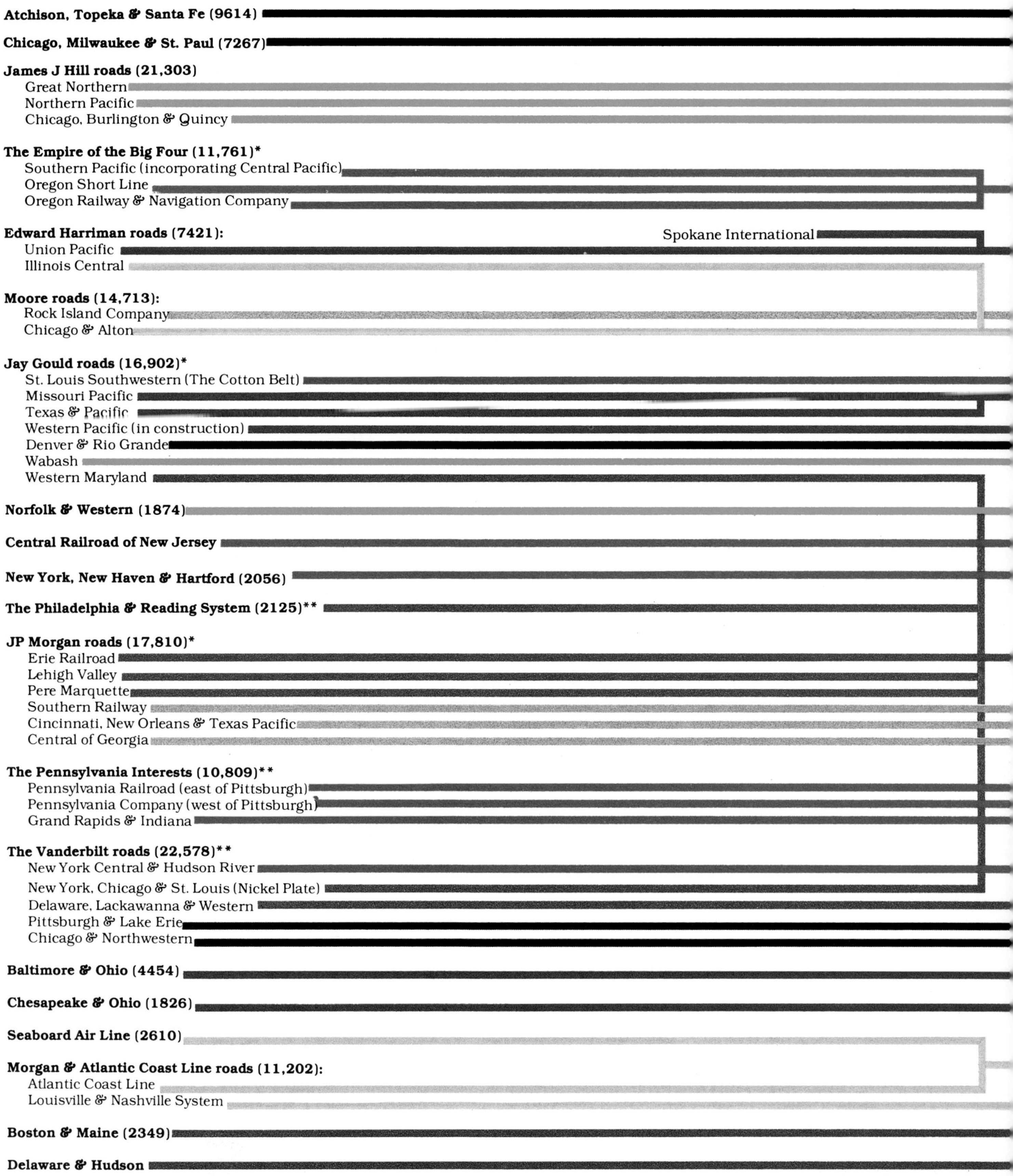

**Atchison, Topeka & Santa Fe (9614)**

**Chicago, Milwaukee & St. Paul (7267)**

**James J Hill roads (21,303)**
 Great Northern
 Northern Pacific
 Chicago, Burlington & Quincy

**The Empire of the Big Four (11,761)\***
 Southern Pacific (incorporating Central Pacific)
 Oregon Short Line
 Oregon Railway & Navigation Company

**Edward Harriman roads (7421):**
 Union Pacific             Spokane International
 Illinois Central

**Moore roads (14,713):**
 Rock Island Company
 Chicago & Alton

**Jay Gould roads (16,902)\***
 St. Louis Southwestern (The Cotton Belt)
 Missouri Pacific
 Texas & Pacific
 Western Pacific (in construction)
 Denver & Rio Grande
 Wabash
 Western Maryland

**Norfolk & Western (1874)**

**Central Railroad of New Jersey**

**New York, New Haven & Hartford (2056)**

**The Philadelphia & Reading System (2125)\*\***

**JP Morgan roads (17,810)\***
 Erie Railroad
 Lehigh Valley
 Pere Marquette
 Southern Railway
 Cincinnati, New Orleans & Texas Pacific
 Central of Georgia

**The Pennsylvania Interests (10,809)\*\***
 Pennsylvania Railroad (east of Pittsburgh)
 Pennsylvania Company (west of Pittsburgh)
 Grand Rapids & Indiana

**The Vanderbilt roads (22,578)\*\***
 New York Central & Hudson River
 New York, Chicago & St. Louis (Nickel Plate)
 Delaware, Lackawanna & Western
 Pittsburgh & Lake Erie
 Chicago & Northwestern

**Baltimore & Ohio (4454)**

**Chesapeake & Ohio (1826)**

**Seaboard Air Line (2610)**

**Morgan & Atlantic Coast Line roads (11,202):**
 Atlantic Coast Line
 Louisville & Nashville System

**Boston & Maine (2349)**

**Delaware & Hudson**

\*The holdings of the Big Four, C P Huntington, Leland Stanford, Mark Hopkins and Charles Crocker, came under the control of Edward Harriman upon the death of the last of the Big Four (Huntington) in 1901.

\*\*The Philadelphia & Reading System was owned by the Vanderbilt and the Pennsylvania interests.

# The Largest US Railroads: 1986

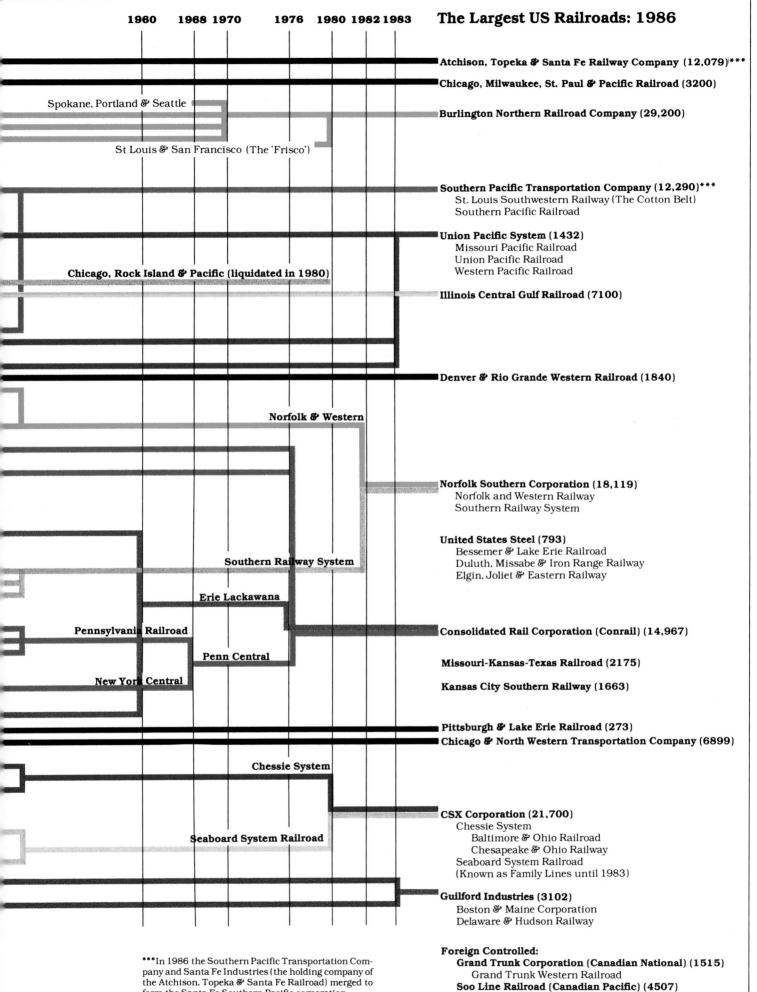

**Atchison, Topeka & Santa Fe Railway Company (12,079)\*\*\***

**Chicago, Milwaukee, St. Paul & Pacific Railroad (3200)**

Spokane, Portland & Seattle

**Burlington Northern Railroad Company (29,200)**

St Louis & San Francisco (The 'Frisco')

**Southern Pacific Transportation Company (12,290)\*\*\***
St. Louis Southwestern Railway (The Cotton Belt)
Southern Pacific Railroad

**Union Pacific System (1432)**
Missouri Pacific Railroad
Union Pacific Railroad
Western Pacific Railroad

**Chicago, Rock Island & Pacific (liquidated in 1980)**

**Illinois Central Gulf Railroad (7100)**

**Denver & Rio Grande Western Railroad (1840)**

**Norfolk & Western**

**Norfolk Southern Corporation (18,119)**
Norfolk and Western Railway
Southern Railway System

**United States Steel (793)**
Bessemer & Lake Erie Railroad
Duluth, Missabe & Iron Range Railway
Elgin, Joliet & Eastern Railway

**Southern Railway System**

**Erie Lackawana**

**Pennsylvania Railroad**

**Consolidated Rail Corporation (Conrail) (14,967)**

**Penn Central**

**Missouri-Kansas-Texas Railroad (2175)**

**New York Central**

**Kansas City Southern Railway (1663)**

**Pittsburgh & Lake Erie Railroad (273)**
**Chicago & North Western Transportation Company (6899)**

**Chessie System**

**CSX Corporation (21,700)**
Chessie System
Baltimore & Ohio Railroad
Chesapeake & Ohio Railway
Seaboard System Railroad
(Known as Family Lines until 1983)

**Seaboard System Railroad**

**Guilford Industries (3102)**
Boston & Maine Corporation
Delaware & Hudson Railway

**Foreign Controlled:**
**Grand Trunk Corporation (Canadian National) (1515)**
Grand Trunk Western Railroad
**Soo Line Railroad (Canadian Pacific) (4507)**

1960  1968 1970  1976  1980 1982 1983

\*\*\*In 1986 the Southern Pacific Transportation Company and Santa Fe Industries (the holding company of the Atchison, Topeka & Santa Fe Railroad) merged to form the Santa Fe Southern Pacific corporation.

# CHAPTER 1

# BUILDING THE AMERICAN RAIL SYSTEM

## Emory Johnson

**U**ntil the 1830s the inland highways of travel and trade were wagon roads, rivers and canals. Compared with Europe, the United States was poorly equipped with these highways. The newness of the country, the sparseness of population, and the undeveloped state of its industries had kept both the government and individuals from devoting time and resources to the building of roads and waterways. In the construction of railroads, the United States was surpassed only by Great Britain, but in the building of highways and waterways she lagged behind by several European countries.

Until near the end of the eighteenth century the country roads constructed in America were built by the local governments—by towns in New England, townships in the Middle Atlantic section and counties in the south. When population and business grew, these highways became so

*Ties across the wilderness (above) await steel bands that will bind the nation from coast to coast. Lines of oil tank cars (left) await delivery to market upon those very lines in the 1890s. It was the railroad and its development that allowed the remarkable economic development enjoyed by the North American continent.*

inadequate that individual companies began constructing roads and charging tolls for their use. At the place where tolls were collected stood a gate, turning upon a post, armed with pikes (pointed spikes). Naturally these roads came to be called turnpikes.

The construction of toll roads began soon after 1790, and numerous turnpike companies were chartered by each state, particularly by the middle and New England states. The greatest mileage was built in Pennsylvania, and what was done in that state is typical of what occurred in many other parts of the country. In 1790 a company was chartered to build a turnpike from Philadelphia to Lancaster, and this road, begun in 1792, was completed in 1794. Later this road became a part of a continuous line of turnpikes extending from Trenton, New Jersey, to Steubenville, Ohio, a distance of 343 miles. Before the construction of railroads began in the United States, 102 Pennsylvania companies had built 2380 miles of roads in that state at a cost of nearly $8,500,000. Although these toll roads did not, as a rule, prove to be profitable to the companies which built them, they greatly benefited the people of the

state. Many of these turnpikes evolved into twentieth century highways.

Some turnpike roads were built with funds donated by the states and the federal government at the time when public aid was being given to works of 'internal improvement.' The most celebrated turnpike was the Cumberland Road, or the 'National Pike,' constructed by the United States. Begun in 1806, it was built westward from Cumberland, Maryland, through Wheeling and Columbus, Ohio, and finally, 21 years later after periodic extensions, it reached Vandalia, in central Illinois. The turnpike was to have gone through to Jefferson City, Missouri, but before Illinois had been passed the superiority of the railroad for long-distance traffic had become an accepted fact.

Surveys of canal routes were made in Pennsylvania as early as 1762. In 1772 General Washington called attention to the importance of constructing canals and improving the rivers of the country. He was particularly hopeful that the Atlantic coast section be connected by a through route to the region west of the Allegheny Mountains. It was, however, not until 1825, 26 years after the death of Washington, that the completion of the Erie Canal, connecting the Hudson River and Lake Erie fulfilled his hope. Although numerous companies were chartered during the decade ending in 1812, little was done to improve inland navigation until after the War of 1812, when several corporations energetically began the work of connecting the anthracite coal fields with tidewater by means of canals. The states aided these and other navigation companies, and attention was directed, especially by New York, Pennsylvania and Maryland, to the project of securing routes to the West. New York was the first to succeed with the Erie Canal, which was finished in 1825.

The opening of the Erie Canal roused Pennsylvania to action, and in 1826 she began her system of 'public works,' the main feature of which was a composite rail and water route, completed in 1834, connecting Philadelphia with Pittsburgh. A railroad ran from Philadelphia to the Susquehanna River at Columbia, then a canal extended up the Susquehanna and Juniata rivers to Hollidaysburg. Between Hollidaysburg and Johnstown the canal barges were carried over the mountains by a portage railroad; a canal connected Johnstown and Pittsburgh, at which point junction was made with the Ohio River steamboats.

A corporation aided by the states of Maryland and Virginia began to construct the Chesapeake & Ohio Canal in the Valley of the Potomac at the same time that Pennsylvania undertook her public works, but it was 1850 when the Chesapeake & Ohio Canal reached Cumberland. Between 1830 and 1850 Ohio, Indiana, Illinois and numerous other states constructed canals or aided corporations to build them, but the appearance of the railroad made the further construction of small barge canals inadvisable.

Canal building rapidly fell off after 1840. The panic of 1837 so crippled the financial resources of the states that they were temporarily left without surplus funds to invest in internal improvements; at the same time the railroads were being extended rapidly, taking the traffic that had previously moved by water.

In the beginning the railroad was an improved tramway equipped with a track upon which locomotives could be run. The distinctive feature of the railroad was the substitution of mechanical for animal traction (the use of steam instead of muscle as the power by which vehicles were moved). Although the first locomotives were small and crude, their use in transportation marks one of the greatest advances the world has ever made. Mechanical traction not only freed society from the narrow limitations which muscular force placed upon development, but appeared to be capable of indefinite improvement.

The construction of tramways for cars drawn by horses was a comparatively simple task, and, from 1801 on, tramway companies were frequently chartered in England. The tracks were used mainly for hauling minerals. The Quincy tramway, the first road of its kind in America, was built in Massachusetts in 1826 and sometimes wrongly called the first railroad in America. It was used to transport the stone used for building the Bunker Hill monument. The Quincy tramway was only three miles long and extended from the Quincy quarries to a wharf on the Neponset River. Near the quarry a stationary engine handled cars on the steep incline. For the remainder of the distance horses were used.

The rails used on the tramways and on most of the early railroads of America consisted of wooden beams with a strap of iron nailed to the upper surface, the rails resembling those used for street railways until horse-cars were displaced by the heavier and faster electric cars.

The first successful locomotive dates from 1829, when the celebrated English engineer George Stephenson brought out *The Rocket*. The stationary engine had been introduced by James Watt 50 years before that time, but Stephenson first incorporated in the engine the two features essential to a workable locomotive. One of these features was the multitubular boiler, by which the heating surface could be greatly increased. Stephenson was the first to make practical use of the invention. The other feature was the exhaust draft, a device whereby the exhaust steam from the cylinder created a stronger draft through the firebox and the tubes of the boiler. By combining these two principles in *The Rocket*, Stephenson became the 'father of the locomotive.'

The pioneer American railroad built for general public use was the Baltimore & Ohio, chartered in 1827. Construction was begun in 1828, but apparently not on a large scale because only 13 miles were open for traffic in 1830. Five years later the length of the road was 135 miles.

The first rail of this historic road was laid on 4 July 1828 by Charles Carroll, the only living signer of the Declaration of Independence. As Professor Hadley commented in 1855: 'One man's life formed the connecting link between the political revolution of the last century and the industrial revolution of the present.'

The construction of numerous other roads was begun shortly after work commenced on the Baltimore & Ohio. A South Carolina road, the Charleston & Hamburg, was chartered in 1829, and in 1834 it had 137 miles in operation. For a short time it was the longest line in the world under one management. The parent company of the New York Central system, the Mohawk & Hudson, was chartered as early as 1826, and began construction in 1830. The 17-mile line from Albany to Schenectady was opened in 1831, and five years later Albany and Utica had been connected by rail. In 1842 Buffalo was reached, and by that time lines had been built from New York and Boston to Albany, so that the east and west of that period had been joined by easy communication.

Between 1830 and 1835 railroad building was pushed more rapidly in Pennsylvania than in any other state, and 200 miles were opened. The first division of the great Pennsylvania Railroad system was the Columbia Railroad, by which Philadelphia was connected with Columbia, on the Susquehanna River, in 1834. The road was built by the state after its construction was authorized in 1828. This railroad was a link in the through route consisting of canals and railroads that connected Philadelphia with the Ohio River at Pittsburgh in 1834. The line to connect Philadelphia with New York, the Camden & Amboy, was chartered in 1830 and completed in 1837. The road from Philadelphia to Baltimore, the Philadelphia, Wilmington & Baltimore, was chartered in 1831 and finished in 1837. The Reading Railroad, built mainly for the transportation of coal, was chartered in 1833 and opened for traffic five years later.

In Massachusetts the chartering of railroad companies began in 1830, and in 1835 three lines radiated from Boston. One ran south to Providence, another north to Lowell, and a third west to Worcester. This third line reached Albany and western connections just at the close of 1841.

Americans began to build locomotives in 1830 at about the same time that they became engaged in railroad building. The English locomotives were expensive, could not be secured promptly and when obtained were not well adapted to the light rails, steep grades and sharp curves of the American tracks. The traffic conditions caused the engines and cars to be built according to designs different from those followed in Great Britain, and the differences in equipment set the tone for the development of rail car technology for the next century.

## THE GROWTH OF THE AMERICAN RAIL SYSTEM

In 1830 there were just 23 miles of railroad track in use in the United States. During the succeeding ten years the total mileage reached 2818. The roads constructed during these first ten years radiated from several Atlantic seaports although Philadelphia was the most important center in 1840. New York was a larger city, but because it had especially favorable facilities for water transportation, its railway connections were developed somewhat more slowly than were those of Philadelphia.

In 1850 the length of the railways in the United States reached 9021 miles. The growth during the preceding ten years had not been especially rapid outside of the New England states. The decade of the 1840s was not a period of rapid industrial development. Progress was steady, but comparatively slow. Railroad building in the southern states made little headway, and in the Midwest only three important lines were begun. In New England, where the country was the most densely populated, the progress was greater, so that by 1850 nearly all the important trunk lines in that region had been completed.

The ten years following 1850 were far more important in railroad history than the preceding decade. The increase between 1850 and 1860 was from 9021 to 30,635 miles, a result of several factors. The southern and midwestern states were developing, thereby creating a demand for greater transportation facilities. The discovery of gold in California in 1848 until 1857 brought the people of the United States highly prosperous times. Business activity in all lines was keen, and railroad building shared with other enterprises in prosperity.

The year 1850 marks the beginning of a rapid merging of short connecting railroads into long lines under single ownership. The early roads were short, largely because the corporations of the early nineteenth century could not command the capital needed to build long roads or large systems. Some of the short roads were built as part of a through or general system, but many were constructed simply to connect local points. The necessity for providing facilities for uninterrupted travel and shipment over long distances became so imperative that railway consolidations became necessary.

The New York Central and the Pennsylvania Railroads are good examples of these consolidations. Originally eleven companies owned and operated the railroads composing the line connecting Albany and Buffalo, and in

The early evolution of transportation: The conestoga wagon (*left*) was the predecessor of the freight car; the stage coach (*center*) once carried passengers. The *John Bull* engine and train (*right*), built in 1831, which is today displayed at the Smithsonian Institution as the oldest existing locomotive in the United States.

1850 seven distinct companies served between those two cities; the following year they were united under one management. Two years later the Hudson River Railroad became a part of the Central system, and by 1858 five more lines were added to this property. Thus was built the powerful New York Central system.

The Pennsylvania Railroad Company, through construction of roads and the purchase and lease of state lines, established through-connections between Philadelphia and Pittsburgh in 1852. After that the system extended by absorbing other companies and by building new lines, until it comprised properties formerly owned by more than 200 companies.

During the decade following 1850 many of the trunk lines of the large railway systems of the present day were completed. The Erie Railroad joined New York with Lake Erie in 1851, and the Baltimore & Ohio reached the Ohio River the same year. The construction of long lines proceeded rapidly in the states east of the Mississippi River and north of the Ohio. By 1853 it became possible to travel from the Atlantic seaboard to Chicago by rail. In the following year the Chicago & Rock Island connected Chicago with the Mississippi River. Land grants, state subsidies, and prosperous times combined to foster the rapid spread of the railway net in the Midwest. This lasted until 1857, when the good times were interrupted by a panic. Railroad building was then so seriously interrupted that it had not regained its previous activity when the Civil War stopped nearly all industrial progress for half a decade.

The construction of railroads in Illinois and beyond the Mississippi River was greatly stimulated by federal land grants. In 1850 the first large grant was made to the Illinois Central Railroad. Many other grants were made during the next few years. This policy of giving lands to aid in railroad construction was followed by the United States for nearly thirty years, and it caused the railway lines in the central and far western states to be built earlier and more rapidly than they otherwise would have been. The states also made large contributions of public funds to induce corporations to construct railways.

The United States government made especially liberal gifts to the companies that undertook the great task of building roads across the dry plains and high mountains to the Pacific coast. The first line to reach the Pacific in 1869 was constructed mainly by the Union Pacific and Central Pacific railroad companies. These and other Pacific railroad companies received large gifts of public land. The companies that constructed the first lines to the Pacific also obtained large loans from the government in the form of United States bonds.

During the decade of the 1860s the mileage of the railways in the United States increased from 30,635 to 52,914. The rate of growth was slow except during the last two years of the period. From 1868 to the panic of 1873 was a period of intense speculation and of very rapid railway construction. Indeed the severe business crisis of 1873 was largely the result of building railways too rapidly and of overcapitalizing those lines. During those five years 28,000 miles were added to the railway net of the country, while in the five years following 1873 only 11,500 miles were built.

In 1880 there were 93,296 miles of railroad in the United States and in 1890 there were 163,597. In a single decade 70,000 miles of railroad had been built in the United States. This marvelous achievement was unparalleled in

By the late nineteenth and early twentieth century the steam locomotives that ran on the rail lines of the south were linked to the trunk lines of the north. After all, there was coal in Kentucky and West Virginia and it was natural that the coal roads there should feed into the coal road net of Pennsylvania and points north. *Below:* A Savannah & Atlanta (ex-Florida East Coast) 4-6-2 steam locomotive No 750 at Emory Gap, Tennessee after its arrival on The Autumn Foliage Run from Chattanooga.

the economic history of any other country of the world. Within ten years the people of the United States built as many miles of railroad as the people of the three leading countries of Europe had constructed in 50 years. The building operations were carried on in all sections of the country, but the largest increases were made in the central and western states, where settlers were rapidly taking possession of the unoccupied agricultural and grazing sections of the vast public domain, and where vast mineral wealth was causing cities and states to be established on the great Rocky Mountain plateau. Capitalists, confident of the growth of the country, and assisted by generous aid from the United States and from local governments and individuals of the sections to be served, constructed railroads to create the traffic upon which the earnings of the roads must depend. In many cases the railroads built during the 20 years following the Civil War were pioneers entering unsettled regions beyond the Mississippi and Missouri rivers and opening the highways by which immigration was able rapidly to occupy the prairies and mountain valleys of the West.

After 1890 railroad construction was not as rapid—completing less than 30,000 miles for the decade ending in 1900. It seems that by 1890 the most urgent needs for railways had been met and that the country had been so well covered with the railroad net that only minor extensions were necessary. Moreover, the financial depression which began in 1893 and lasted for nearly five years compelled the railway companies to practice rigid economies and to extend their systems slowly. During the five years from 1894 through 1898 the annual construction averaged less than 2000 miles, a yearly increase of only a little more than one percent.

In 1906, there were 222,000 miles in the United States, nearly 40 percent of the railway mileage of the world. The mileage in the United States exceeded that in all Europe by more than 15 percent. By 1929 the total mileage had increased to only 229,530. By 1939 it had decreased to 220,915 and by 1980 to just 164,822. Thus the turn of the century truly marked the point at which America's railroads turned from expansion to management of existing lines.

The magnitude of the railway system of the United States at the turn of the century was only partially indicated by the mileage figures. The par value of the capital stocks and bonds comprising the capitalization or 'securities' of the railroads amounted to $14.57 billion in 1906. Not all of these securities had a selling value, and it is impossible to say just how much capital was actually invested in our railroads at that time. Poor's Manual of Railroads for 1900 states the cost of the railroads in the United States to have been in excess of $10 billion, and estimates on the basis of Interstate Commerce Commission (ICC) data that the value of all railroad assets in that year were about $12.5 billion. Commenting on these figures, the Report of the ICC of 1902 says:

'Accepting these estimates provisionally, and also the estimate of the total wealth of the United States in 1900 at about $90 billion, it appears that investments in railroad property form from one-seventh to one-fifth of the aggregate capital. This is based upon the assumption that railroad securities at par represent the value of the property. Judged by market values at the present time, this amount would be considerably increased, approximating perhaps

The men who made it possible. This group photographed in an 1889 Southern Pacific construction shop represent the flesh and blood who wrestled the sooty, steamy, white-hot steel for the cause of the railroads.

A Great Nothern Railroad train crossing Two Medicine Bridge, Montana in 1891. Near the boundary of present day Glacier National Park, Two Medicine Bridge is just east of the Continental Divide at Marias Pass.

the estimate . . . that the railroads formed about one-fifth of the total wealth of the country. If we accept the estimate recently made in a foreign financial journal of the cost of railroad property the world over at $33 billion, it would seem that the American railroads constitute more than one-third of the railroad property of the world.'

Comparisons with the capital invested in other forms of business are suggestive. The capital stock and surplus of all the 6137 national banks in the United States in 1906 equaled $1,325,000,000—less than one-tenth the probable value of the American railroads. The total capital and the surplus funds of all the banks—national, state, and private —and of the loan and trust companies in the United States in 1906 amounted to $2,796,000,000, about one-fifth the value of the railroads. Indeed, with the exception of agriculture, there was no single class of industry that equaled the railroads in the amount of invested capital and in the value of the annual business done.

## THE RAIL SYSTEM OF THE UNITED STATES AT THE TURN OF THE CENTURY

Of the 230,000 miles of railroad lines in service in the United States at the end of 1907, many were double- or multitracked. If the total length of track in the various roads and in their freightyards were measured, there would have been about 330,000 miles of railroad track. This vast mileage was owned by about 2440 corporations, many of which were subsidiary to others, but (according to the reports of the Interstate Commerce Commission) there were over 1000 operating companies. In 1980, there were just 300.

By dividing the United States into several natural territorial sections, classifying the railroad lines or systems according to those sections and grouping the railroads according to ownership, it is possible to get a general picture of what we term the American railway system.

At the turn of the century the most general and most frequent grouping of the railroads of the United States territorially was into three sections: one section north of the Ohio and James rivers and east of the Mississippi, another the region south of the Ohio and east of the Mississippi, and the third the country west of the Mississippi. A basis for this grouping was to be found in differences in production, density of population and other economic and social conditions prevailing in these three sections of the country. There were also sufficient differences in the freight business of the railroads in these sections to cause distinct classifications of freight to have been worked out for each of the three regions. Within each of these large groups there were distinct subdivisions, due in part to diversity of physical conditions, and in part to the fact that the railroads in different portions of the country had come to be owned by a limited number of groups of people.

The railway system of the United States as a whole could have been divided into seven groups, each a nearly distinct section of the country. The first of these territorial groups of railroads comprises the New England states. The railroads in this section differed from those of other parts of the country, because they served the region where population was densest; where the passenger business as com-

pared with the freight was larger than in any of the other states; and where the local freight business as contrasted with the through freight was of greater importance. Boston was and is the hub of this region and the roads north of Boston are quite distinct from those south of that city. The interchange of traffic between the two sections is comparatively small, and the railroad lines in the two sections are under the control of different managements.

The region west of New England and the middle Atlantic seaboard, north of the Ohio and James rivers, and east of the cities of Chicago and St Louis comprised another section of the country within which there was considerable unity in the operation and ownership of the railroad systems. The railroads in this group had the heaviest freight traffic of any roads in the country. Most of them were built from the East toward the West, to bring the agricultural, forest and mineral products of the great Midwest to the Atlantic seaboard for American and European markets. Most also provided the manufacturing industries of the northeastern section of the United States with a western outlet for the products of the mills and factories. The railroads in this group were often called the 'trunk lines,' because the first through or trunk lines in the United States were built here.

Within this trunk-line territory there was a distinct subdivision of lines whose business it was to transport anthracite coal from the Pennsylvania mines to the seaboard. Some of the hard coal mined in Pennsylvania was handled by the trunk lines, but the larger part of this coal was mined and transported by other than the trunk-line companies.

The traffic conditions in the region south of the Ohio River and east of the Mississippi differed from those in other parts of the country. The Allegheny Mountains separated the South into two parts—one tributary to the Gulf and the other to the Atlantic seaboard.

To the west and north of Chicago and St Louis, and including the chief grain-raising states of the United States the railroads were called 'granger' lines, after a term that originated in the 1870s when the farmers of the Midwest

The *Goliath* (*far left*), photographed in Nevada in 1880 with friends, was built in 1867 and broken up in 1905. The dogsled appears to be leading in this good-natured race (*above*) near Lake Tahoe, California.

Union Pacific steam locomotive No 4003 doubleheading with another locomotive pulling out of Emkay, Wyoming in 1958. These last vestiges of the steam age were soon replaced with the electric diesel locomotives of today.

organized their 'granges,' or societies. The granger roads radiated from two major hubs, the chief of which was Chicago, although St Louis had always been an important point for the collection and distribution of the traffic from and to the agricultural Midwest.

South and west of St Louis there was a large number of railway lines, some of them having St Louis and Memphis connections, and others being more distinctly tributary to Gulf ports. A large part of the roads in this system had been controlled by the notorious railroad baron Jay Gould and were often spoken of as the Gould roads.

West of these regions lay the territory occupied by the transcontinental or Pacific roads. These transcontinental lines had connections with Chicago and points on the Mississippi, and were divided into two rather distinct groups, the Northern and Southern. Within the Northern section are comprised the Great Northern, the Northern Pacific and the Chicago, Burlington & Quincy. The Southern section includes the Union Pacific, Central Pacific, Southern Pacific and the Atchison, Topeka & Santa Fé.

The largest share of the great railroad mileage in this country was already in the hands of a limited number of large interests. Between these groups of capitalists there had developed a community of interest or harmony of action that was seen as restraining the competition in rate-making that had formerly prevailed among separately managed railway systems.

Many of the major railroads in the United States at the turn of the century had a greater mileage and a larger volume of traffic than the railroads in any European countries with the exception of Great Britain, France, Germany, and Russia. Indeed, there was probably more freight handled over the group of roads controlled by the Pennsylvania interests than over the railroad system of any European country.

In France a large number of corporations were chartered in the beginning of railroad construction, but after a few years these companies consolidated into six large ones, among which the country was divided. In Great Britain much the same thing occurred, and a few large companies came to occupy each a fairly definite part of the country. Eventually, however, the railroads of these two countries fell under centralized national government control.

Although the United States included a vast stretch of territory, the country was well supplied with railroad facilities. There were two ways by which the supply of railway facilities was most frequently measured. One of the methods ascertained the ratio between the railroad mileage and the number of square miles of territory in the country or in the section being considered—that is, it determined the number of miles of railroad per 100 square miles of territory. Another measure was the ratio of mileage to population, or the number of miles of railroad per 10,000 inhabitants. The number of miles of railroad per 100 square miles was greater in the 'trunk-line' territory, the section between New England, Chicago and St Louis, than in any other part of the United States, the number being about 19. New England was second, with 11.6 miles per 100 square miles of territory; and the granger territory third, with 11.73; after which came the southern district, then the southwestern, and finally the western sections served by the transcontinental lines. In the United States as a whole there were 7.55 miles of railroad for each 100 square miles of territory in 1900.

The steam turbo-engine locomotive of the Chesapeake & Ohio. These monsters marked the beginning of the end of the age of steam. Destined to be outdated by the electric diesels of the mid-1950s, only three of these steam turbos were built in the late 1940s and early 1950s.

# CHAPTER 2

# RAILROAD AND LOCOMOTIVE TECHNOLOGY IN THE NINETEENTH CENTURY

## Emory Johnson

Although this book is concerned with the history of American railroads rather than with the technical or engineering phases of the subject, a brief account of the development of the technology of railroading, especially in its formative years, is important to our understanding of this history.

The railway machine consists of three parts: the track, the locomotive, and the car. Each had crude beginnings and, with the exception of the introduction of diesel and electric locomotives, had evolved by the end of the nineteenth century to a point very close to the state of the art 80 years later.

At the beginning of railroad construction, tracks of various designs were built. The builders' primary objective was to secure a solid structure that would not permit the rails to spread. In relation to the weight of the rolling stock and volume of traffic the track was heavy and expensive. This was particularly true in England and on some American railroads begun before 1835, during which time American practice was more influenced by the British.

Three kinds of rails were used. The most common consisted of strong wooden beams, surfaced with strap iron. The first iron rails used were cast iron, and, because of

The locomotive technology that dominated the nineteenth century featured small hard-working engines which were steam driven and coal or wood powered. A Nils Huxtable photograph of a 4-6-4 (*opposite*) stopping at one of the many water tanks that dotted the railroad lines. Horatio Allen (*above*) was the man who introduced the steam locomotive to North America in 1829.

Early track designs (*top to bottom*); Wooden stringers surfaced with straps of iron; granite sills plated with straps of iron; cast iron rails resting on granite blocks; rolled iron U-rail.

their brittleness, their length did not exceed 3½ feet. Rolled rails were soon substituted for cast iron ones, and the length was increased to 15 feet. The weight per yard of these rolled rails sometimes exceeded 40 pounds. Until 1844 all the rolled iron rails used in the United States were imported from England.

The road bed of the Columbia Railroad from Philadelphia to the Susquehanna River, constructed by the State of Pennsylvania between 1828 and 1834, illustrates the various types of construction followed in the early days of railroad building. This double-track road was 81.6 miles in length. For six miles of this distance the rails consisted of granite sills plated with flat iron bars. Sixteen miles of track had rails consisting of wooden string-pieces plated with thin bars of iron. These wooden string-pieces were laid upon wooden crossties, placed four feet apart upon a secure foundation of broken stone. On two miles of the track rails made of iron were supported upon stone blocks. As a precaution against spreading of the rails, stone sills were placed across the track at intervals of 15 feet. The remainder of the track was constructed with iron rails resting upon stone blocks, and with wooden cross-sills every 15 feet. Throughout the entire length of this road there was a horse-path between the rails.

The roads constructed in this manner were needlessly expensive, and because of their rigidity were more destructive to rolling stock than the railroad tracks developed later. American builders soon adopted the kind of track with which we are now familiar: rails placed upon wooden crossties, resting either directly upon earth or upon a thin ballast of gravel or broken rock.

Builders tended early to substitute iron for wooden rails, but as late as 1850 several railroads in the United States, particularly in the southern states, still had wooden rails surfaced with thin plates of iron. The earlier iron rails rolled were in the shape of an inverted U. The T-rail, universally employed since the late nineteenth century, was not much used during the first 20 years of railroad construction, and the use of steel instead of iron was not common until after 1870, when the cost of rolled steel had become low enough to permit its use in the manufacture of rails.

The weight of the rail used has been steadily increased until at the end of the nineteenth century new rails being laid weighed from 85 to 110 lb to the yard. One hundred lb to the yard became the standard upon most tracks where traffic was heaviest. For some time past the standard length of rail had been 30 feet, but by the 1890s some track was being laid with rails 60 feet long. A rail 60 feet long weighing 100 lb to the yard weighed exactly one ton. The use of these heavy rails was made necessary by the increased weight of locomotives and cars and by an increase in the speed of passenger trains and freight traffic. Along with the improvements in the track, the bridges and other structures were gradually strengthened to meet the necessities of modern transportation methods. Therefore in spite of the relative cheapness of material, the roadbed of 1900 was much more expensive than that of 1850. With few exceptions, the early roads had a single track, and, indeed, today those with a relatively small volume of traffic have only one track. As the business over a line increased, a second track usually became necessary, and some roads found difficulty in handling their business with four-track lines.

The amount of traffic that can be handled over a railroad was greatly increased by the use of the telegraph for dispatching trains, by the adoption of electric and other signals and by the possibility of running both passenger and freight trains at higher speeds. The higher speeds resulted from not only more powerful locomotives, but also power brakes which were operated from the engines and kept the train under easy control. Even the necessity for stopping to take on water for the engine was eliminated by placing, between the rails, long shallow troughs from which the tank of the tender could be filled while the train was in rapid motion. The efforts to economize in time and cost of service were directed as much to the improvement of the track and roadbed as to the development of the other elements of technology by which rail transportation was accomplished.

The *Tom Thumb*, **built by Peter Cooper, was a one-horsepower experimental engine whose boiler tubes were made from musket barrels. On 28 August 1830 it hauled the B&O directors on a short jaunt, thereby becoming the first passenger locomotive in service in North America.**

## THE IRON HORSE

The Baltimore & Ohio was the pioneer railroad, but the Charleston & Hamburg road in South Carolina was the first one constructed solely for the immediate use of steam traction. Horses preceded locomotives on the Baltimore & Ohio, the Philadelphia & Columbia, the Mohawk & Hudson and other early lines. The first locomotive actually run on an American railroad was the *Stourbridge Lion,* imported from England in 1829 to be used near Honesdale, Pennsylvania, but the engine proved too heavy for the trestles, and was not put into service.

Locomotive building in the United States began in 1830 but experiments were begun the previous year by Peter Cooper and others. Peter Cooper expected financial gains from the successful completion of the Baltimore & Ohio, and when it seemed uncertain whether locomotives could be run on a road having grades and sharp curves, Cooper designed a little engine called the *Tom Thumb,* which weighed barely a ton. The *Tom Thumb* succeeded, in

August 1830, in hauling 4½ tons around curves and up grades at a speed of 12 to 15 miles an hour, demonstrating the possibility of using steam locomotives on American railroads.

The first locomotives constructed in the United States for actual service on a railroad were built in New York City at the West Point Foundry Works. Locomotive No. 1 was the *Best Friend,* built in 1830, and put into service that year on the Charleston & Hamburg Railroad. The following year the *West Point* was delivered to the same company. The third locomotive to come from the West Point Foundry Works was the *De Witt Clinton,* also built in 1831, and put into use on the Mohawk & Hudson Railroad between Albany and Schenectady.

Machinists in New York, Baltimore, York, Pennsylvania, and elsewhere continued to study and experiment, so that within two years from the time when the first tracks were laid, American builders had demonstrated their ability to construct locomotives adapted to the requirements imposed by American conditions. Among the firms which early undertook locomotive construction was the one founded in Philadelphia by Matthias Baldwin, whose first engine, *Old Ironsides,* appeared in 1832. Up to 1 June 1908, the Baldwin Locomotive Works had constructed 3K,803 locomotives, and was building 2600 to 2700 each year. Baldwin was the most important builder of steam locomotives in the United States for over a century, but it failed to successfully make the transition to diesel, and went out of business in the 1940s.

The influence of George Stephenson, of England, and of his celebrated locomotive the *Rocket,* was felt in the United States, but considering the undeveloped condition of American industries in 1830, a surprisingly small number of English engines were imported. The needs of American railroads were mainly supplied by American foundries and shops. Neither were British models followed to much extent; American designers followed new lines in order to meet novel conditions. They were so successful in making engines that would work on curves and climb grades that American locomotives soon began to be sold in England.

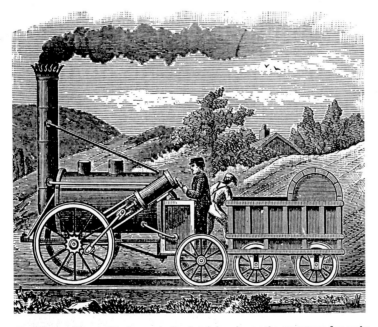

Englishman George Stephenson's *Rocket* (*above*) was the prototype for early American locomotives, but American designs eventually were exported to England. The historic race (*right*) between the *Tom Thumb* and a horse-drawn car used on the Baltimore and Ohio Railroad took place on 25 August 1830.

AAR-8

As compared with the steam and diesel locomotives that became familiar in the twentieth century, those built in 1830 seem tiny and curiously designed. The first locomotives constructed for actual service weighed from three to five tons; the weight of the *De Witt Clinton,* for example, was 3½ tons. The English imports were double that weight and proved too heavy for the tracks with rails of wood surfaced with strap iron. The *John Bull* engine, imported in 1831 for use on the Camden & Amboy line connecting New York and Philadelphia, weighed 10 tons, and was the heaviest engine yet run in the United States. Indeed, its great size was a positive disadvantage to the company for some time.

The American locomotives and cars, unlike the English and those on the Continent (where English models were generally followed), adopted a swivel truck. After the first few years practically all American locomotives had eight wheels, four driving wheels under the rear part of the engine and a four-wheeled truck carrying the fore part of the boiler. The truck was fastened to the engine by a bolt which permitted the truck to swing or swivel through several degrees around sharp curves. The swiveling truck idea seems to have occurred to several people about the same time. Ross Winans, of Baltimore, used it under a passenger coach in 1831. Later in the same year he placed a truck under the forward part of a locomotive. Also in 1831, the truck principle was applied to two locomotives built in New York. One was designed by Horatio Allen, chief engineer of the Charleston & Hamburg Railroad, and the other by John B Jervis, chief engineer for the Mohawk & Hudson. The engine planned by Jervis was more in accordance with subsequent designs, and to him the greater credit is due.

The American or Campbell type locomotive had four connected driving wheels and a four-wheeled truck. The first engine of this design was built in 1836 by James Brooks for Henry R Campbell, both of Philadelphia. This rapidly became the prevailing design for the passenger service, and remained so throughout the nineteenth century.

One essential feature of the locomotive awaited introduction until 1837—the use of equalizing beams by means of which the weight on the driving wheels ceased to be affected by the inequalities of the elevation in the track. After 1837 locomotives were constructed so that each driving wheel had a vertical motion independent of the other wheels, and could move without greatly changing the pressure imposed by the wheel on the track. Equalizing beams were first used in the *Hercules,* designed by Joseph Harrison, Jr and constructed by the Baldwin Locomotive Works.

*DeWitt Clinton* (*below*) was put into service in 1831 and hauled cars that looked like stagecoaches. The *Atlantic* locomotives, known as the grasshopper type, were built in 1832 by Phineas Davis (*above*).

4. In steam and ready to go after less than 17 hours.

3. After ten hours, the locomotive's eight wheels are under and the cab is up.

2. After five hours of work the boiler is in position.

1. Construction begins on a 4-4-0 in the Altoona Pennsylvania plant of the Baldwin locomotive works.

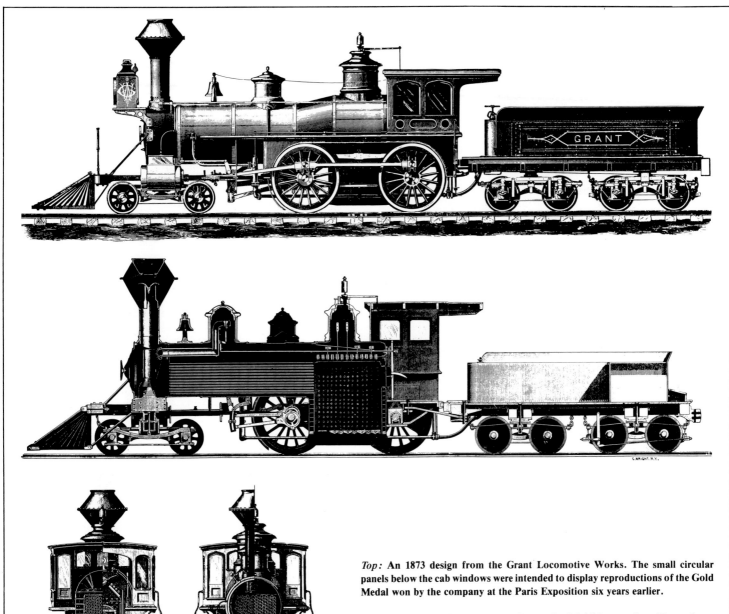

*Top:* An 1873 design from the Grant Locomotive Works. The small circular panels below the cab windows were intended to display reproductions of the Gold Medal won by the company at the Paris Exposition six years earlier.

*Center:* The internal arrangement of a standard 4-4-0 locomotive, this one from Baldwin who built most of the locomotives in the United States in the mid-nineteenth century. Among these were literally hundreds of 4-4-0s.

*Below:* Back cutaway view of the Grant 4-4-0 *American* class (*left*) and front cutaway view of the same locomotive (*right*).

The differentiation in designs for freight and passenger locomotives became evident after 1840. The Campbell engine was the model generally followed for the passenger service, but for handling freight traffic heavier and more powerful locomotives, having six, eight, or ten driving-wheels (all connected), were necessary. There were three major classes of heavy locomotives: the mogul, with six connected drivers; the consolidation, with eight drivers; and the decapod, with ten coupled driving-wheels. In 1844, Ross Winans of Baltimore constructed a locomotive with eight connected wheels. Four years later he brought out the first 'camel' type of engine, so named because the engine-driver's cab was placed above the middle part of the boiler. The construction of mogul and consolidation locomotives became common after 1870.

During the last half of the nineteenth century a great many important improvements were made in locomotives. Among the most valuable innovations was the introduc-

tion of compound locomotives, by which the steam, in passing from the boiler to the exhaust, was used in two cylinders in succession. By that means a greater amount of power is derived from a given quantity of fuel.

The steam locomotives in use in the early twentieth century weighed as much as 25 of the engines used at the beginning of railroading. A locomotive weighing 200,000 lb was not considered notably heavy, and some with their tender weighed 500,000 lb. In 1850 a locomotive weighing more than 50,000 lb was considered large, and a train load of 200 tons would have been a heavy one to handle. Fifty years later 2500 to 3000 tons were hauled over long distances by the largest types of freight engines. The achievements in increased speed of locomotives were less pronounced, but the schedule speed of 60 to 65 miles an hour for passenger trains, regularly maintained on many American roads in 1900, was double the rate possible in 1865, and the discomforts and risks were less.

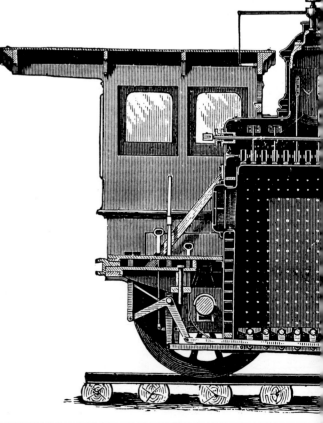

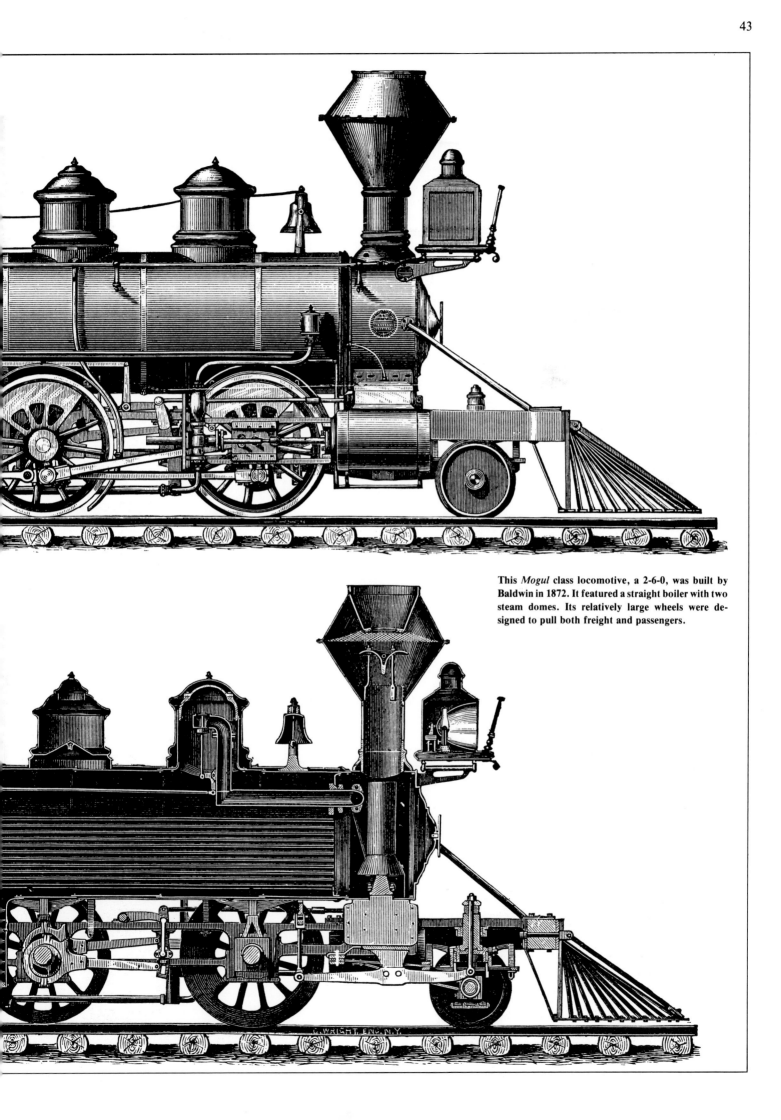

This *Mogul* class locomotive, a 2-6-0, was built by Baldwin in 1872. It featured a straight boiler with two steam domes. Its relatively large wheels were designed to pull both freight and passengers.

# COACHES & ROLLING STOCK

The improvements in travel and traffic resulted quite as much from the progressive adaptation of the vehicle to the service to be performed as from betterments in the roadbed and the locomotive. The passenger coaches first used were similar to the stagecoaches. Carriage builders in making vehicles for the railroad followed the designs with which they were familiar. Indeed, the passenger coaches of Europe, with their compartments entered from the side, indicated that the stagecoach influenced their style. Coaches of the European type were used on a few of the early American roads.

The construction of coaches for American railroads, differing totally in design from those used on highways, began with the opening of the first lines. The first railroad coaches were not unlike the caboose in appearance, but after 1830 longer vehicles mounted on two four-wheeled trucks began to be used, and the typical American coach soon came to differ from the European coach. It was longer, had the doors at the ends and had a central aisle. This form of coach was probably adopted because the curves in American tracks required the use of trucks under the cars as well as under the engines.

Many improvements in design were necessary to produce the comfortable coaches that became the standard after about 1890. Better ventilation was secured by raising the central half of the roof and inserting 'deck-lights.' This was first done in 1836, but it was several years before the raised roof became a feature of all passenger cars. For thirty years the jolting caused by the loose coupling of cars was a great discomfort to travelers, but automatic couplers eliminated the problem.

The sleeping car originated with George M Pullman, who built the *Pioneer A* in 1864. Cars had been fitted up with tiers of bunks on each side as early as 1837, but the discomforts of such accommodations were so great that sleeping cars did not become popular until the Pullman and Wagner services became available. The sleeping car was soon followed by the buffet or hotel car, drawing room and dining cars. The necessity for passing from one car to another suggested the vestibuling of trains. The idea was as old as 1852, when a man by the name of Waterbury first designed a vestibuled car. Some individual cars were fitted with vestibules that year, but the first vestibuled train was designed and built by Pullman and was run on the Pennsylvania Railroad in 1886.

The air brake, first successfully applied to passenger trains in 1868, was one of the most valuable of all the inventions by which the improvement of the transportation service has been brought about. In 1887 the air brake had been developed for use on freight trains, and by the turn of the century the law required all trains in the United States to be equipped with air brakes controlled by the engineer. The days of the hand brake were past. The power brake greatly lessened the risks to employees and decreased the danger of travel, making possible much greater speed for freight as well as passenger trains.

Many appliances came into use that contributed to the comfort and safety of the passenger. The railroad companies wanted the traveler to have the conveniences of living and the facilities for transacting business that he would have at home or at a hotel.

The freight car was developed in many designs for the accommodation of the numerous kinds of traffic to be handled. Starting with only crudely constructed open and box cars mounted on four wheels with a loading capacity of three to five tons, the freight equipment of railroads came to include a large variety of cars provided with many mechanical appliances for saving labor costs and minimizing damages to property in transit, and capable of carrying loads of over 50 tons. Many of the improvements in car construction, such as the swiveling truck that had four or more wheels, improved couplings and air brakes, were as applicable to the freight car as to the passenger coach.

Specialization in freight cars grew with the growing volume of traffic. Special cars were developed for carrying cattle, dressed meats, oil, coal, coke, iron ore, fruit, milk and many other commodities. It seemed as though a special car was brought into use whenever a new kind of traffic developed that could not be handled by ordinary box or flat cars. The invention of the refrigerator and heater cars was incidental to this specialization, and proved to be of great value. The distribution of perishable commodities throughout the entire country could be carried on during all seasons of the year, to the great advantage both of the producer and consumer.

With the construction of stronger tracks and with the use of steel rails the railroad companies took advantage of the economy resulting from the use of large cars. Compared with the weight of the cargo, the larger the cars became, the less they weighed. The larger the cars, the greater the live load the engine could haul. In 1880, 20 tons was the standard carload, but by 1900 the standard box and open car in the United States was built to carry 30 tons. Many cars used in carrying coal, ore and other heavy commodities were loaded with 50 to 55 tons of cargo. In 1939 the average freight car capacity still stood at 50 tons, but by 1970 it had increased to 67 tons, and by 1983 to 82 tons.

The construction of cars with a capacity of 50 tons or more had been facilitated by the large use of steel, both in the truck frames and in the body of the car. Indeed, a large share of the cars built for heavy traffic were constructed entirely of steel throughout most of the twentieth century. Just as the small wooden sailing vessel gave way to the large steel steamship, so the wooden freight car was displaced by steel cars of greater strength and capacity.

The first sleeping car designed by George Pullman (*opposite*) was a converted coach. Another Pullman offering was 'The Olympian' barber shop (*above*). The railroad companies were convinced during their heyday that passengers on their lines should enjoy all the comforts of home, if not all the comforts of luxury hotels. One needed to watch out for barbers with straight-razors on the curves.

# CHAPTER 3

# THE DEVELOPMENT OF RAILROAD SERVICES IN THE NINETEENTH CENTURY

## Emory Johnson

The volume of freight transported by North America's railroads increased rapidly with the progress of civilization and the diversification of public need.

During the year ending 30 June 1906, the railroads in the United States reported a freight traffic of 1,631,374,219 tons. This is a greater tonnage than shippers actually turned over to the roads, because the same freight is often handled by more than one road and duplications result from taking the total of all the traffic of all the companies. After duplications are deducted, the traffic actually received from shippers during that year amounted to 896,159,485 tons. By 1929 this figure was up to 1,339,-091,000. Except for the period of the Great Depression, when total tonnage dropped below a billion, annual ton-

nage has remained relatively stable throughout the twentieth century. In 1944 it stood at 1,491,491,000, in 1970 at 1,484,919,000 and in 1984 at 1,429,388,000. To handle that vast tonnage of traffic required nearly 40 thousand freight and switching locomotives and nearly 2 million freight cars in 1906; 57 thousand and 2.6 million in 1929; and 25 thousand and 1.5 million in 1984.

The mines from which the coal, iron ore and other minerals were taken furnished more than half the tonnage handled by the railroads, but as this traffic was carried at low

**The image of a steam engine puffing through the countryside (*opposite*) conjures up memories of a bygone era. The name of George M Pullman (*above*) was synonomous with luxurious hotel-like coaches symbolic of the time when train travel was unquestionably first class.**

rates per ton the receipts from this business amount to much less than half the total freight revenue of the railroads. Manufacturers supplied over one-seventh of the tonnage, the products of the forest above one-ninth and the products of agriculture about one-twelfth. The remainder of the traffic, comprising somewhat less than one-eighth of the total, consists of animal products, general merchandise and miscellaneous unclassified commodities. There were no figures obtainable regarding the value of the goods which the railroads transport, but if their value did not average more than $25 a ton, their total worth would have been nearly $22 billion in 1906.

Until 1887 nearly every large railroad had a classification of its own, but by 1906 most business was handled by one of three classifications. In the section east of the Mississippi River and north of the Ohio and Potomac—that is, in the New England and trunk-line territories—a classification called the 'Official' was in force. Its construction, revision and supervision were under the charge of a committee with headquarters in New York. South of the Ohio and east of the Mississippi the 'Southern' classification was in operation under the control of a committee located at Atlanta. In the country west of the Mississippi the 'Western' classification prevailed, administered by a committee in Chicago. Some of the through business to and from the Pacific coast points was done under a classification issued by the Transcontinental Freight Bureau, whose offices were in Chicago.

Freight was usually spoken of as through and local. In a popular sense through freight meant that which was transported a long distance, and local freight that which was moved only a short distance. The railroad companies, however, used the words in a more technical sense. By local freight they meant that which originated and terminated upon the same line—that is, freight carried between two points on the same road. Through freight was that

**Early wood-burning locomotives (*opposite*) at work hauling pieces of giant redwood trees for lumber that built the nation. This load was headed for San Francisco. Men such as these (*above*) from an 1878 machine department shop kept the engines chugging, trains rolling and railroad clients smiling in satisfaction.**

EXCELSIOR
REDWOOD CO.
EUREKA, CAL.

DIA. 11 FT. 9 IN.
LENGTH 18

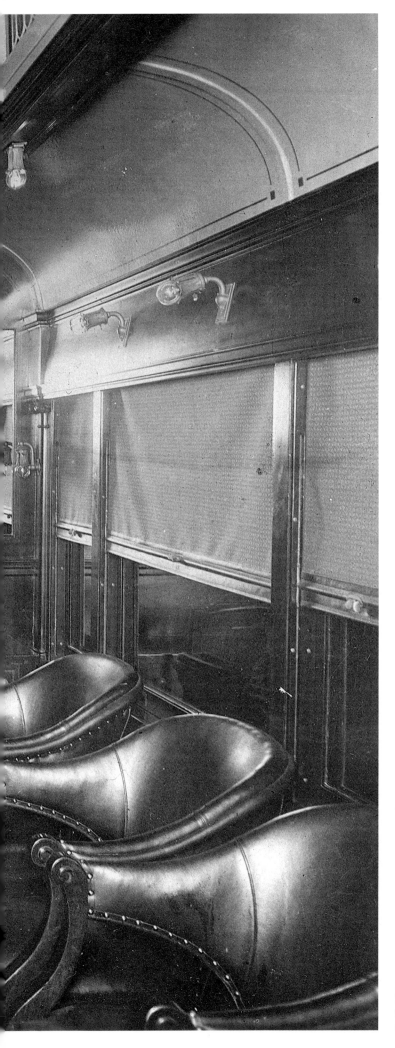

which came to the railroad company from some other railroad, or originated at some point on the line and was turned over to some connecting carrier. More simply, through freight was transported by more than one carrying company. In general, the technical use of the terms corresponded with their popular meaning, but not always. Some freight may have traveled hundreds of miles, passed state boundaries and moved between great centers of population, without leaving the original line. At the same time, through freight may have moved only a short distance.

## THE PASSENGER SERVICE

The service of transporting people naturally differed from freight service. Goods were shipped, while people traveled of their own volition, controlling, in most instances, the time and direction of their movements. In the nineteenth century freight rates and passenger fares were charges levied by the same railroads for dissimilar services, and to a large extent were determined by different considerations.

One important difference between the two branches of the service was that most freight was moved in carloads or trainloads, whenever the car was loaded or the train made up, while the passenger business was performed by trains that ran on fixed schedules. However, some commodities, like milk and fresh fruit, were dispatched by trains which ran strictly according to schedule, and the collection and distribution of the traffic at the local centers of production or consumption were usually accomplished by 'way-freight' trains which had a more or less definite time of arrival and departure. Frequently in the nineteenth and early twentieth centuries the 'milk' trains and way-freight trains had passenger coaches attached, and thus performed a mixed service. The larger share of the freight traffic, however, was handled in trains whose time of departure was determined by the volume of goods offered for shipment.

Among the results following from the pursuit of these different aims in the two main branches of the railroad business was an increase in the average freight train load, but no gain in the average number of persons per passenger train between 1890 and 1906. There was an increase in the number of people carried and in the distance traveled by them, but the growing demand for frequency of service, speed and comfort resulted more in an increase of trains than in a gain in train load.

The number of passenger trips taken on American railroads in 1900 was 576,865,230, and in 1906 797,946,116. The greatest previous number was for 1893, when the Columbian Exposition at Chicago caused the figures for that year to reach 593,560,612. The aggregate length of the trips taken in 1906 was over 25,000,000,000 miles, the average journey per passenger or the average length of a trip being 31.5 miles. The increase in speed of trains and in the comforts of travel were accompanied by a greater amount of long-distance travel, the average trip having lengthened over 7 miles from 1890 to 1900. The average length of a rail passenger's trip continued to increase grad-

*Opposite:* **This observation car boasts leather upholstery, fine wood paneling, brass spittoons — all the dash and sparkle associated with fine living in the nineteenth century. Though it was originally built in the 1800s, electric lights were added to this car about 1910.**

ually until 1951, when it reached a peace-time peak of 71.4 miles (the World War II peak average was 104.5). It declined to 37.7 by 1970 and has remained relatively constant ever since.

In the United States, passengers in the nineteenth century did not divide themselves into classes as was customary in most foreign countries, but the railroads furnished different grades of service corresponding in a general way to the classes found on foreign roads. Most of the travel in America was on first-class tickets, but most companies also sold second-class tickets. On the routes over which travel justified them, excursion and immigrant trains were run which provided inferior accommodations at rates cheaper than second class. Beyond first-class accommodations were those furnished in the parlor cars and sleeping cars, called extra-fare cars.

Most American railroad companies, unlike those in foreign countries, placed the sleeping-, parlor-, and dining-car services in charge of a separate company. The Pullman Palace-Car Company, of Chicago, owned and operated most of the cars in use from the beginning of this service in 1865 until 1955. For many years the Vanderbilt-controlled Wagner Palace-Car Company, of Buffalo, built and managed from one-fourth to one-third of the sleeping-, parlor-, and dining-cars. In 1899 the two companies con-

solidated under the name of the Pullman Company, which controlled nearly all the extra-fare cars. The Chicago, Milwaukee and St Paul, the Canadian Pacific, the Great Northern, the New York, New Haven & Hartford systems, and a few other companies, ran their own cars exclusively, but their total numbers were relatively few.

The railroads paid the Pullman Company mileage (about one cent per car mile in 1906) for the use of the coaches, and the Pullman Company, in addition to this revenue from mileage, received the extra fares paid by the passengers for the privilege of riding in the parlor- or sleeping-car. On some especially fast trains the railroads charged more than the usual first-class fare, to cover the additional expense of running the trains at a high speed.

The parlor- and sleeping-coaches were much heavier than the ordinary first-class day coach, and had accommodations for fewer people; hence the profits received by the railroads from the parlor- and sleeping-car traffic were really smaller than those obtained from the day coach service. Someone said that 'the man who sits up all night in the day coach helps pay for the fare of the man who rides in the Pullman car.'

The railroad companies found it to their advantage to rent the parlor- and sleeping-coaches instead of owning them, because the Pullman Company, having control of a

great number of cars, was able to supply the railroad with just the number of cars required. When one railroad company or one section of the country had a large demand for coaches, some other company or section probably didn't need more than the usual quota, and the Pullman Company was able to distribute the cars economically according to the needs of the service.

The 'resort' traffic and suburban traffic (what is now called commuter traffic) was zealously stimulated by reduction in fares and an attractive service. With the growth of wealth in the United States and the increase in the number of those who could afford recreation, the summer travel between the cities and the seashore and mountain resorts rapidly expanded during the early years of the twentieth century. Likewise the change from city to suburban residence for a part or all the year accelerated rapidly as the inconvenience, discomfort and expense of getting to and from the city was lessened. In stimulating suburban residence the trolley was as influential as the steam railroads, and its competition in some instances compelled the railroad companies to make their service more attractive by reducing fares and offering better accommodations. The trolleys in some cases took so much of the short-distance suburban traffic away from the steam lines that they were compelled to curtail or abandon part of their service.

*Above and below:* Coaches designed for passenger sleeping comfort by George M Pullman who got the idea after he endured a particularly rough trip on a typical railroad coach. In 1867 Pullman formed the Pullman Palace Car Company that produced not only sleeping cars, but 'hotel cars' which included small kitchens, dining cars, smoking cars, card rooms, libraries and even barber shops.

# CHAPTER 4

# THE BIG FOUR AND THE TRANSCONTINENTAL RAILROAD

## Bill Yenne

The story of American industrial expansion in the nineteenth century is the story of the visionary men who guided the nation during its growth years. These men created the framework upon which men of lesser ambition were able to build their lives, their fortunes and their own smaller empires. The great industrial giants of America's period of expansion built the nation's infrastructure, her cities, her factories, her railroads. Without the railroads the Industrial Revolution would never have spread across Europe, and without the railroads the United States would never have sprawled across the North American continent.

When gold was discovered at Sutter's Mill in the western slopes of the Sierra Nevada in January 1848, thousands of

people flocked to California in the ensuing gold rush. California became a state of the Union in 1850, and in 1854 Sacramento was made its capital. Included in the hordes who swept across the wilderness and around Cape Horn were dozens who came to build vast fortunes in the new land.

Theodore Dehone Judah, a civil engineer from Troy, New York, arrived in Sacramento in 1854 at the behest of the Sacramento Valley Rail Road Company (SVRR). With the Sacramento business community behind it, the SVRR had been incorporated in 1852 with plans for a railroad to connect that city with the gold fields of the Sierra, and Judah was the man picked to engineer the line. He was prepared to do the job, but his vision was fixed on a larger idea: a transcontinental line that would connect California to the rest of the nation.

His first western railroad complete, Judah became one of the leading exponents of a transcontinental, or 'Pacific,'

**Perhaps the biggest of the Four, Leland Stanford (*opposite*) became president of the Central Pacific in 1861 and governor of California the following year. After building the Central Pacific and Southern Pacific, he served as a US Senator. Central Pacific workers (*above*) toiled in the Sierra Nevada earning small wages for themselves and massive fortunes for the Big Four.**

*Above from left:* The Big Four who joined forces to build the Central Pacific Railroad across the Sierra Nevada and at the same time built fortunes for themselves: Collis P Huntington, Leland Stanford, Charles Crocker and Mark Hopkins. These former small-time Sacramento businessmen developed wealth beyond their dreams.

*Opposite:* The grand mansion built atop San Francisco's Nob Hill by 'uncle' Mark Hopkins was destroyed by the 1906 fire and earthquake. Hopkins was satisfied to live in his Sutter Street cottage but constructed the mansion to please his young spoiled bride. He died in 1878, the year the mansion was completed and never had to live there anyway.

railroad as it was known then. When Asa Whitney first suggested such a railroad in 1845, his was a decidedly minority voice. However, by the time Theodore Judah arrived in Washington, DC, in late 1856 to lobby Congress for funding, the idea had grown in popularity. Senator Thomas Hart Benton of Missouri had placed the idea before Congress in 1849, and Pacific railroad conventions had been held in Memphis, New Orleans and Boston that same year. It seemed as though the gold rush had won many converts to the dream of a railroad to the West.

The only question, apparently, was which route would the new road take. The central route to the Pacific followed the major overland routes of the day and was the shortest distance between San Francisco and chief western embarkation points like St Louis and Kansas City. Advocates of a northern route pointed out that the nature of the navigable Mississippi/Missouri River network made Puget Sound 700 miles closer than San Francisco. The southern route, too, had many advocates. In 1853 Secretary of War (and later President of the Confederacy) Jefferson Davis of Mississippi presented a 13-volume study of nine possible southern routes, which, it was pointed out, were largely free of snow and high mountain passes. The Gadsden Purchase of 1854 made these routes all the more attractive.

## THE CENTRAL PACIFIC

In Sacramento, Theodore Judah had been introduced to four merchants who had gone west in the wake of the gold rush to set up shop in California's capital. On 28 June 1861 they formed the Central Pacific Railroad, forerunner of the empire that was called the Southern Pacific. The Central Pacific was incorporated under the laws of California and dedicated to building a railroad across the Sierra via Dutch Flat. Leland Stanford became president of the new firm and Collis Huntington became its vice-president. The frugal Mark Hopkins was named treasurer. Judah became chief engineer and Charles Crocker formed Charles Crocker and Company, a wholly owned subsidiary that would undertake construction of the Central Pacific.

Personal relations among the Big Four (they preferred to be called 'the Associates') were not always the best, and were frequently the worst. These men were nevertheless uniquely and ideally suited for the partnership. Each contributed something to a whole that was greater than the sum of its parts: the greatest commercial empire that had yet been seen on the western side of the continent.

On 1 October 1861, having spent his summer in the Sierra, Theodore Judah reported to the directors of the Central Pacific that a practical route had been found. On 6 January 1862, Leland Stanford was inducted into office as governor of California, and he found himself in a unique position to put resources behind the building of the Central Pacific. In his inaugural address, Stanford told a Sacramento crowd, 'Within a short time the territory of Nevada has sprung into great importance [with a silver strike]; her vast undeveloped wealth will attract and give employment to an immense population of industrious and thriving people, ensuring her a brilliant and important destiny. From California she will necessarily derive most of her supplies. The most difficult link of the Pacific railroad which must pass through this Territory lies in California. It is not necessary at this late date to go into a general argument to prove the importance of a railroad connecting the Pacific and Atlantic Oceans, especially now, when its military necessity is so much more than ever apparent. I allude to it briefly because I think the time has arrived when, in consequence of local business, the most difficult and important part of the work can be accomplished without direct pecuniary aid from the national government. May we not therefore, with the utmost propriety even at this time, ask the national government to donate lands and loan its credit in aid of this portion of that communication [the Pacific railroad] which is of the very first importance, not alone to the states and territories west of the Rocky Mountains, but to the whole nation, and is the great work of the age.'

## THE UNION PACIFIC

Across the continent another Republican, President Abraham Lincoln, shared the vision. Presiding over a nation embroiled in a struggle for its survival, Lincoln could see that keeping California and the wealth of California and Nevada in the Union was essential. With the Union at war with the South, the southern transcontinental route was clearly not available, so the central route long

The 90-foot high Secrettown trestle in the Sierra Nevada of California is filled with dirt by Central Pacific workers. The mostly Chinese workers toiled with meager tools but managed to blast a trail over the rugged mountains for the rails of the first transcontinental railroad.

favored by Judah was selected. Lincoln signed the Pacific Railroad Act on 1 July 1862, creating the Union Pacific Railroad Company to build a line westward from Omaha, Nebraska. The act authorized the Central Pacific to 'Start at or near San Francisco or some point on the navigable waters of the Sacramento River and build eastwardly to the western boundary of California, and . . . continue construction until meeting the line of the Union Pacific.'

## SILVER SPADE AND GOLDEN SPIKE

On 8 January 1863, Governor Leland Stanford, wielding a silver spade, broke ground at Front and K streets in Sacramento, and the dream was on its way to becoming a reality. After Theodore Judah completed his surveys and as the railroad was gradually built westward, Judah's role began to diminish. Though he still referred to it as 'my little road,' it clearly belonged to the four 'associates' who were financing and building it. Animosity developed between Judah and Huntington, so Judah decided to go east to seek the financing necessary to buy out his partners. He arranged a series of meetings in New York and left San Francisco by steamer in October 1863. When he crossed through the jungles of Panama, he contracted yellow fever, and on 2 November he died in New York at the age of 38.

On 7 October 1863, the Central Pacific's first locomotive arrived in Sacramento; on 9 November, having been dubbed *Governor Stanford,* it made its first run. On 25 April 1864, the first Central Pacific passenger service to Roseville began, and by 3 June the line had been extended to Newcastle. As the line reached into the mountains, the going became more difficult.

Construction of the Union Pacific had finally gotten under way on 5 November 1865, nearly three years behind the Central Pacific, but the work was moving considerably faster. Laying tracks across the wonderfully flat expanses of Nebraska prairie bore no similarity to the difficulties encountered in the Sierra. While the Central Pacific had its sights set on completing its line east across Nevada and part of Utah to Salt Lake, Union Pacific surveyors had laid out a route westward all the way to the California border.

The Sierra summit tunnels, begun even before the tracks reached Cisco, took two painful years to complete. These years, 1866 to 1868, included the two worst winters on record; men who weren't maimed in nitroglycerine mishaps ran the risk of freezing.

In July 1868, the Central Pacific had finally broken out of the mountains, and Charles Crocker stared in relief and anticipation at the relative flatness of Nevada. The 150-mile crossing from Newcastle had taken the railroad 41 months. They would cross the 555 miles to the Salt Lake in 10.

The final mad dash was on. Both railroads wanted to reach the lake first, and Leland Stanford personally made five trips to Salt Lake City to expedite the process. The Central Pacific crews, meanwhile, were laying more than a mile of track each day. The question of where they would meet was one of speed, until Congress stepped in on 10 April 1869 and dictated that 'The common terminal of the Union Pacific and Central Pacific railroads shall be at or near Ogden . . . and the Central Pacific Railroad Com-

pany shall pay for and own the railroad from the terminus aforesaid to Promontory Summit [north of Salt Lake], at which point the rails shall meet and connect and form one continuous line.'

In the meantime, the Union Pacific's chief engineer, General G M Dodge, was making a great deal out of his 'Irish terriers' having laid six miles of track in a single day. On 28 April 1869, Central Pacific foreman J H Strobridge invited Dodge to have a look at what his Chinese Central Pacific crews could do. A train stood by before daybreak with two miles of rails, and the Central Pacific gangs went to work. Before dawn, the two miles were down. In one instance 240 feet were laid in one minute and 15 seconds. By the end of the day, two million pounds of rails were spiked, gauged and bolted. There were 10 miles and 56 feet of track laid that day, more than had ever been laid, or would ever be laid again, in so short a time. As General Dodge looked on, a Central Pacific locomotive rolled back and forth over the section.

As the sun set on those 10 miles of track and the hundreds that preceded it, the end was very near at hand. On 10 May 1869, the Central Pacific locomotive *Jupiter* moved toward Promontory pulling the private car of Leland Stanford. On the track ahead was the Union Pacific's *No 119* and its vice president, T C Durant. Stanford had actually arrived on 8 May and had waited in the rain for two days while Durant was delayed. (His train had been kidnapped by some unpaid contractors and was held until the account was settled.)

The rain stopped as the two locomotives paused within sight of one another, and the last rail was put into place. This was followed by speeches and the presentation of a golden spike to Governor Stanford. Nevada offered a silver spike and a speech, and Arizona presented a gold, silver and iron spike and another speech. Stanford responded with a speech. In place of the silver spade he had taken up in Sacramento six years before, he brandished a silver hammer. Telegraph lines that had been strung parallel to the two railroads were poised to carry the news east to Omaha and Chicago, and west to Sacramento and San Francisco. Both the spike and the hammer were wired into the telegraph so the moment of their contact could send a tiny spark of electricity exploding across the nation, poised breathless for this monumental occasion.

A hush fell over the assembled crowd as Leland Stanford swung the silver hammer at the first gold spike. The hammer plunged downward toward the final notch in the steel belt that would bind the nation . . . and missed. Stanford's second blow connected, but it was anticlimatic. Having seen the first blow fall short, a telegraph technician had tapped his key and the celebrations in Chicago and San Francisco had already begun.

*Jupiter* moved forward the last few feet of the 690-mile distance from Sacramento, while *No 119* inched ahead on the last of its 1086-mile trek from Omaha. As their cowcatchers clanged together, the champagne flowed and the Central Pacific and Union Pacific construction superintendents were photographed shaking hands. The gold and silver spikes were unceremoniously pulled, returned to Stanford and replaced with steel ones. Judah's dream had

*Left*: **The famous picture of the ceremony at Promontory, Utah on 10 May 1869. Representatives from the Union Pacific and Central Pacific join hands, a gesture symbolic of the joining of their two rival railroad lines by a spike made of California gold.**

Southern Pacific leads the way across the parched American desert into the Golden West in this photo taken near Santa Rosa, New Mexico. Included in the train are an Atchison, Topeka & Santa Fe coal car and refrigerated cars of the Pacific Fruit express, a joint venture of the Southern Pacific and Union Pacific.

opened the way to the fruition of a whole nation's dreams.

The changes wrought by completion of the transcontinental were far reaching and immediate. Less than a week after Leland Stanford's parlor car receded across the desert toward the Sierra and Sacramento, the first regularly scheduled freight service from Chicago to Sacramento was inaugurated, on 15 May 1869. The West may not yet have been won, but it had certainly been served notice.

## THE SOUTHERN PACIFIC

Another road of interest to the Big Four existed largely on paper, but it owned the land grants to build south from San Francisco and San Jose to Los Angeles and San Diego. This road, which had been organized in 1865 by some of the same San Francisco financiers who had earlier turned down participation in the Central Pacific, was the original Southern Pacific Railroad.

The Southern Pacific had received notice from Congress on 27 July 1866 that it would be the western link of a second transcontinental line then under consideration. On 4 February 1868, the Southern Pacific bought the San Francisco & San Jose Railroad coveted by the Big Four, and in August 1868 Southern Pacific President Timothy Guy Phelps announced his intention to start building his line south to San Diego, where it would then turn east to 'the California line, and to the Mississippi River.'

On 25 September 1869, the Big Four purchased the Southern Pacific. The following year the Central and Southern Pacific operations were merged, although a full merger did not take place for another 15 years, at which time the operations of the entire network came under the Southern Pacific name.

In 1883, the Southern Pacific's Sunset Route, connecting New Orleans to California by way of Texas, was completed. By 1884, Southern Pacific owned every mile of standard-gauge railroad in the state of California, a 4711-mile system radiating from the bustling San Francisco yards to the far corners of the state and 800 miles beyond. When the line connecting Portland, Oregon to the California network was completed in 1887, Southern Pacific's route map covered a quarter of the United States, an empire unparalleled by any other railroad company.

*Below:* The *Governor Stanford,* the first of Central Pacific's locomotives, was put into service in 1863. In this 1916 photo the locomotive is seen heading into the Stanford Museum on the campus of Stanford University.

*Above:* The original Southern Pacific headquarters in San Francisco. This building built by the Big Four was destroyed in the fire resulting from the great earthquake of 1906.

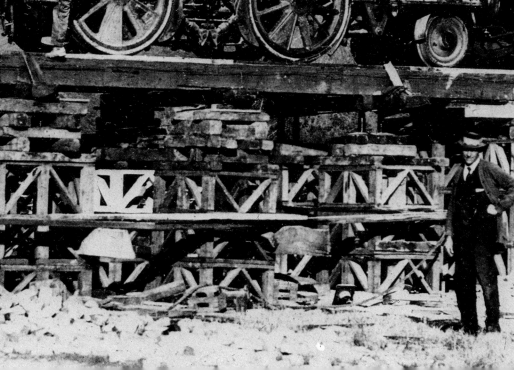

# FEDERAL LAND GRANTS AND THE WESTWARD EXPANSION OF AMERICA'S RAILROADS

### Purpose of the Grants

In 1850, when the first railroad land grant was made, there were vast areas of public domain amounting to nearly 1.4 billion acres. Congressional debate on the first land grant act made clear its objective, which was to provide the western frontier with transportation that would make settlement possible. Senator William R King, afterward vice president, said that, 'unless some mode of the kind proposed be adopted, it [the unsettled land] will never command ten cents.'

Senator William H Seward, who later became secretary of state, added: 'The best and highest interests of the people of the United States . . . is to bring them [the lands] into cultivation and settlement in the shortest space of time and under the most favorable auspices.'

Railroads were neither the first—nor the last—to receive land grants. Developers of wagon roads and canals received 10,007,687 acres, and thousands of individual farmers later were given homesteads of up to 640 acres each. The railroads received a total of 131,250,534 acres—specifically for providing the necessary security for borrowing construction money.

Under the first land-grant act—involving areas in Illinois, Mississippi and Alabama—railroads received alternate sections of land on either side of the proposed rail routes. Title to the remaining alternate sections was retained by the federal government. Later acts, involving lands west of the Mississippi River, followed a similar pattern.

Prior to 1850, the government offered land for sale at $1.25 an acre. There were few takers. When the first land-grant legislation was passed, the government immediately advanced the price of its retained lands to $2.50 an acre, or double the former price. And, with a railroad assured, the land was eagerly bought up by settlers.

The land grants—and the railroads they fostered—made a great contribution, not only to the West, but to all of America. These railroads converted vast areas yielding no tax revenues into taxable properties for the benefit of states through which they passed and of the municipalities which sprang up along them. As title was cleared to property serving as security for loans, much of this land was sold—usually at bargain prices—to stimulate development which would help generate business for the wilderness railroads. On land that the railroads retained, taxes—often at discriminatory rates—have been paid for a century or more. The transportation system that evolved from the land grant era remains the most efficient and economical ever developed and continues to give impetus to agricultural and industrial development. Perhaps most important of all, the

*Below:* A St Paul & Pacific 4-4-0 nicknamed *Wm Crooks* was the first locomotive to serve the Northwest. The St Paul & Pacific evolved into part of the Northern Pacific Railroad, which in more recent years has itself evolved into part of the Burlington Northern Railroad Company. The collapsing of small, regional railroad lines into segments of huge corporate enterprises has been typical of North America's railroad history.

*Overleaf:* Employees of the Southern Pacific's San Francisco ticket office pose for this portrait taken during the company's golden years between 1890 to 1917.

De Land
Clerk

Holbrook
Clerk

Giffin
Head Clerk
Foreign
Interline
Bureau

Stevens
Chief Clerk

Fuller

Holton
Ticket Auditor

Robinson
Head Clerk
Local

Marks
Head Clerk
Statistical

Employes
Ticket Auditors Office S. P. Co—
Fourth and Townsend Streets
San Francisco.

grants that made transcontinental rail service feasible helped unite the country at a critical point.

Railroads were not given the land grants; they had to pay for them. Most railroads receiving land were required by law to haul government freight and personnel at reduced rates averaging 50 percent, and mail was hauled at a 20 percent reduction. For competitive reasons, other railroads, including those which received no land, entered into 'equalization agreements' granting similar rate reductions on government business. When the reduced rate requirements were finally repealed by Congress in 1945, a Congressional committee reported:

*'It is probable that the railroads have contributed over $900 million in payment of the lands which were transferred to them. . . . Former ICC Commissioner J B Eastman estimated the value of the lands at the time they were granted was not more than $126 million.'*

Reduced rates applied to the vast government traffic carried during World War II, and remained in effect until 1 October 1946, raising the total estimated value of the railroads' contributions to $1.25 billion or about 10 times the original value of the lands received.

The railroad land grants accomplished the objective set for them—and more. Two and a half centuries after the first permanent settlement on the Atlantic Seaboard, large areas west of the Mississippi River were vacant or sparsely settled. Within less than one generation after the first railroad land grant, railroads—both with and without the aid of grants—touched off and made possible the great surge of development that transformed the West from a wilderness into a burgeoning community. Land grants made it possible to do what never had been done before: provide transportation ahead of settlement.

## The Last Frontier

When the land grants were initiated, all of the nation's rail trackage lay east of the Mississippi. Thereafter, the lines began reaching farther westward, the first being the Pacific Railroad (now part of the Missouri Pacific) which was build west from St Louis in 1850. Others soon followed, and the maturing nation was about ready to stretch rails to its last remaining frontier.

The push toward California was strong. It was the nation's western doorway through which could flow the glamorous goods of the Orient. Driving rails to the Pacific would make these goods more readily available to the nation's eastern populace. Then, too, there was the lure of gold, whose discovery in California in 1849 promised wealth to those who could find it and no smaller reward to those who could link the East with opportunities which the gold rush had created in California.

Thus, between 1850 and 1860, the nation's rail mileage more than tripled. By the beginning of the Civil War, there were 31,246 miles of road. Many new lines were being contemplated, but the imagination of railroaders centered on one that would link East to West. The 'Pacific railroad' had the potential to dwarf what had gone before. The contemplated transcontinental railroad would call for a line two and a half times as long as any ever built.

In July 1862, with the nation torn by internal strife, President Lincoln signed the Pacific Railroad Act—a step later described by General William T Sherman as the 'only thing positively essential to the binding together of the republic.'

The act authorized two railroads to build the great line to the Pacific. The Central Pacific (now a part of the Southern Pacific) was to head east from Sacramento; the newly chartered Union Pacific would drive westward from the Missouri River. As each mile of track was completed, the government would grant 10 (later increased to 20) sections of land. Also provided for were US bonds, to be loaned to the railroads in amounts dependent on the difficulty of the terrain crossed. Despite these incentives, so gigiantic was the task, particularly in wartime, that it took three years of gathering investors and other preparations before the Union Pacific was able to put down its first rails beyond Omaha. In 1866, with only 40 miles of track down, the impetus of competition gave new spirit to Union Pacific's westward drive. That June, Congress repealed earlier legislation forbidding the Central Pacific from building more than 150 miles east of the California-Nevada border.

President Abraham Lincoln (*far left*) signed the Pacific Railroad Act in 1862 that authorized the building of the transcontinental railroad. The construction of a permanent bridge (*below*) parallels the temporary bridge laid on the snow near Citadel Rock situated along the transcontinental line.

Since the land grant acreage was awarded on the basis of completed trackage, the great undertaking was transformed into a race.

To speed things up, the Union Pacific hired the Casement brothers, Jack and Dan, who had built much midwestern trackage during the war. Dedicated to the job at hand, liked and respected by their men, the Casements made rail-laying into a science. Many of their workers were newly arrived in America from Ireland. Followed by a construction and supply train, complete with sleeping quarters, and flanked by a herd of cattle to supply fresh beef, the men were eager to pursue the extra rewards of tobacco and money promised for good performance. By the fall of 1866, Casement crews were putting down track at the rate of 65 miles a month.

Problems, though, were many and severe. Indians, incensed at the coming of the iron horse, tore up rails and burned ties as the Union Pacific battled its way across the prairie. Saloon girls, gamblers, outlaws and troublemakers followed along like pilot fish, creating their own set of problems. Through it all, including the freezing winters and blazing summers, the railroad surged westward.

The Central Pacific, meanwhile, continued to drive eastward. Its Chinese laborers—initially recruited when new silver mines lured other workers—had learned quickly, pushing rails eastward through the mountains and across the Nevada desert to Utah's western border by 1869. When Charles Crocker, CP's construction boss, heard that the Union Pacific crews had topped his previous record by laying eight miles of track in one day, he bet $10,000 on the ability of his own crews. The Chinese workers, he said, could lay 10 miles of rail 'between daylight and dark.' After careful planning, his crews swung into action, laying 10 miles and 56 feet in less than 12 hours. Even the Casements were impressed.

Finally, on 10 May 1869, Central Pacific and Union Pacific locomotives sat a shoveltoss of coal apart at Promontory, Utah, just north of the Great Salt Lake. Plans for the heroic joining had been laid well ahead of time. The Central Pacific president and a former Governor of California, Leland Stanford, would join with Union Pacific Vice President Thomas Durant in driving home a final gold spike with a silver sledge hammer.

History would probably like to recall that both men applied mighty jolts to the trembling spike, but the truth is far less dramatic. Neither man could even hit the spike, much less drive it home. It was left for Jack Casement—all 5 feet 4 inches of him—to slam in the historic spike. The transcontinental railroad had been built.

## An Explosive Growth

It had taken more than half a century from the time the nation's first railroad was chartered to build a transcontinental railroad. It took only 12 more years to build the second, this one coming to a junction in New Mexico and providing the first direct line to Southern California. Two years later, St Paul was linked to the Pacific Northwest, and New Orleans got a connection to the West Coast.

The system grew rapidly after that. Five more years saw the completion of a southern route between Chicago and

The Union Pacific paymaster's car, surrounded by some of the many thousands of workers who built the transcontinental railroad. About one man in four was a tracklayer who earned an average of three dollars a day.

California. Five more and the Great Lakes were downline from Puget Sound. Another route to the Pacific opened in 1909. An unparalleled explosion of growth marked the decades of the 1870s and 1880s, as 110,675 miles of road were added to the rail system.

To stimulate business along the spreading network, the railroads actively sought immigrants to colonize the western regions. The potential of the American West was advertised widely, not only in the United States, but in Europe as well. Many responded to the call, singly and in groups. One group responding to such colonization efforts, the Mennonites, brought with them the seeds of the now famous Turkey Red wheat. The area in which they settled came to be known as the breadbasket of the world.

In seeking passengers for their western routes, railroads also became early exponents of 'See America First'—and, in the process, played a major role in the establishment of national parks. Indeed, the importance of railroad support for national parks was well recognized by the preservationists of the late 1800s and early 1900s. Thus, railroads were among the pioneers in the environmental movement.

By 1916, the nation's rail system was at its peak, with 254,000 miles of road linking city to town and town to hamlet. As the economy shifted and more and more highways were built and as railroad technology improved and routing became more efficient, the system was gradually reduced to its present size. The freight of a still growing nation is now moved over a system nearly 170,000 miles in length.

## The Age of Regulation

The beginning of Reconstruction and the opening of the West put the railroad industry and the nation on a course that was ultimately to make the federal government a total regulator of the railroads. In the years after the Civil War, speculators with more interest in profits than transportation helped sour public opinion against those who were truly interested in providing sound rail service. The eagerness of developing areas to attract railroads tended to make entry into the field easier and gave access to those who, in more normal times, might not have been so readily accepted as business associates. Then, too, the general business climate of the day included practices that would now be far less acceptable.

This was the time when major industrial empires were being erected, built by men who set titanic goals for themselves and brooked no opposition in their drive to reach them. Some of these men were later to be dubbed 'robber barons.' Their activities no doubt produced many of the legal constraints imposed on their enterprises.

The promise of a new land and the unlimited markets which the railroad could provide attracted many farmers to the West. As farm prices began to decline—partly as a result of increased production brought on by the rapid settlement of the West—the farmers turned on railroads, charging that rates were so high little profit was left for the producer. They complained in particular that rates were higher where a railroad monopoly existed than between competitive points. The 'Granger laws' of the 1870s were the result. The National Grange of the Patrons of Hus-

James J Hill drives a golden spike at Bend, Oregon on 5 October 1911. Hill was called 'the empire builder' and was known for his savvy in turning financial crises into opportunities. In both the United States and Canada, his role in railroad expansion brought much growth to large undeveloped areas of North America.

The *General Sherman* (*right*), Union Pacific's first locomotive. A work train (*below*) rides on temporary tracks in downtown Auburn, California. During the time of Reconstruction, the 1887 Interstate Commerce Act attempted to regulate railroad practice without enforcement authority. It wasn't until the Transportation Act of 1920, however, that railroad activities were actually regulated.

bandry was formed in 1867, originally for social and educational purposes. Later, the Grange became interested in economic and political matters and, by 1875, there were 20,000 local granges with a membership of 800,000. The state of Illinois in 1871, followed by other states in later years, passed legislation regulating passenger fares and freight rates based on distance.

Hastily and emotionally drawn, these laws included provisions that were so drastic they could not be enforced. Meanwhile, the growth of the rail network and depressed business conditions growing out of the Panic of 1873 combined to change railroad pricing practices. Rate wars had already broken out and, as the railroads pursued their new philosophy of high volume at low unit cost, charges of discrimination among shippers and commodities as well as between shipping points grew louder.

By 1880, the focus of pressure for regulation had begun to shift to the national level. In 1885, a special Senate committee led by former Illinois Governor Shelby M Cullom recommended that an independent commission be formed to regulate the nation's railroads. The following year, the Supreme Court reversed itself and laid the legal foundation for such a commission by ruling that a state could not regulate rates on shipments passing beyond its own borders. On 4 February 1887, the Interstate Commerce Act was signed into law by President Grover Cleveland. The era of regulation had come.

The Act gave the Interstate Commerce Commission (ICC) responsibility for regulating the railroads with an eye toward eliminating some of the most criticized practices of the time, such as rebates to favored shippers and higher charges for noncompetitive hauls. The Commission, however, lacked any real enforcement authority. It was not until the Hepburn Act of 1906 that the tide of power turned in the Commission's favor. After the passage of the Transportation Act of 1920, the ICC's regulatory authority covered virtually every area of railroading.

At that time, the railroads still enjoyed a virtual monopoly of intercity freight transportation. Over the next 50 years, however, they saw modes of transportation that barely existed in 1920 develop into full-grown railroad competitors. By 1970, the railroads' share of traffic had dropped to 37 percent—with significant erosion of earnings—while their competitors reaped the profits of the remaining 63 percent.

—*Association of American Railroads*

# AMERICAN RAILROADS IN THE CIVIL WAR

The idea behind the building of railroads has been a peaceful one—the expansion of commerce and industry. But peaceful inventions find their place in violent times and, over the years, the railroads have shown their value to a nation at war—with itself and with others.

As the nation moved toward the Civil War, an 1860 railroad map would show that two-thirds of America's 30,000 miles of rail lay in the North. Just what sort of an advantage this gave the Union can be gleaned from the words of General Sherman, who noted that 'no army dependent on wagons can operate more than a hundred miles from its base, because the teams going and coming consume the contents of their wagons.'

Such knowledge was not lost on Lincoln's administration. After the president had appointed Herman Haupt, formerly general manager of the Pennsylvania Railroad, to run the railroads in occupied Virginia, Secretary of War Edwin M Stanton was forced to threaten with dismissal from the service any Union officer who interfered with railroad operations. Despite their displeasure at the thought, the officers would have to take orders from a railroad man whose expertise had brought him into the Army as a colonel.

Railroads north and south bustled during the US Civil War moving troops and supplies. The Union trains (*above*) were stored near the Capitol, visible in the background, to prevent their falling into rebel hands. The famous *General*

On 2 June 1861, 3000 Union troops were moved by two Baltimore & Ohio trains in an overnight pincers movement that captured Philippi, West Virginia, but narrowly missed destroying the Southern forces, who barely had time to flee when warned of the coming blow. It was the first military victory in which the railroads played a major role.

The Civil War was also the occasion for a daring raid that turned into an historic chase. In April 1862, two civilians and 18 Union soldiers, operating under cover in Big Shanty, Georgia, stole *The General,* a locomotive owned by the Western & Atlantic Railroad, and headed north. Their plan was to burn railroad bridges and thus cripple the Confederate supply link between Atlanta and the front at Chattanooga, Tennessee. The conductor of the train to which *The General* had been attached gave chase, along with the engineer and a W & A foreman—first on foot, then on a push car, and finally on commandeered locomotives. The dogged pursuit prevented the raiders from doing serious damage, and they finally abandoned *The General* just beyond Ringgold, Georgia.

(*below left*) was captured by the Union and then recaptured by the Confederates during the Civil War. It is exhibited today at Union Station in Chattanooga, Tennessee. Troops (*below right*) guard a trestle passing.

—*Association of American Railroads*

# CHAPTER 5

# THE VANDERBILTS: THE FIRST FAMILY OF EASTERN RAIL TYCOONS

## Fletcher Johnson and Allen Fowler

The way to wealth is as plain as the way to market. It depends chiefly on two words, industry and frugality; that is, waste neither time nor money, but make the best use of both. Without industry and frugality nothing will do, and with them everything.

—*Benjamin Franklin*

**V**anderbilt is a name which, in the late nineteenth-century United States, became almost synonymous with boundless wealth. This wealth was acquired, however, not by any lucky stroke of fortune, a fortunate deal at a gambling table, or the wholesale swindling so often gilded with the name of speculation, but by a combination of un-flagging industry and rare perception of the fitness of means to ends—usually commendable means and ends almost invariably for the welfare of the community. The family was of Dutch origin and first came to the United States early in the last century. For many years the family

home was on Staten Island, where its members pursued a hardy and laborious outdoor life. Strong wills, and clear perceptions were transmitted from generation to generation without impairment. The first famous Vanderbilt, named Cornelius, but best known as the Commodore, was the eldest son of an eldest son. His successor in the administration of the great fortune he amassed was also an eldest son, and in turn his eldest son became the foremost figure of the generation that welcomed the twentieth century.

Cornelius Vanderbilt was born on Staten Island in 1794, the son of a thriving farmer, who owned his farm, and carried his produce to the New York markets in his own sailboat. Cornelius was a sturdy lad, a leader in athletic feats on land and water, a daring rider and great lover of

Cornelius Vanderbilt (*above*). When he died in 1877, the Commodore's personal fortune was estimated to be more than $100 million. New York's Grand Central Depot (*left*) in 1883. The view is of the north end of the station from the rail yards near 46th street.

**Grand Central Station, crossroads of the world in the heart of New York City. Designed in 1899, Grand Central was to accommodate over a million passengers a month. This magnificent structure was the crowning jewel of the Vanderbilt empire begun by Cornelius Vanderbilt who led his family from farming to fortune.**

horses. He would not endure the restraints of a schoolroom, and so acquired his rudimentary education on the farm and on the bay. When he had earned enough money to buy a sailboat, he began business on his own account. When he was eighteen he had saved $500 of his own earnings, and a year later he was married to his second cousin, Sophia Johnson. He soon became the captain of a small steamboat running between New York and New Brunswick, New Jersey, and ultimately placed himself at the head of a considerable coasting trade. As a result of this change of business the family moved to New Brunswick and opened a hotel. By the year 1853 he was a wealthy owner of steamships and having built the ship *North Star* for the purpose, went with his family on a voyage to

Europe. A few years later he built the Staten Island Railroad and began withdrawing his money from steamships for railroad investments. In 1860 he bought the Harlem Railroad at below $7 a share, and a few years later he became its president when its shares were worth $30. In 1864 the same shares were worth $285. This was the foundation of the great Vanderbilt fortune. The consolidation of the New York Central and Hudson River roads followed, and the entire system became the property of Commodore Vanderbilt.

He began at once improving the property. Useless expenditures were stopped, waste was checked, improved depots were built, tracks were relaid, and business was encouraged and developed all along the line. When Commodore Vanderbilt died on 4 January 1877, he was one of the richest men in America, his fortune amounting to more than $100 million, almost entirely in railroads.

William H Vanderbilt, the Commodore's eldest son, was born at the New Brunswick hotel and was educated at the

Columbia grammar school in New York City. For a time he worked in a ship chandler's shop, and at the age of eighteen became clerk in a bank at $150 a year. When he was twenty years old, he married Miss Kissam, and the young couple went to live on East Broadway in New York City. After a time he became tired of city life and bought a 75-acre farm on Staten Island, intending to settle down to humble rural life. His father appears to have had at this time a contemptuous opinion of his abilities. The young farmer needed capital to improve his property, but the Commodore refused to advance it to him, thinking it would likely be wasted. So William borrowed $6000 from a friend and gave as security a mortgage on the farm. A few months later his father found it out.

'Is it true,' he asked, 'that you have mortgaged your farm for $6000?'

'Yes,' was the young man's reply.

'You don't amount to a row of pins!' thundered the old man, furiously. 'You never were worth your salt, and never will be. You'll never be able to do anything, except bring disgrace upon yourself and upon every one connected with you. I'm not going to have anything more to do with you. You can hoe your own row, and go to the devil as you please.'

It was in vain that the younger man tried to explain that the money was needed for improvements which would make the farm vastly more profitable than before. The enraged Commodore merely growled and grumbled and raged the more; but the next day he sent the young man a check for $6000, with the curt command to 'Pay off that mortgage, right off!' The young man happily disappointed his father's gloomy prophecies. In a few years he was the owner of 350 fertile acres, which yielded him an annual profit of $12,000. Still the Commodore distrusted him, and thought he never would rise above the rank of a successful farmer, although he had to confess that as a farmer he was uncommonly successful.

In 1853 father and son went on the 'North Star' voyage to Europe together. Walking the deck one day in mid-ocean, the Commodore noticed his son smoking a cigar.

'Bill,' said he, 'I'll give you $10,000 if you'll quit smoking.'

'I don't want your money,' replied the son, 'but if you say quit smoking, I'll do it,' and he threw his cigar overboard.

Later, the younger Vanderbilt became associated in the Staten Island Railroad. When his father allowed the railroad to become bankrupt, Bill was made its receiver and soon restored it to prosperity and became its president. This convinced the Commodore that Bill might amount to something after all. Soon after this a younger son, George Vanderbilt, died in Europe. He had been the Commodore's favorite child, and had been educated at West Point for a soldier; he was one of the most brilliant and physically powerful young men ever entered at that school, lifting with ease on one occasion a dead weight of 900 lb, but his health was ruined by his arduous services in the Civil War. Cornelius Vanderbilt, Jr, the second son of the Commodore, was leading a reckless life, and had become estranged from his father. The old gentleman therefore began to look upon William as his successor in the management of the great fortune he was building up. From month to month he trusted him more thoroughly.

In 1865 William H Vanderbilt became vice president of

William H 'Bill' Vanderbilt, eldest son of the Commodore and heir to the estate, was a major figure in American railroad history.

the Hudson River Railroad, and four years later held the same office over the consolidated Hudson River and New York Central system. On his father's death he succeeded to the presidency of this great railroad, and also of the Harlem Railroad and the Lake Shore & Michigan Southern Railroad. Under the Commodore's will, William H Vanderbilt received the bulk of the enormous estate. The will was disputed by other members of the family but was sustained by the courts. From that time until the fall of 1881 William H Vanderbilt's history was the history of American railroad enterprise. In that period of unusual railroad activity, he was sufficiently enterprising to place himself in the forefront. Among his other accomplishments, he acquired possession of the Canada Southern Railroad.

In 1877 during the great railroad strikes there were 12,000 men employed on the New York Central and Hudson River lines, and their wages had just been reduced 10 percent. Vanderbilt at once sent out word that $100,000 would be distributed as a gratuity among the men and the 10 percent restored to their wages as soon as increasing business justified such a step. The result was, while other railroad systems were paralyzed, that these lines worked without interruption and with fewer than 500 of the 12,000 men going on strike. From time to time William was forced to engage in rate wars with competing trunk lines. These he conducted vigorously and with invariable success and established the policy of protecting his lines and all their branches from the attacks of rivals. In November 1879, he sold a block of 250,000 shares of stock to a foreign syndicate. The transaction greatly increased public confidence in the stability of his roads and raised the price of all stocks in which he was interested. From the proceeds of this sale and other funds he purchased $53,000,000 of government bonds.

William K Vanderbilt (*left*) discusses the sport of kings (horse racing) with a kindred spirit in 1915. Grand Central in 1872 (*right*) as viewed from 42nd street and Park Avenue. This building was the predecessor to the later monument which became the glory of the Vanderbilt empire (*see page 82*).

Realizing the uncertainty of life and feeling his own health weakening, William then began putting his fortune into such a shape that it could readily be transfered to his heirs at his death. The sale of stock and purchase of government bonds was an important step in this direction. In 1881 he began transfering the active management of his railroads to his sons, Cornelius and William K. It was under the management of William K Vanderbilt that the Nickel Plate road, which had been built as a competing line, was purchased outright in 1883. In that year on 4 May, William H Vanderbilt finally surrendered the presidencies of all roads with which he had been identified. 'In my judgment,' he said, 'the time has arrived when I owe it as a duty to myself, to the corporations and to those around me upon whom the chief management will devolve, to retire from the presidency. I do not mean to sever my relations or abate the interest I have heretofore taken in these corporations. It is my purpose and aim that these several corporations shall remain upon such a basis for their harmonious working with each other and for the efficient management of each as will secure for the system both permanency and prosperity.' The next day William Vanderbilt, with his son George, and his uncle, Jacob H Vanderbilt, sailed for Europe. James H Rutter, long conspicuously identified with the roads, was elected president of the New York Central, and on his death was succeeded by Chauncey M Depew.

William H Vanderbilt died on 8 December 1885. He was one of 13 brothers and sisters, and to him had been born nine children, of whom only one died in early life. His eldest child, Cornelius Vanderbilt, succeeded to the chief management of the great railroad systems, although the second son, William K, was prominently identified with them in official capacities. The third son, Frederick W, was also deeply interested in some of the roads. The youngest, George W, devoted himself chiefly to a literary career, and became one of the most liberal and discriminating collectors of books in America. On his death Mr Vanderbilt divided the bulk of his fortune among his four sons, handsomely providing, however, for all other members of the family, and arranging for the bulk of the fortune to be kept intact as a family possession. His successors have faithfully followed out his plans and wishes in all respects.

When William H Vanderbilt was already worth millions he continued to live in a house which had been given to him by his father at Thirty-eighth Street and Fifth Avenue. From there he moved to a larger, yet still unpretentious, house on the same avenue. After his father's death, however, he determined to build what should be the finest private residence in the city. A block of ground was purchased at Fifth Avenue and Fifty-first Street, and the ablest artists and architects were instructed to spare no expense in designing and executing the great work. They were empowered to ransack the world to furnish the palace. On this ground two great houses of brownstone connected by

a wing were constructed; one for Mr Vanderbilt, and one for his two daughters, Mrs William Sloane and Mrs Elliot Shepard. Outwardly they closely resembled each other, but within differed widely in arrangement and furnishing. The one intended for Mr Vanderbilt himself cost without its priceless picture gallery more than $2,000,000. It represented a year-and-a-half's work of more than 600 men on the interior decorations alone. Sixty sculptors were brought from Europe on large salaries, and kept at work for more than a year. The great front doors of solid bronze were exact copies, reduced in size, of Ghiberti's famous bronze gates in Florence.

William Vanderbilt inherited his father's love for horses. One of his favorite recreations was to go on the road behind a team of swift trotters. He purchased the famous trotter, Maud S, for $20,000 as well as such horses as Aldine, Early Rose, Small Hopes, Lysander, Leander, and Charles Dickens. In 1877 he went to England to see the great Derby race, and said afterward that the sight of 300,000 persons watching a horse race was well worth a trip across the ocean. Whenever he visited Saratoga or Sharon Springs, or other watering places, he always took a number of his favorite horses with him. He built them a stable in New York, at Fifty-second Street and Madison Avenue that cost more than $60,000, exclusive of the land. Its walls within were finished in polished cherry, ash, and black walnut, and the metal work was largely sterling silver. His sons did not altogether inherit this taste, and generally preferred yachting. William K Vanderbilt spent much of his time cruising about the world in his steam yacht, 'Alva.'

The name of Vanderbilt has been pleasantly connected with many great deeds of benevolence. William H Vanderbilt gave vast sums every year for charitable purposes, but so quietly that few persons knew of it besides himself. His father had already given a great deal through the Rev Charles F Deems, a Methodist minister to whom in early life he became much attached. He had given Dr Deems a fine church in New York City and had endowed Vanderbilt University in Nashville, Tennessee with more than a million dollars. To the latter institution William H Vanderbilt also gave liberally, and continued to contribute through Dr Deems to many of his charities. He secured the transportation, at a cost of more than $100,000, of the famous obelisk known as Cleopatra's Needle, from Egypt to New York and had it set up in Central Park. It was formally presented to the city of New York on 22 February, 1881, with Secretary of State William M Evarts delivering the oration.

His four sons continued to practice the liberal generosity inaugurated by him, and were frequent givers to causes that promoted the welfare of the general public. The younger Cornelius Vanderbilt conspicuously identified himself with the work of the YMCA and was for years at the head of a branch of that institution existing among the employees of his railroads.

# CHAPTER 6

# COAL ROADS AND TRUNK LINES: THE EASTERN RAILROADS COME OF AGE

## Jules Bogen

The Transportation Act of 1920 ushered in a new era of railroading in the United States. The consolidation provision of the act encouraged mergers that were formerly opposed by the federal authorities and under the plans of the Interstate Commerce Commission, the anthracite railroads were to be absorbed by other carriers. The story of the growth of the anthracite railroads forms one of the most fascinating chapters in the economic history of the United States. Indeed, even in the 1980s, coal still constituted the single largest and most important commodity carried on America's railroads.

Five great railroad companies grew on the anthracite carrying trade, and three others secured a large part of their traffic from hard coal mines which they reached by branch lines. This valuable mineral resource of the northeastern part of Pennsylvania had a far-reaching effect upon transportation in the trunk-line region, and the wealth it brought its owners has in turn played an important part in the exploitation of other natural resources and in the development of the West. The existence of an enormous deposit of the most valuable type of coal in a relatively accessible location so near the Atlantic seaboard has played no small role in shaping the economic history of the United States.

**Baltimore & Ohio Railroad Engine No 7400 (*left*), a Baldwin-built articulated 2-6-6-2, well suited for the large heavy loads carried on the northeastern trunk lines. *Above*: A 4-6-4 of the Richmond, Fredericksburg & Potomac Railroad.**

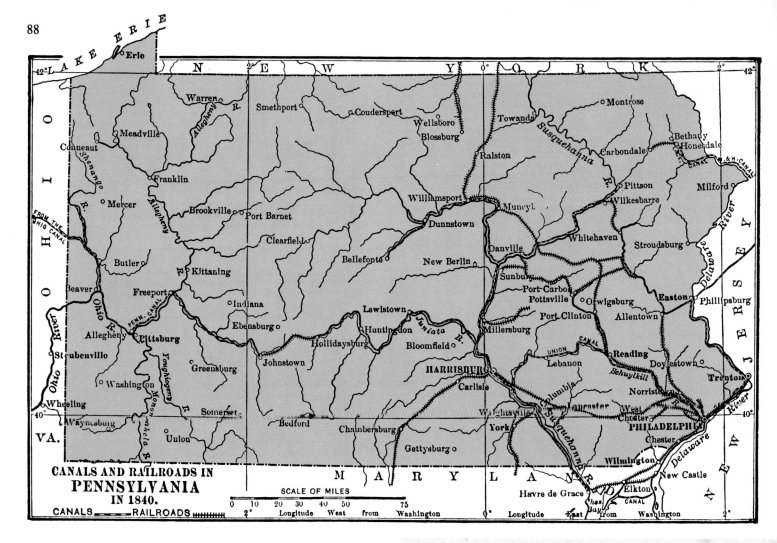

### CANALS AND RAILROADS IN
### PENNSYLVANIA
### IN 1840.

CANALS _____ RAILROADS ┼┼┼┼┼┼

SCALE OF MILES

0    10    20    30    40    50         75

Pennsylvania (*above*) was at the heart of early American railroad development because of its location between the coal fields and the major centers of industry. This wood-burning 2-4-0 (*right*), photographed in 1861, was the 1000th locomotive of the PRR fleet.

During the early years of railroad building, the canals formed the through routes, the railroad lines acting as feeders and covering the short distances from the mines to the canals along the rivers. Short mine railways had been known in England since the early nineteenth century, and the first gravity lines in northeastern Pennsylvania were not too different from the more primitive of these, though their methods of construction and operation were independently developed by American engineers. The first pioneer line was the 9-mile gravity road built to connect the Summit miners of the Lehigh Coal & Navigation Company with its canal at Mauch Chunk. The highly creditable financial showing of this gravity railroad demonstrated the feasibility of railroads as canal feeders, and resulted in the construction of several similar lines. In 1829, the Delaware & Hudson Canal Company opened its railroad from Honesdale to Carbondale, 16 miles long, joining its mines with its water route to the Hudson. This also was a gravity road, although its greater length necessitated more advanced methods of construction.

Railroad building in the anthracite region was also determined by a peculiar factor in the coal trade of the Schuylkill region. In the northern and middle coal fields, the canal companies combined transportation and mining privileges and wanted no outsiders to open competing mines. The Schuylkill Navigation Company, launched as a general traffic highway, had no mining powers, and so, under its charter, could not engage in the coal business. To make the largest returns from its natural transportation monopoly,

the canal company cut its tolls to stimulate private initiative to develop the coal lands it could not itself exploit. As a result, numerous mines were opened which had to be connected by short feeder railroads with the canal.

The largest and most progressive of the mine railroads was the Mine Hill & Schuylkill Haven Railroad Company, chartered in 1828, which was later absorbed, along with practically all the other feeder lines of Schuylkill County, in the Philadelphia & Reading system. By 1847, 315 miles of canals and 503 miles of railroad had been built in the anthracite regions, at a total cost of $29,970,000. All the railroads were feeders of the canal with the exception of the Philadelphia & Reading, which had been completed in 1842.

The Philadelphia & Reading, until 1861, was little more than a link in the transportation chain whereby coal was moved from the Schuylkill coal fields into Philadelphia.

## VANDERBILT, THE NEW YORK CENTRAL AND THE READING

In the 1880s William H Vanderbilt acquired a substantial interest in the company. The battle between the trunk lines was particularly keen at the moment, and the shrewd head of the New York Central saw the importance of the Reading as a means of bringing the Pennsylvania Railroad to terms, while also securing for the New York Central lines the coal and coke traffic in which it was weak. The

3,000,000 tons of anthracite which the Reading annually shipped to the West was desirable business for the Vanderbilt system.

With the aid of Vanderbilt, Reading President Franklin B Gowen again proceeded upon a program of expansion to strengthen his railroad's position in the anthracite traffic and acquire new sources and outlets for its business. He revived immediately the project first broached in 1879, on the eve of receivership, to lease the Central Railroad of New Jersey for 999 years.

The new traffic connections secured by cooperation with the Vanderbilts also involved a heavy financial burden. The plan developed by Gowen and Vanderbilt involved nothing less than the transformation of the Reading from a local coal road into a system of trunk-line proportions. There were four important elements in this program:

1. Construction of the Jersey Shore, Pine Creek & Buffalo from Williamsport (the northwestern terminus of the Philadelphia & Reading) to Stokesdale (the point from which Buffalo could be reached over the West Shore). The Reading would thus become a link in the shortest line to Chicago. It was to take a one-third interest in this line.

2. The Beech Creek, Clearfield & Southwestern Railroad was projected into the rich Clearfield bituminous coal region. A 900-year contract was executed with the Philadelphia & Reading whereby the Beech Creek's entire tonnage to the southeast was thrown on the Reading lines,

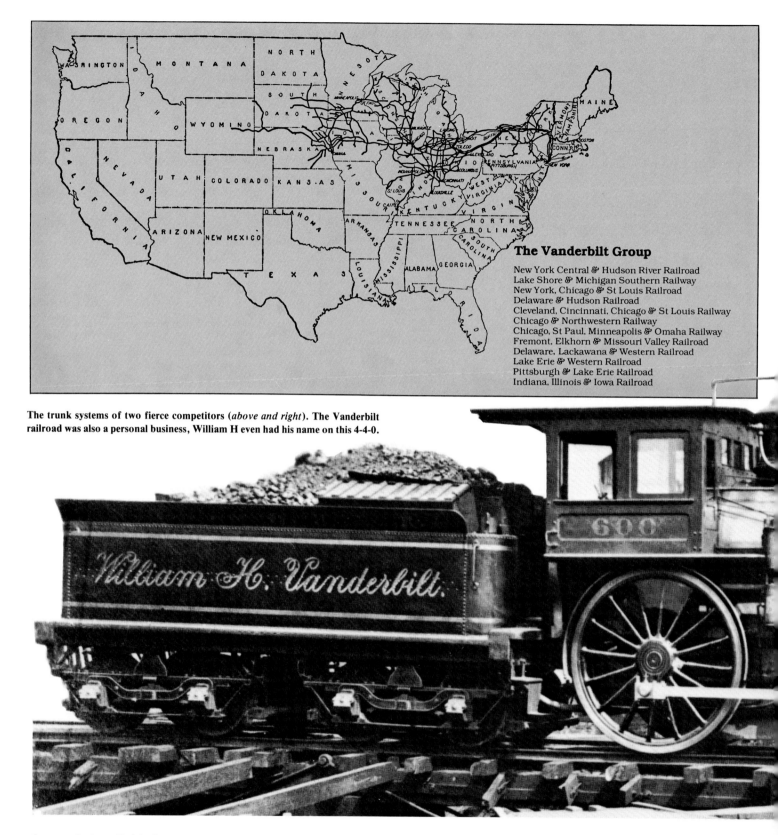

**The Vanderbilt Group**

New York Central & Hudson River Railroad
Lake Shore & Michigan Southern Railway
New York, Chicago & St Louis Railroad
Delaware & Hudson Railroad
Cleveland, Cincinnati, Chicago & St Louis Railway
Chicago & Northwestern Railway
Chicago, St Paul, Minneapolis & Omaha Railway
Fremont, Elkhorn & Missouri Valley Railroad
Delaware, Lackawana & Western Railroad
Lake Erie & Western Railroad
Pittsburgh & Lake Erie Railroad
Indiana, Illinois & Iowa Railroad

The trunk systems of two fierce competitors (*above and right*). The Vanderbilt railroad was also a personal business, William H even had his name on this 4-4-0.

charges being divided pro rata between the two roads. This opened up to the Reading an extensive soft-coal business to supplement its anthracite trade.

3. A syndicate headed by Vanderbilt was formed to build a new line from the Reading at Harrisburg to Pittsburgh, to be known as the South Pennsylvania Railroad Company. By holding out the promise of lower rates, aid for the project was obtained from Andrew Carnegie and other leading Pittsburgh industrialists, who charged the Pennsylvania with monopolistic practices. From Pittsburgh the new line was to reach the West over the Pittsburgh & Lake Erie, which the Vanderbilts had acquired in

1882. This railroad was to constitute virtually a western extension for the Reading.

4. The Baltimore & Ohio, then also engaged in a struggle with the Pennsylvania Railroad, was building a line from Baltimore to Philadelphia, and negotiated a traffic agreement whereby the Philadelphia & Reading's Bound Brook route to New York was to constitute its outlet to the metropolis. The Schuylkill River East Side Railway was jointly built to connect the two systems in Philadelphia.

Construction of these new lines was begun immediately. The immediate effects on the Reading were unfortunate.

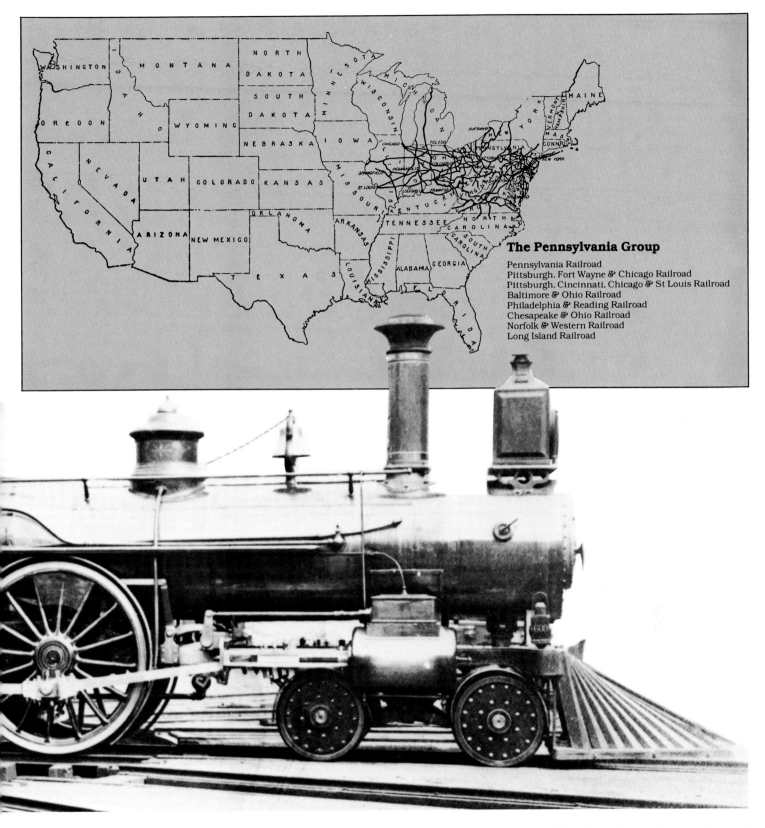

**The Pennsylvania Group**

Pennsylvania Railroad
Pittsburgh, Fort Wayne & Chicago Railroad
Pittsburgh, Cincinnati, Chicago & St Louis Railroad
Baltimore & Ohio Railroad
Philadelphia & Reading Railroad
Chesapeake & Ohio Railroad
Norfolk & Western Railroad
Long Island Railroad

The new work further depleted its weak treasury, and forced it to incur new floating liabilities to carry out its part of the scheme, while receiving little immediate returns. Furthermore, this aggressive stand only stimulated the Pennsylvania Railroad to follow a policy of reprisals by paralleling several of the chief Reading lines, which proved quite embarrassing to the latter. In May 1884, the Pennsylvania started the Pennsylvania Schuylkill Valley Railway, giving the main line of the Reading parallel competition for the first time. In order to retain its full coal traffic, the Reading was compelled to purchase additional coal lands on the route of the new Pennsylvania line. At the end of 1883, Gowen escaped from this precarious situation by resigning, after recommending that the surplus earnings of the year be paid out as a dividend. One of his last acts was the purchase of the Philadelphia & Atlantic City Railway, giving a direct line to the Jersey coast, but involving the obligation to spend a large sum for the reconstruction of its narrow-gauge line, which had the doubtful distinction of being the fastest example of railroad construction on record, the entire line having been built in three months' time.

The Reading's floating debt became unmanageable during the monetary stringency of 1884, and for the second time a receiver was appointed on 2 June of that year, scarcely three weeks after the formal discharge by the courts of the old receivership of 1880–82. Soon thereafter interest on the junior bonds and lease payments to the Central Railroad of New Jersey ceased, throwing the latter into a new receivership. At the same time, the animosity between the trunk lines ended, and the building of the South Pennsylvania Railroad, on which Gowen had placed such high hopes, was halted by an agreement between the Vanderbilts and the Pennsylvania Railroad. William H Vanderbilt, who was holding the 50,000 shares of Jersey Central bought on margin for the Philadelphia & Reading, threw the stock on the market for what it would fetch, placing the burden of the loss, amounting to $1,163,409, on the Reading. The natural assumption was that 'he must have lost some of the interest he manifested in the company . . . when he advanced $3.5 million on the Jersey Central stock.'

## J P MORGAN STILLS THE
## READING-PENNSYLVANIA FEUD

A drastic cutting of fixed charges was immediately necessary to restore the vast Reading property to financial health. At first foreclosure suits were started, but fears of losing control of the coal properties brought about a reorganization under the old charter. In 1887 J P Morgan formed a strong syndicate, with a subscription of $15 million in cash, and by adopting his usual method of ending the expensive competition, he made peace between the Reading and the Pennsylvania and provided for cooperation with other anthracite lines in limiting production and maintaining prices. The burdensome lease of the Jersey Central was happily ended by a suit of minority stockholders of that road, who claimed they had not been consulted when the lease was made, and separate receivers were appointed for it.

Thus ended the first important effort of the Reading to establish itself as a strong, independent, fully rounded railroad property. Only a small part of the program advanced by President Gowen in 1883 had been consummated. Connections to the west and north, and to the south with the Baltimore & Ohio, had in fact been established. The Reading had, as a result, become an important terminal road, carrying grain and other products to Philadelphia for the New York Central, Erie, Lehigh Valley and Lackawanna. On the other hand, the direct line to Pittsburgh and the west had been abandoned, and the position of the company in the anthracite trade, after the loss of the Jersey Central, was unchanged. Peace with the Pennsylvania was obtained by an agreement by which the Reading was to turn over to the former's new Schuylkill Valley line 1 million tons of anthracite annually for a period of 10 years. A voting trust, headed by J P Morgan, was formed to give the bankers control for five years. The second Reading receivership terminated on 1 January 1888.

The most important result of the reorganization was the passing of control of the company to a group of bankers, headed by J P Morgan, who were then chiefly interested in

bringing about harmony among other carriers in trunk-line territories. The new president of the company was a New York banker, Austin Corbin. This conservative policy was criticized as weak and was particularly irksome to the Gowen contingent, who argued that the Reading was strong enough to play a lone hand and act as the aggressor, rather than the dependent, in railroad strategy. A group of financiers, including Gowen, decided to buy up control of the railroad in the open market and use it as the nucleus for an eventual combination of all the anthracite railroad companies into a gigantic monopoly.

A beginning towards closer control and harmony of the anthracite roads had already been made under Corbin's administration and was the cornerstone of J P Morgan's policy. The real difference in the plans of men like Morgan and Corbin and those of the syndicate was in the financial methods and the deliberateness with which the project was to be carried out.

## A A McLEOD'S HOUR IN THE SUN

Five months after his elevation to the presidency in November 1890, A A McLeod began the vigorous expansion policy of the syndicate. He organized the Port Reading Railroad Company to acquire extensive terminal property near Perth Amboy, New Jersey, and build a 20-mile line from Bound Brook, giving the Reading direct access to New York harbor for the first time. The construc-

tion of a new terminal nearer the center of Philadelphia, approved by the City Council 26 December 1890, involved a heavy capital expenditure which was met by the issue of $8.5 million in new bonds. McLeod next proceeded to improve the company's western connections. He developed a new route from Harrisburg to Pittsburgh to take the place of the defunct South Pennsylvania line, by buying a railroad to Shippensburg and making a tripartite agreement with the Western Maryland and the Baltimore & Ohio to reach the great iron and steel center.

McLeod then announced his plans to secure control of virtually the entire business of mining and transporting anthracite coal, as well as additional outlets for the sale of this commodity. On 11 February, he announced the lease of the Lehigh Valley Railroad for 999 years from 1 December, 1891. The next day, he leased the Central Railroad of New Jersey and, to avoid a New Jersey law forbidding the leasing of a domestic to a foreign corporation, made the recently formed Port Reading Railroad the formal lessee and had the Reading guarantee the contract. Private parties acquired for the Reading a controlling interest in the Lackawanna. Through these transactions, the Reading secured control of 72 percent of the coal output of the anthracite region, based on 1891 figures. Up to this point, McLeod appeared to have had the passive approval of the road's bankers, including J P Morgan and Anthony J Drexel, but later ventures were undertaken in the face of opposition from these interests.

New England was a leading market for anthracite, and

At its peak, the Pennsylvania Railroad was the largest in the United States in terms of revenue and tonnage. Incorporated in 1846 for service between Harrisburg and Altoona, the PRR eventually expanded to Chicago, St Louis, New York and Washington DC (see the trunk map on page 91). A vigorous competitor of the New York Central, the PRR built tunnels under the Hudson River to gain access to New York City and erected the Pennsylvania Station as a response to the NYC Grand Central. The PRR introduced the first high-speed electric traction system which could be used on any steam rail line in the United States. This electric traction was first used on the Burlington and Mount Holly branch of the Amboy division of the PRR. In June of 1885 motor coach No 1 (below) and passenger coach No 281 made the first experimental trip. Regular passenger service was inaugurated in July of that year.

McLeod decided on the fantastic scheme of taking over several railroads in the region to control the fuel movement. He first acquired a controlling interest in the Poughkeepsie Bridge Company and the Central New England & Western, and reorganized them as the Philadelphia, Reading & New England, which permitted Reading trains to run on its own trackage into Hartford and other New England points. The next step was the purchase of a controlling stock interest in the Boston & Maine on margin, through F H Prince & Company of Boston, by the interests then in control of the Reading. At first, 15,000 shares of Boston & Maine stock was purchased with the intention of later leasing the company, but it was decided instead to cement control by absolute stock ownership and 9034 additional shares were acquired in the open market.

Having secured a practical monopoly of the anthracite coal business, and extensive lines for distributing the coal to the east, north and west, the indefatigable McLeod turned to the bituminous coal fields to secure additional traffic for his railroads. He contracted in May 1892, with the Buffalo, Rochester & Pittsburgh and the New York Central & Hudson River Railroad, as lessee of the Beach Creek line, to make the Reading the sole carrier of the large soft-coal tonnage of the former destined for points in the east and south. McLeod's effort at a monopoly was harrassed from every side. The public press and political leaders raised a loud outcry against it, and the authorities in Pennsylvania and New Jersey sought to break the leases of the Lehigh Valley and Central of New Jersey.

While McLeod's rapidly built structure was thus crumbling like a house of cards because of legal difficulties, financial troubles made short shrift of the rest. The Reading's holdings of Boston & Maine and New York & New England stocks were sold by the brokers and bankers holding them at a loss of $1,472,004. The two Reading companies had a floating debt of $10 million, and the severe winter of 1893 made business so unprofitable that a deficit after interest of $1,401,805 was shown for both in the first quarter alone, while the Lehigh Valley failed to earn its lease rental by $616,351. These losses hastened the collapse of the combination, already practically insured by the withdrawal of the Jersey Central and the appointment of receivers. McLeod resigned and was succeeded by Joseph S Harris, head of the Lehigh Coal & Navigation Company,

A group of railroads forming a route from Portsmouth, Virginia to Atlanta, Georgia had come to be called the Seaboard Air Line Railway. The system expanded through acquisition of the Florida Central & Peninsular Railroad. In 1967 Seaboard merged with the Atlantic Coast Line (formerly part of JP Morgan's Empire) and became the Seaboard Coast Line. Included in the merger was the Louisville & Nashville Railroad. Seaboard is a leading transporter of fruits and vegetables from central Florida to the Northeast. Much of this produce is carried on the famed Orange Blossom Special, an integrated road-rail-road service. Locomotive No 249 was the Orange Blossom Special of 1935. Seaboard and the Chessie System merged in 1982 to become the CSX Corporation.

an executive of known ability and conservatism. In August, the Lehigh Valley lease was abrogated with the permission of the court, and the Philadelphia, Reading & New England lease was given up at the same time.

The long receivership that followed, from 1893 to 1897, put the Reading back upon the policy of conservative intensive development from which McLeod had forcibly diverted it in 1890. Once again J P Morgan was given the leading hand in reorganization. The company gave up its old charter and a new corporation, the Reading Company, was formed to own all the stock of the Philadelphia & Reading Railway Company and the Philadelphia & Reading Coal & Iron Company, as well as securities of constituent railroads, equipment and real estate not used for railroad purposes. A new voting trust of all stock of the company was formed, with J P Morgan, F P Olcott and C S W Packard as trustees.

The Reading rapidly recovered under its new management, but control was definitely placed in 1904, when the question once again became acute with the dissolution of the voting trust following the payment of dividends on the first preferred stock for two consecutive years. Action was hastened also by the desire to prevent Jay Gould, then building up his transcontinental system, from getting the road. Large purchases of Reading stock had been made in the open market early in 1902, in the interest of the Pennsylvania Railroad, and turned over to the Baltimore & Ohio, which it controlled. In January, 1903, President Loree of the latter announced that control of the Reading had been bought at a cost of $50 million for 1,213,300 shares. One-half of this was then turned over to the Vanderbilts for the consideration of a short-term note of $25 million, the stock being lodged in the treasury of the West Shore. It was planned to pool the Reading holdings of these two interests with shares of the Lehigh Valley and other anthracite lines in a jointly controlled holding company, but this plan was discarded with the adverse decision in the Northern Securities case, and the West Shore and Baltimore & Ohio each retained a 40 percent interest in the Reading, while the balance of power was held by the Widener interests of Philadelphia. The control of the Reading was definitely 'taken out of the street' for the first time in its history. The Reading was now firmly under trunk-line control.

# THE DELAWARE, LACKAWANNA &
# WESTERN RAILROAD COMPANY

While the Schuylkill coal field was situated in a region which was comparatively populous when the Reading Railroad was built, the northern coal region, in the Lackawanna and Wyoming valleys, was little more than a wilderness early in the nineteenth century. This area had suffered severely during the Revolution from Indian massacres, and at the end of the war it was largely deserted. A railroad from the Lackawanna valley to the east had been proposed from time to time over the years. In 1846 Seldon Scranton, the Pennsylvania coal man, was approached by New York interests then engaged in completing the New York & Erie Railroad about a contract for 'T' rails to complete the Delaware division of the Erie in time to get a $3 million donation from the state. It was necessary to get the rails quickly, without the customary waiting for shipments from England. After the completion of the Erie contract, Scranton expanded his activities rapidly. He built three additional blast furnaces within the following decade and bought up about 7000 acres of coal and timber lands. Scranton and his allies, now the dominant interest in the Lackawanna region, needed improved means of transportation to market. The building of the Erie made them look to the North for the easiest route, and in 1847 they purchased the charter of the old Ligetts' Gap line, which had been kept alive by renewals. Work on the northern Ligetts' Gap line, involving almost a continuous descent from Scranton to Great Bend, was begun in the spring of 1851 under the supervision of Colonel George W Scranton. The line was opened on 20 October of the same year, and George W Scranton became general agent for the line. Additional stock and $900,000 of mortgage bonds were sold to the original subscribers to equip the railroad.

The northern division, the name of which was changed to the Lackawanna & Western Rail Road Company in 1851, was consolidated with the Delaware & Cobb's Gap Rail Road Company in 1853 to facilitate financing. The combined company was called the Delaware, Lackawanna & Western Railroad Company. The enabling act permitted the payment of interest at six percent on stock subscriptions until the completion of construction, the amount being charged to cost of construction. This gave a better market to the stock although inflating book accounts. The capital stock was then $1.4 million and $1.5 million additional was sold immediately to complete the southern division to the Delaware Water Gap. A first mortgage on this division of $1.5 million was placed in 1855, and 20-year, seven percent convertible bonds were sold under it. The next year, a second mortgage issue of $2.6 million was sold.

The southern division was opened for traffic in May 1856. The entire line was broad, six-foot gauge. This gauge, it was believed, gave a greater capacity to the equipment, and so reduced the cost of operation. Having ample financial support, the Lackawanna directors proceeded systematically to give it a strong strategic position through adequate traffic connections to the tidewater and interior markets, especially to New York. A connecting link to reach the Central Railroad of New Jersey was incorporated in 1851 as the Warren Railroad.

During the first five years of operation, the coal traffic accounted for more than two-thirds of the total freight business. The coal department showed a consistent profit but failed to increase its earnings with the growth in volume of business. The operating ratio was approximately 50 percent. Shortly after its opening, the Lackawanna passed through the one dark period in its history and its one involuntary default. The direct cause was the lack, brought on by excess construction expenses, of working capital with which to tide over the panic of 1857. The Lackawanna rapidly increased its earning power after the panic of 1857, and in 1860 paid a dividend of 18 percent in stock scrip to make up for the suspension of dividends during the three previous years. Railroad earnings alone in 1859 amounted to $1,062,436. The company adopted a policy of secrecy regarding its earnings after 1857. It did not report income from coal mining at all for fear that competitors would utilize the information to their advantage and because it was unwilling to publicize the large profits secured by the company from the coal business.

The Civil War resulted in great prosperity for the Lackawanna, as for the other anthracite mining and transportation companies. In 1864, with the tremendous profits accruing from wartime prices for coal, earnings were large enough to justify a payment of 15 percent in cash and 70 percent in stock. This great prosperity radically changed the financial structure of the company.

The great profits realized in the anthracite trade during and after the Civil War stimulated a demand for coal lands which was intensified by the efforts of the competing railroad companies to secure control of an adequate reserve for future transportation. About 1865 the Central Railroad of New Jersey and the Delaware & Hudson began to aggressively buy privately owned coal lands in the northern coal field, which the Lackawanna served. As a measure of self-defense, the Lackawanna was compelled to build up immediately a larger coal estate to safeguard its chief source of traffic.

# JAY GOULD AND
# THE LACKAWANNA

By the late 1870s, Jay Gould, the notorious financier, owned a group of western railroads whose eastern terminus was the Wabash at Buffalo. Gould also then virtually controlled the Central Railroad of New Jersey. This latter line, however, proved of little aid in giving him a through outlet to the Atlantic coast, and so he sought a road which would carry the Wabash business to New York. The Lackawanna, although it got no nearer Buffalo than Binghamton, seemed the most likely property, and he accumulated a substantial interest in it. By 1880, the road was commonly referred to on Wall Street as a Gould property, and in 1881 and 1882 he was on the board of directors. It would be incorrect, however, to suppose that Gould had more than a small interest in the line. The dominant stockholder in the company until his death in 1882 was Moses Taylor, veteran president of the National City Bank. His son-in-law, Percy Pine, was vice president, and other capitalists in the National City Bank group made up the bulk of the board.

Gould succeeded, however, in getting the cooperation of the National City Bank interests in a joint venture to build a line from Binghamton to Buffalo, in order to fill the gap. In August 1880, a charter was taken out for the New York, Lackawanna & Western Railroad. The project was carried out through the Central Construction Company, which was to be paid in mortgage bonds and capital stock of the new road. The initial $2 million of the capital stock of the construction company was taken for the most part by directors of the Lackawanna. Its contract was considered so valuable that construction company shares were quoted at a premium of 26 percent soon after issuance. The road was completed over the entire 207 miles from Binghamton to Buffalo within two years at a real cost of $12 million but it was turned over to the railroad at a book value of $22 million, its capitalization being $12 million in six percent first mortgage bonds and $10 million in stock. These securities were distributed to stockholders of the Central Construction Company, who realized a handsome profit.

Shortly after its completion, the line was leased by the Delaware, Lackawanna & Western, as the financial weakness of the Wabash, then near receivership, prevented it from assuming any further financial obligations. The lease established the Lackawanna as a through line from New York to Buffalo, but minority stockholders protested loudly at the cost. The $10 million of capital stock, upon which five percent was guaranteed, represented the profit to construction company stockholders, and, together with the premium at which their mortgage bonds sold, gave them a profit of nearly 100 percent. The minority stockholders claimed they should have been given a prior right to subscribe to the construction company securities. They failed to uphold their contention by legal action, however.

In entering the competition for trunk-line business after the Buffalo line was completed, the railroad had a difficult struggle. The trunk-line pool was then functioning under the leadership of Commissioner Albert Fink. The Lackawanna had a very small general freight tonnage and preferred to compete openly for a time in an effort to secure a better bargaining position for the road later in entering the pool. He made an alliance with the Grand Trunk whereby the latter got its full proportion of through rates to the West, even though the rate quoted on the Lackawanna was reduced. Wholesale cutting of rates was accomplished by reducing the classification of a long list of commodities. As the coal business gave the Lackawanna a good basis for

Jay Gould (*above*) was born in 1835. Once a blacksmith's helper, Gould went on to become one of the nineteenth century's greatest rail barons. In 1867 he obtained a seat on the board of the Erie Railroad. A year later he went head to head with the Vanderbilts over control of the Erie and won. He was finally ousted from the Erie board in 1872, but gained control of the Union Pacific two years later. He later controlled the *New York World* newspaper and the Western Union Telegraph Company, along with the railroads shown below, which constituted the core of his empire at the time of his death in 1892.

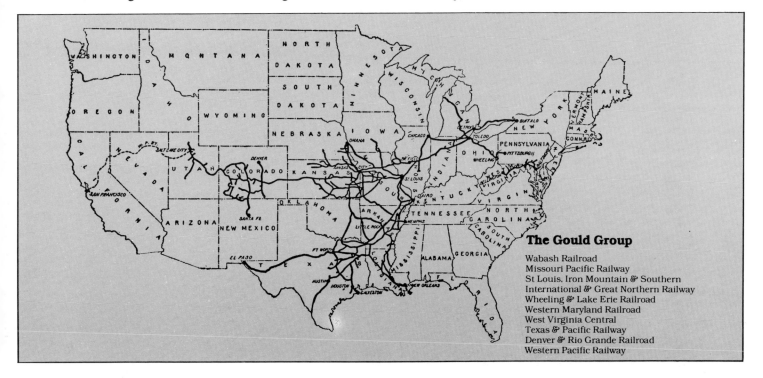

## The Gould Group

Wabash Railroad
Missouri Pacific Railway
St Louis, Iron Mountain & Southern
International & Great Northern Railway
Wheeling & Lake Erie Railroad
Western Maryland Railroad
West Virginia Central
Texas & Pacific Railway
Denver & Rio Grande Railroad
Western Pacific Railway

At its peak, the Atlantic Coast Line extended from Richmond, Virginia to Florida and as far east as Alabama. ACL's history is one of growth through acquisition and merger. The system began in 1833 as the Petersburg Railroad which operated between Petersburg, Virginia and Weldon, North Carolina. In the early 1900s ACL acquired several small lines in Virginia, North Carolina and South Carolina to extend its route system from Richmond, Virginia to Charleston, South Carolina. In 1902 a combined rail-steamship line was acquired and, at the same time, control of the Louisville and Nashville RR obtained thereby extending ACL to Florida, Georgia and Alabama. In 1967 ACL merged with Chessie to become part of the Seaboard System Railroad. These locomotives, 4-8-4 No 1800 and (overleaf) 4-6-2 No 2006 were built by Matthias Baldwin for ACL.

profitable operation in any case, it could carry this struggle to the limit without endangering its solvency, while threatening the very existence of the trunk-line pool.

The trunk-line situation was further complicated by the competition of the New York, West Shore & Buffalo, which had been competed at the same time as a competitor of the New York Central from New York to Buffalo. For a time, there seemed to be the danger of a disruption of trunk-line harmony, but through the persuasion of Commissioner Fink the Lackawanna was finally induced to enter the pool in 1884—at the same time that the West Shore announced bankruptcy. It was allocated 12.6 percent of the west-bound business. From that time, the Lackawanna built up a stable traffic with the West, interchanging chiefly with the Grand Trunk and Wabash. The coal traffic remained the major reliance of the road.

In 1892, when President McLeod of the Reading was carrying on his spectacular effort to combine practically all the anthracite and northern New England systems into a single monopoly, the Reading interests acquired a substantial block of stock of the Lackawanna. The early collapse of his plans, however, again left the system independent under Rockefeller-National City Bank control. Signs of Vanderbilt-Morgan interest in the property, however, began to appear shortly afterwards, probably as an aftermath of McLeod's stock purchases. In 1893, Vanderbilt bought 40,000 additional shares which, added to the 40,000 he already owned, gave him a 15 percent interest. The New Jersey Central held 50,000 shares, and was represented on the board by three directors. The Vanderbilt representation assured the operation of the property in harmony both with the anthracite coal understanding brought about through the Temple Iron Company and the trunk line community of interest. It gave the New York Central a voice in the control of every New York state railroad except the Erie, which was held by the allied Morgan banking group.

An unusual type of locomotive was the Camel class first built by Ross Winans in 1848. The name Camel stemmed from the cab being located atop the boiler. These were powerful locomotives designed to pull heavy, coal-laden trains through difficult mountain terrain. This Lehigh Valley 4-6-2 locomotive No 2006 was of the Camel class and probably carried anthracite coal from Mauch Chunk to Easton, Pennsylvania.

## THE LEHIGH VALLEY RAILROAD

Construction began in 1853, under a contract made with Asa Packer on 27 November 1852. Packer was to build the entire line, receiving payment in stocks and bonds of the road. When the road was partially complete, he used the securities already received to borrow $200,000 from Commodore Stockton, head of the Camden & Amboy Railroad, on condition that the latter enterprise be given representation on the Lehigh Valley board.

The name of the company officially became the Lehigh Valley Railroad Company on 7 January 1853. Work progressed steadily, and, with the aid of funds received from the Camden & Amboy and the Jersey Central, Packer completed the road from Easton to Mauch Chunk on 12 September 1855. However, construction costs had absorbed all available cash resources, and he had yet to build up a coal tonnage large enough to justify further invest-

ment. He decided to stay within his resources in getting the railroad in operation. Rolling stock for the coal trade was leased from the Central Railroad of New Jersey. A contract was made with the prosperous Beaver Meadow Company to furnish its own cars for coal, and a similar contract was made with Packer's own company, Packer, Carter & Company, an important miner and shipper of anthracite.

The Lehigh Valley, unlike the other anthracite railroads, was largely a one-man concern. Asa Packer, although he did not assume the presidency until 1862 (and then only temporarily), held a controlling stock interest and often merged his personal activities with the operation of the road. His relation to it was similar to that of the Vanderbilts with the New York Central. Even before the completion of the Lehigh Valley, he planned a railroad network which would cover the whole Lehigh region and feed a growing volume of coal traffic to the Lehigh Valley.

The prosperity brought on by the Civil War stimulated

the comprehensive expansion program on the Lehigh Valley. In July 1862, the Penn Haven & White Haven was put under contract. As the Civil War brought large profits to the Lehigh Coal & Navigation Company also, it was decided in 1864 to build a railroad to Easton paralleling the Lehigh Valley all the way along its course. Asa Packer made a personal effort to avoid an open war between the two companies by offering to prorate traffic between them. When this effort failed, he openly consolidated his system and boldly met the competition of the Navigation Company.

The railroad steadily increased its traffic and earning power. By 1863, its coal tonnage for the first time had passed the million-ton mark. In 1866, with the merger of the Beaver Meadow and Lehigh & Mahanoy companies, it reached 2,037,714 tons. In 1863, the general merchandise tonnage had amounted to 447,848 tons. By 1867, it had reached 1,050,442 tons. Gross earnings kept pace with the increase in traffic, and net earnings rose from $448,502 in 1862 to $1,391,274 in 1864 and $1,963,010 in 1866.

Asa Packer died in 1879. He held at his death 25 percent of the capital stock of the company in which he had been the dominating figure since 1852. Having a personal fortune of some $17 million, he had used it freely to advance the interests of the railroad which he had sponsored. His will sought to perpetuate the independent operation of the company. He provided that his Lehigh Valley holdings be held intact and directed the trustees to subscribe to new stock to which they were entitled whenever additional shares were offered, thus maintaining his proportionate interest in the company.

During the decade following the death of Asa Packer, the Lehigh Valley expanded its operations but little. This period was chiefly noted for consolidating the gains already made and for preparations made to facilitate further future expansion.

In 1889, the final link to New York harbor was constructed, a line being built to Newark and then over Newark Bay to join the National Docks Railway, in which the Lehigh Valley had bought a half-interest at Jersey City. The whole of the extension to New York Harbor was reincorporated in 1891 as the Lehigh Valley Terminal Railway Company, and a $10 million mortgage was placed on the property and the bonds sold to help defray the cost.

The financial position of the Lehigh Valley was complicated by the lease of the company in 1892 to the Reading. The Lehigh Valley had been paying five percent dividends since 1888, but only a small margin remained after this payment; in 1891 only $266,231. At the same time, the company was finding it increasingly difficult to finance additional improvements. Therefore, when President A A McLeod offered to lease the road for a guarantee of five percent for the first six months, six percent for the second six months, and seven percent thereafter with one-half of surplus earnings up to a maximum rental of 10 percent, the directors quickly accepted and signed the lease on February 11. The Lehigh Valley Coal Company was not included in the lease, so that its larger earnings could be expected. The effects of McLeod's reckless program were disastrous. Although the Pennsylvania courts upheld the lease, the Reading could not meet the rental requirements. The Lehigh Valley earnings fell off, and within six months the Reading had to advance $1,412,420 on account of deficiencies. After some efforts to modify its terms, the arrangement was abandoned and the Lehigh Valley returned to its owners.

Coal fueled the fires that refined the ore which built American industry. Trains played the pivotal role of supplier of those raw materials. As industry grew, the demand for coal and ore increased and the railroads expanded accordingly. The steel of which rails and locomotives were made came from the materials which trains carried. This Camel 4-4-0 No 196 (*above*) of the P&RR carried coal from the Schuylkill coal fields to Philadelphia. The DM&IR 2-8-8-4 steam locomotive No 231 (*below*) carried iron ore from northeastern Minnesota mines to ports on Lake Superior.

Chicago & Northwestern 4-6-0 steam locomotive No 1385 passing some automobiles of the 1920s era. Trains and cars such as these were the transportation which shortened distance in a great nation. This wonderful old train was restored by the Mid-continent Railway Museum at North Freedom, Wisconsin. The train is operated on the museum's four-and-one-half-mile track and system-wide over the C&NW.

## THE HAND OF J P MORGAN

**O**n 18 February 1895 Lehigh Valley dropped to 20⅛ per share. The forcing out of the Packer stock would have been a severe blow to the company, and would have endangered the recovery and stabilization of the anthracite industry which J P Morgan was trying to work out following his reorganization of the Reading and Erie roads.

Morgan stepped in at this point to relieve the situation. Through Drexel & Company he arranged to fund for a period of years all the indebtedness of the Packer estate, thus removing the 'Packer paper,' then amounting to $2.7 million, from the market. In return, the voting power on this stock was to be exercised by J P Morgan & Company, and an option was to be given the latter to buy 37,500 shares at $25 and 37,500 shares at $27.50. The Morgan interests also were to have the option of bidding first on the 75,000 remaining shares of this stock should the trustees decide to sell them also.

The advent of Morgan control was followed by a radical change in policy. Applying here the same methods of liberal physical rehabilitation and intensive development of facilities which they applied to the Reading, the new controlling interests made a remarkable transformation of the property. Elisha P Wilbur resigned the presidency and was succeeded by Alfred Walter. The executive offices of the company were removed to New York, representing the end of control by independent Philadelphia capital.

The results of President Walter's policy were immediate and substantial. The average trainload had been 383.87 tons in 1898; it had been increased to 466.83 tons in 1902, a figure better than that of the New York Central. The volume of traffic was simultaneously increased by the better facilities offered and the prosperity of the country. The anthracite traffic was supplemented by a growing volume of soft coal, as well as by the rapidly expanding Lehigh cement industry. In 1895, 318,062 tons of cement, brick and lime had been carried. In 1901, this total rose to 1,018,926. Grain and flour moved rose from 1,277,861 tons in 1895 to 2,411,321 tons in 1901. Pig iron and ores moved rose from 435,320 tons to 756,921 tons.

As a result of new accounting methods, the report of 1903 showed a surplus of 8.1 percent earned on the capital stock. It was then decided to open the way for future bond financing. The six subsidiaries in New York were merged into the Lehigh Valley Rail Way Company and the six in New Jersey into the Lehigh Valley Railroad Company of New Jersey. In 1904, with continued improvement in earnings, dividends were restored after a lapse of 11 years. Greater efficiency, combined with the growing volume of traffic and the higher freight rates resulting from the permanent harmony established by J P Morgan in eastern

**Pennsylvania Railroad 2-8-2 steam locomotive No 2861. This big locomotive was designed and built by the Baldwin Ironworks of Philadelphia.**

territory, caused a growing balance of earnings for the common stock and the sky-rocketing of market quotations for the shares.

## TRUNK-LINE CONTROL

During the early period of rehabilitation, the controlling interest in the Lehigh Valley had been held by J P Morgan & Company, who had substantially increased their original investment, taken over from the Packer estate, by open market purchase. It was originally intended that Lehigh Valley holdings be combined with the controlling interest in the Reading owned by the Lake Shore and Baltimore & Ohio, along with other securities, in a holding company to be jointly owned by the Vanderbilts and the Pennsylvania Railroad. This plan was given up, and instead various lines continued to hold their Lehigh Valley stock, thus insuring the operation of the property in harmony with the other roads in its territory. After 1907, in response to an aroused public opinion and the hostile attitude of the Roosevelt administration, the railroads sold out their Lehigh Valley holdings. In 1908, the Lake Shore and the Erie disposed of their stock and the Lackawanna the following year. Judge William H Moore became the largest stockholder in the company. The control of the property remained with the Morgan-First National Bank interests after the Moores passed from the scene with the collapse of the Rock Island Company in 1914.

The Lehigh Valley achieved to a fair degree that independence of anthracite tonnage which all the coal roads had sought to attain. The common stock advanced in 1927 to $125 per share of $50 par value, in response to the evidence of an established earning power and the expectation of merger developments. Both the New York Central and the Pennsylvania Railroad, as well as the Nickel Plate, evinced a willingness to absorb this strong bridge line from New York to the Lakes, with its large coal traffic originated on its own lines (see chart on pages 14–15).

## THE CENTRAL RAILROAD COMPANY OF NEW JERSEY

The Philadelphia & Reading, the Lackawanna and the Lehigh Valley had all been built from the coal fields towards outside markets. The development of the Central Railroad of New Jersey (also called the Jersey Central) was in a reverse direction, and only late in its history did it acquire a railroad into the coal region proper. From an early date, however, the coal traffic was the purpose of its construction and the chief reliance of its management.

Norfolk & Western's J-611 steam locomotive which was taken out of storage at the Roanoke Transportation Museum and restored at the Southern Railways Birmingham, Alabama steam shops. The 'J' is the last survivor of the streamlined locomotives which were built in the N&W shops around 1950. This grand old train now pulls steam excursions.

The Camden & Amboy had been begun in 1830, and projects for new lines appeared in increasing number. The northern part of New Jersey attracted railroad enterprise for two reasons. First, the region was relatively populous and produced a substantial amount of agricultural produce for transportation to New York. Second, the level topography made railroad building cheap, and it was easy to visualize further extensions to the West. The Elizabethtown & Somerville Rail Road Company was chartered in 1831 and construction began three years later. In 1849, with a large network in place, the railroad was acquired by the Phelps Dodge interests, and its name was changed to Central Railroad of New Jersey.

During the 1839–54 period the Central Railroad of New Jersey was primarily a passenger railroad for local traffic. Passenger receipts exceeded freight revenues until 1854. Until October of 1855, the only important connection of the Jersey Central was the New Jersey Railroad, which carried its passenger cars to Jersey City at a fixed charge of 15 cents per passenger. But two important sources of traffic loomed up to give the road a bright future. One was the coal business which was looked for from the Lehigh Valley and the Lackawanna. In 1853, work was begun on the Warren Railroad, a connecting line to reach the Lackawanna at the Delaware Water Gap. The second was through-freight business from the West. The Catawissa Rail Road and the Sunbury & Erie were then under contract and together gave the Jersey Central a 462-mile route to Lake Erie which promised a rich tonnage. The Lackawanna also promised a good through traffic from the Erie and other western New York roads. With the successful sale of the new stock during 1853, work was begun on double-tracking the road, in preparation for a heavy coal traffic.

The operating methods of this early period were very primitive. Locomotive power had been introduced in 1838 on the Elizabethtown & Somerville, but yellow pine wood had been exclusively used for fuel until 1853, when oak was largely substituted. With the beginning of the coal traffic on the Jersey Central, an anthracite-burning locomotive was placed on the road, and only after 1861 was coal used generally as locomotive fuel. The saving over the use of wood was estimated at from three to four cents per mile.

The long-expected coal business finally came in 1856, with the simultaneous opening of the Lackawanna, the Warren and the Lehigh Valley railroads that year. At first the Lackawanna gave the greater part of the coal tonnage, but the Lehigh Valley surpassed it in 1865. Together they turned over a steadily increasing volume of coal, which passed the million-ton mark in 1863. The coal was carried under permanent traffic agreements with the two connecting railroads, the Lackawanna and the Lehigh Valley.

The Central Railroad of New Jersey acquired temporary importance at this time as a link in the shortest route to the West, that of the Pennsylvania Railroad. It began advertising this route in 1862, after completing arrangements for the carriage of its cars without transfer from New York harbor to Pittsburgh. The line of the Jersey Central was used to Easton, whence the Lehigh Valley provided a link to Allentown, the Reading lines to Harrisburg, and the Pennsylvania Railroad to Pittsburgh. Passenger trains covered the entire distance in 16 hours and five minutes. The Pittsburgh, Fort Wayne & Chicago furnished the final link in this so-called 'Allentown Route' to Chicago, which accomplished the entire run in 36 hours. This line built up the business of the Pennsylvania in the West but was abandoned when the Pennsylvania leased the Camden & Amboy in 1871.

By the end of 1870 both the Jersey Central and the Lehigh & Susquehanna sought to affiliate themselves with complementary railroads to secure a through line from New York harbor into the coal regions. It was only a matter of months before a plan was worked out to do this. On 28 March 1871, a lease of the Lehigh & Susquehanna by the Jersey Central was approved, the rental consisting of one-third of all receipts of the leased lines. The equipment was sold to the Jersey Central.

**A Pennsylvania Railroad 4-6-2 *Pacific* steam locomotive designed and built by the Baldwin Ironworks. This type became one of the standard freight locomotives in the United States during the latter nineteenth century.**

## THE LACKAWANNA MERGER

While the lease of the Lehigh & Susquehanna greatly strengthened the position of the Jersey Central, it did not make up for the loss of the large general business previously turned over to it by the Lackawanna. Furthermore, while the Jersey Central still carried the Lackawanna's coal business, an agreement reached on 16 March 1872 consolidated the two enterprises.

This merger brought under joint control 893 miles of railroad. The Jersey Central's own coal land holdings were small, and it had its only substantial assured coal tonnage through the Lehigh Coal & Navigation Company, which profited from any increase in the gross earnings of the leased Lehigh & Susquehanna. The Lackawanna controlled 25,000 acres of the richest anthracite lands, which were valued at from 15 to 20 millions, although taken into the merger at a book value of $5 million, including improvements.

The stockholders of the Jersey Central, however, defeated the merger proposal upon a second presentation by a vote of 112,600 to 5917, and the project was given up. By 1874 an agreement was made between the Lackawanna and

the Jersey Central ending all interchange between the two roads on 1 April 1875.

The Jersey Central, until 1875, was practically a single line without branches from Jersey City to Wilkes-Barre, depending primarily upon two types of freight traffic, coal and merchandise received from connections for the haul from New York harbor. Passenger business until 1881 gave a larger revenue than general freight business, as the road traversed a large suburban area in northeastern New Jersey. The first important addition to the railroad, after the lease of the Lehigh & Susquehanna, was the construction of a line along the Jersey shore, the New York & Long Branch, to serve the resort area.

The opening of the Delaware & Bound Brook Railroad in 1875 from Jenkintown to Bound Brook made the Jersey Central a link in a new short line from New York to Philadelphia, and also threw over its lines the tremendous coal business of the Reading. An agreement was immediately made with the North Pennsylvania and the Bound Brook railroads to operate the through route as one railroad. In 1879, the two smaller roads were leased by the Reading, and the control of the strategic Bound Brook route (which also became the entrance of the Baltimore & Ohio into New York), was shared by the Reading and Jersey Central alone.

The largest gain in mileage was secured in 1879, through acquisition of the New Jersey Southern. This system, an outgrowth of the old Raritan & Delaware Bay Railroad, was chartered in 1854 and had twice failed. It was reorganized by Jay Gould and leased to the Jersey Central for interest upon its mortgage bonds, part of which had already been bought up by the Jersey Central. The sole liability incurred, therefore, was a guarantee on $630,000 of bonds left in the hands of the public. This acquisition gave the Jersey Central a new line along the Jersey coast extending down to the southern tip of the state. It also opened up possibilities of developing an air line along the coast for Baltimore and southern points, though this route never attained any importance.

The Jersey Central, since its incorporation, had been a conspicuously independent property. Until the resignation of President Johnston in 1876, he had both controlled and managed the road. Now, with its credit impaired and its capital stock available at low prices, its valuable railroad and terminal properties attracted new interests, who sought to control it in the interest of other railroads. A three-cornered contest developed for control in 1880 which resulted in a bitter fight and litigation. One of the contestants, Jay Gould, finally was forced out by the combination of the two others—President Gowen of the Reading and President Garrett of the Baltimore & Ohio.

## JAY GOULD STRIKES A DEAL

Having accumulated a large stock interest, Jay Gould was elected to a place on the board of directors of the Jersey Central in 1880. He was then engaged in a new attempt to establish himself in trunk line territory, although his Wabash road got no farther east then Toledo. He now planned to use the Reading to Sunbury and the Philadelphia & Erie thence to Erie, Pennsylvania, as major connecting links to join the Jersey Central and Wabash, but the acquisition of the Philadelphia & Erie by the Pennsylvania Railroad made him change his plans. On 8 June 1881, he signed a tripartite agreement between the Jersey Central, Wabash, St Louis & Pacific and Pennsylvania, whereby the lines of the last were to furnish part of a new through route from New York to Chicago. The Jersey Central was to be used to Red Bank, Pennsylvania, and the Pennsylvania from Red Bank to Youngstown, Ohio. The Wabash was to be extended to Youngstown by a new 70-mile link.

Early in 1882, President Gowen of the Reading opened a campaign to gain control of the Jersey Central as a New York outlet for his system and an important addition to its strength as a coal producer and transporter. Having secured the support of the Vanderbilts for this plan, he began accumulating shares in the open market. The Baltimore & Ohio also desired a line from Philadelphia to New York to extend its new Philadelphia, Wilmington & Baltimore Railroad. President Garrett joined with the Reading on an understanding that Baltimore & Ohio interests would be protected, and together they secured 92,000 shares of Jersey Central in the open market. With this 50 percent interest in hand, the Jersey Central directors were confidently asked to resign.

Gould, using his traditional methods, did not reply but resorted to the legislature. He put through a bill authorizing railroads generally to issue additional stock for the purpose of redeeming outstanding bonds, and thus threatened to flood the market with new shares that Gowen and Garret had to buy to retain control. Of the bonds, $8 million were callable, thus permitting immediate issue of 80,000 new shares at par. Governor Ludlow vetoed the bill, but it was passed over his veto owing to pressure by the combined Gould and Pennsylvania Railroad forces. Gowen then resorted to the courts, and secured an injunction against new stock issues on the ground that new stock

As if awaiting the starting gun, a group of locomotives line up under billowing clouds of steam. The keystone logo formed the background for the locomotive numbers, and symbolically told the story of the Pennsylvania. For nearly half a century the PRR was the heart of the American railroad system.

offerings had not received the approval of a two-thirds vote of stockholders required by the charter.

The Jersey Central had not issued an annual report since 1875, and no stockholders' meeting had been called since the receivership in 1876. Hence, the old board could maintain control until forced out by drastic action. Gowen was never averse to the latter. He discovered an old statute permitting five stockholders to call an annual meeting when the directors had failed to do so, and under the statute published in the press the required ten-day notice. Gould applied to the chancellor to forbid it as irregular, and a decision was handed down which delayed the date, but ordered than an election be held on 23 June 1882, the first in eight years. E C Knight then voted 98,000 shares for the Garret-Gowen ticket, which was also supported by President Sloan of the Lackawanna, and Gould finally was forced out. Each of the victors now obtained his objective. The Baltimore & Ohio secured a New York outlet under a traffic agreement constituting the Bound Brook route its virtual New York extension. The Reading, on 29 May 1883, after the return of the railroad to the company by Receiver Henry S Little, leased the Jersey Central for 999 years with a guarantee of six percent upon the $18,563,200 of capital stock. The Reading deposited $3 million of its own securities to secure the floating debt of the receiver, Henry S Little. The Lehigh & Wilkes-Barre Coal Company, whose property was not included in the lease, was to ship at least 40 percent as much coal as the Philadelphia & Reading Coal & Iron Company in any one year.

The lease was vigorously opposed by the Pennsylvania Railroad, which joined with William B Dinsmore, president of the Adams Express Company and a leading stockholder, in attacking it as contrary to the interests of stockholders. The lease's legal status was very much in doubt throughout its short life. The Reading found that under prevailing conditions it was little more than an opportunity to contribute to the treasury of the Jersey Central. That road failed to earn even its fixed charges, and the dividend rental was a clear loss of $1,113,792 annually to the already overburdened Reading system. Gowen made an attempt to retain the lease, but on the failure of the Reading to make interest payments due on Jersey Central bond issues a petition was filed with the United States Court to end the lease. The Reading opposed this action, but the matter was ended when the chancellor of New Jersey declared the lease void. On 15 October 1886, the application of the Jersey Central directors for separate receivers was granted, and John S Kennedy and Joseph S Harris were appointed by the court. The road was now subject to two receiverships, as Henry S Little, the receiver under the receivership of 1876, had never been dismissed by the court, since a part of the floating debt had been left unpaid.

When the new receivers took over the property, they found a total current indebtedness against it of $2,596,870. They had taken steps to assure friendly relations with the Philadelphia & Reading by executing a traffic agreement providing for full interchange between the two roads at Bound Brook. They found the physical condition of the property 'good and quite equal to that existing at the time of the lease.' Although hampered by a series of strikes in the coal fields and at the terminals, the receivers were able

to resume independent operation without adverse effects on the business of earning power of the railroad.

The Jersey Central had long been on hostile terms with the Lehigh Valley Railroad, as the efforts of the latter to secure a New York terminus at the 'West line grant' interfered with the claims of the American Dock & Improvement Company. Lehigh Valley interests had bought a large block of shares of the Jersey Central at the low prices prevailing, and as a result of this community of interest, effected a settlement of the 15-year-long suit. A traffic agreement was made providing for harmonious relations in the future.

The Jersey Central, after the sale by court order of its coal subsidiary in 1915, took steps further to establish its position as a great terminal railroad property. In 1917, it consolidated 23 operating railroad subsidiaries into the parent company. The sum of $32.5 million received for the coal subsidiary was largely spent on improving the railroad property, which had been brought up to a high level of efficiency without increasing the bonded debt or the capital stock.

Under the Reading segregation decree of 22 May 1923, control of the Jersey Central was turned over to trustees, pending a favorable disposition of the stock holdings of the Reading, and both railroads divorced their coal properties. The two roads taken together were desired by the New York Central and the Baltimore & Ohio. However, the New York Central withdrew after the death of its president, A H Smith, in 1924, leaving the way open for the Baltimore & Ohio to acquire the Jersey Central and the Reading as the eastern end of its system.

As it turned out, both the Jersey Central and the Reading remained independent until their respective bankruptcies in 1967 and 1971. In 1976, both properties were funneled into the Consolidated Rail Corporation (Conrail).

## THE DELAWARE & HUDSON COMPANY

The Delaware & Hudson Canal Company was an established and prosperous miner and transporter of anthracite before any of the railroads already described had been projected. For a number of years its canal enjoyed a monopoly of the coal business from the northern region. Like the Lehigh Coal & Navigation Company, it acquired control of a railroad system after the Civil War, when intensified competition made it difficult for canals to compete with the more efficient railroads, but, unlike that company, it succeeded in maintaining its independence. It became the most independent of the anthracite carriers, and for a time in the early twentieth century, it looked as though the road would one day go on to form the nucleus of a new great east-west trunk line from New York to Chicago. Through its 1983 merger with Boston & Maine, it would ultimately become part of a north-south trunk line.

At the close of the Civil War, the Delaware & Hudson Canal Company was one of the most prosperous concerns in the country, although it faced intense competition from a number of competing transportation companies, all after a proportion of the reduced volume of coal transported in the post-bellum years. Accordingly, the Delaware & Hudson followed a policy of expansion to maintain its position

**This big 2-8-0 consolidated steam locomotive of the 'Ma & Pa' Railroad ran between Hanover and York, Pennsylvania.**

in the industry and strengthen its ability to compete with the other large organizations in the field.

The first move was the acquisition of new coal lands. In this respect the company was probably the first to engage actively in that general buying movement which, during the decade after the Civil War, transformed the numerous small mining operations in the anthracite field into a few large coal estates, owned chiefly by large rail and canal transporting companies. The large profits from anthracite mining during the Civil War encouraged a number of new corporations to enter the business, and these often combined railroad transportation with their coal-mining privileges.

The greatest competitive weakness of the Delaware & Hudson at that time was its lack of interior markets. The coal placed on the canal was practically all carried through to tidewater, and the shipments to New England also were carried by vessel from the Hudson River. The tidewater markets were then plentifully supplied by other companies, and keen competition and sharp reductions in price resulted. This situation did not, however, apply to interior markets, such as those reached by the Philadelphia & Reading, Delaware, Lackawanna & Western and other anthracite lines, for there a virtual monopoly was often enjoyed. These companies could therefore rely upon interior markets to make up the loss suffered by sales of coal at low prices at tidewater, while the Delaware & Hudson had to bear the full brunt of such keen competition without aid from other less competitive markets. To remedy this condition, the management took energetic steps to acquire facilities for reaching western and northern points of large coal consumption.

## THE DELAWARE & HUDSON BECOMES A RAILROAD

The Lackawanna had built up a good market in western New York state, hitherto inaccessible to the Delaware & Hudson. The Albany & Susquehanna was then completing its line from the state capital to Binghamton, through this rich area, and the Delaware & Hudson signed a traffic agreement with it to have it carry its coal to Albany, as well as to distribute anthracite at intervening towns. In consideration of this contract, $500,000 of Albany & Susquehanna second mortgage bonds were purchased, but this line was still incomplete. To fill the wide gap still remaining between the Albany & Susquehanna and the Delaware & Hudson Railroad, negotiations were opened with the Erie for the construction of a branch line from Carbondale to Lanesboro, on its main line, thus giving the Delaware & Hudson Company's railroad an outlet to the railroads of

New York state and New England. The Erie had secured a charter for this route in 1851, under the name of the Jefferson Railroad. On 2 September 1868, a contract was signed whereby the 37-mile line was to be built by the Erie out of funds to be obtained from the sale to the Delaware & Hudson Canal Company. These bonds had come into the treasury of the Erie as a result of the famous fight for control between Gould, Vanderbilt and New England interests in 1868. This line was completed in 1870.

During the next few years the Delaware & Hudson acquired a railroad system reaching to the Canadian border, giving it extensive markets in the interior of New York state, many of them hitherto untouched, as well as connections into New England and Canada. This railroad system was built up in a way far different from that followed by the other coal roads. Existing lines, having practically no previous relation with the coal traffic, were leased and welded together into a north and south system which touched few important cities and possessed at first relatively little general merchandise traffic. Eventually, however, it became an important line for coal traffic for Canada and New England, as well as a vital link from trunk-line territory into the northeast.

The first line to be acquired in this way was the Albany & Susquehanna, which had been projected in 1851 by Albany citizens to divert Erie railroad traffic from New York City to Albany. The Erie was the only important route of travel in the state which did not touch the capital, and a line from Binghamton to Albany was therefore sought to draw business to Albany from the new road through the southern tier of counties. This proposed line was only 143 miles in length, as compared to 224 miles over the Erie to New York City, while its grades were favorable compared to the Erie, which wound its way over steep grades through very rough country at its eastern end. It was also expected that considerable anthracite would eventually be carried over the new line, as the Lackawanna Railroad was then being built north in the direction of Binghamton, and connections could be made with the North Branch and Delaware & Hudson canals.

The city of Albany advanced $1 million of its bonds as a loan to the enterprise. Contracts were then let for the entire line, and, after many delays, the road was completed to Binghamton in January 1869. It was a fairly well-built, broad-gauge road, and naturally expected to interchange business chiefly with the Erie Railroad.

**Big steam locomotives of the Pennsylvania Railroad are seen here in all their power and glory. No 6200 (*below*), designed for heavy loads on Pennsylvania's trunk lines, was a 6-8-6 steam turbine and (*overleaf*) 4-4-2 No 7002 doubleheading with 4-4-0 No 1223 at Cherry Hill, Pennsylvania. The original No 7002 was reputed to have set a world record of 127.1 mph in 1905 with the *Pennsylvania Special*.**

# JAY GOULD AND THE ERIE

The chief purpose in building the Albany & Susquehanna was to deflect trade from the Erie at Binghamton. To prevent this, as well as to get control of markets for anthracite coal to be carried over the Jefferson branch from Carbondale to Lanesboro (then under construction), Jay Gould, the head of the Erie, decided to acquire the new road. He and Fisk bought up all the stock they could reach, raising the quotation from between 20 and 30, to which it had fallen after the long construction period, to nearly par. They then contracted to buy from the towns along the line $450,000 of the stock at par, giving their personal notes in payment. This gave them more than a majority of the $2,000,000 of stock outstanding, but their plans were circumvented by the president of the Albany & Susquehanna, Joseph H Ramsay, aided by the Delaware & Hudson. Ramsay sold 9500 shares of unissued stock—the total authorized capitalization was $4,000,000—to his friends, and thus retained control of a majority of votes. There followed a disgraceful battle of injunctions in connection with a bitterly contested annual meeting. The Gould party finally secured the appointment of 'Jim' Fisk as receiver from Judge Barnard in New York, while Ramsay obtained his legal assistance from Judge Peckham in Albany and had Robert H Pruyn made receiver. At the annual meeting, two sets of directors had been elected, J P

Morgan heading the Ramsay group and Charles Courter the Erie men. The two parties, each supporting a different receiver, then took the law into their own hands. In Albany, the Ramsay party was supreme. Fisk seized the Binghamton property of the company, however, and each party sent out an armed train to secure the road to its interests. Near Binghamton, these trains met. A pitched battle was only halted by the intervention of militia, and Governor Hoffman was compelled to take over control of the property and have the attorney general proceed against all the contestants before Judge E Darwin Smith at Rochester.

The Erie now sought to use other means to attain its object. It offered to lease the road for 99 years at a rental of seven percent upon its bonds and stock, and a 30 percent stock dividend as a bonus. This lease was refused, and in December 1869 Judge Smith handed down his decision supporting the Ramsay party in every contention and assessing costs against Gould and Fisk. Ramsay was reinstated in control, and the next month the road was leased to Delaware & Hudson Canal Company for the life of its charter, at a rental of seven percent on $2,550,000 of stock and $4,450,000 of bonds.

During the seven years following the consummation of the lease, the Delaware & Hudson incurred a loss of $1,402,699 under the agreement. But this loss was in part at least nominal, as the canal company made a profit on the coal moved over the line to markets which perhaps could not have been effectively reached but for the lease. The Albany & Susquehanna was made an integral part of the Delaware & Hudson's growing railroad system by building a connecting railroad from Jefferson Junction, the north end of the new Erie line, to Ninevah, New York, on the Albany & Susquehanna, thus avoiding the detour via Binghamton on the Erie.

The huge *Matt H Shay* was typical of the awesome motive power available on the Erie Railroad in the early twentieth century. Built by Baldwin in Altoona, Pennsylvania, the *Matt H Shay,* was a 2-8-8-8-2 Triplex locomotive, meaning that it was not only articulated, it was articulated into three sections! The *Matt H Shay* was designated No 2603 by the Erie, a former coal road that grew to trunk line proportions and controlled 2315 miles of track by 1906. The railroad later joined the Delaware, Lackawanna & Western to form the Erie Lackawanna which in turn was merged into Conrail in 1976.

## THE RISING STAR OF THE
## DELAWARE & HUDSON

The railroad operations of the Delaware & Hudson rapidly increased in importance after 1880. The railroad system was not materially extended, but was considerably improved. It became an important bridge route into Canada, receiving substantial amounts of interchange freight for Canada and New England. The leased railroads returned a profit for the first time in 1881, and they provedprofitable for the most part thereafter, even as purely railroad enterprises and without allowing for the larger coal earnings they made possible, since they opened up new and highly profitable markets. The company followed a liberal maintenance and improvement policy during these years, despite the occasionally severe coal competition it faced.

The disposition of the canal was becoming a major problem, as this type of transportation was now wholly obsolete. As early as 1866, President Thomas Dickson had advocated its abandonment and the construction of a railroad over its right of way, to give the company an up-to-date route to New York, its chief coal market. This project had been revived in 1880, but again without success. In the meantime the Erie was largely used as an outlet to New York, while the tidewater market steadily declined in relative importance. The canal was severely damaged by flood in 1895 and was not fully repaired again. A new contract for the carrying of coal to New York was made with the Erie in 1897, and the next year the waterway and gravity railroad were finally given up. The name of the company was changed to The Delaware & Hudson Company, the word 'canal' being dropped.

The Delaware & Hudson was now the most conspicuously independent of the large anthracite railroad and mining

companies and the Morgan and Vanderbilt interests, then completing their community of interest arrangement in the anthracite industry, sought to gain a dominant voice in its affairs. At the annual meeting in 1892, the Vanderbilts sought to have a friendly board elected. They failed to capture the whole board but won three places for themselves.

In 1900 the Delaware & Hudson Company had four distinct railroads, each run with a considerable degree of autonomy, and each having a different type of traffic. The Pennsylvania mileage, directly owned by the company, was primarily a coal railroad. The Albany & Susquehanna resembled the other anthracite roads, having a large coal traffic, but also a substantial and growing merchandise business. The Rensselaer & Saratoga was chiefly a general traffic and passenger road, while the New York & Canada, also directly owned, was a relatively undeveloped line, drawing its earnings chiefly from a thin general freight business. The general merchandise business increased 78 percent from 1900 to 1910, while the anthracite business rose 25 percent. By 1924, the general freight had increased by 302 percent and the anthracite business by 109 percent.

With the passage of the Hepburn Act, aimed at segregating coal and railroad properties, the management actively sought to make the railroad as far as possible independent of the anthracite business.

As the importance of coal to the American economy decreased in the twentieth century, the coal roads eventually merged into or became trunk lines. The Lackawanna merged with the Erie in 1960, and they in turn joined the Jersey Central and the Reading in the 1976 merger with Penn Central which resulted in Conrail. The Delaware & Hudson was merged with the Boston & Maine into Guilford Industries in 1983. Though it retained the two individual railroad company names for the individual operating units, Guilford had become a de facto trunk line.

# CHAPTER 7

# THE EVOLUTION OF CANADA'S RAILWAY NETWORK

## Oscar Skelton

**The enduring beauty of Canada's mountains are the everyday vistas of the crews aboard Canadian Pacific locomotives. Notice the round lines of yesteryear's lovely streamlined steam locomotives (*above*) versus the much more angular appearance of the newer diesel electrics (*left*).**

**B**y the end of the 1840s British North America was realizing both the need for railway expansion and the difficulty of financing it. British and American contractors discovered the virgin field awaiting them, and local politicians discovered the cash value of votes and influence. The example set in the United States was powerful. Massachusetts had guaranteed bonds of local roads to the extent of eight million, and though New York's experience had been more varied, the successes were stressed and the failures were plausibly explained away.

The 8 or 10 years which followed 1849 are notable not only for a sudden outburst of railway construction and speculative activity throughout the provinces, but for the beginning of that close connection between politics and railways which is distinctively Canadian. In this era parliament became the field of railway debate. Statesmen began to talk of links of Empire and began to press the claims of their constituencies for needed railway communications. Cabinets realized the value of the charters they could grant or the credit they could pledge, and contractors swarmed to the task.

Francis Hincks, merchant, journalist, and politician, moderate reformer, and Canada's first notable finance minister, took the initiative. As inspector-general in the second Baldwin-LaFontaine cabinet, he brought down the first installment of his railway policy in 1849. He had drawn up two memoranda—one suggesting that the crown lands in the province might be offered as security for the capital to build the road within the province, and the other urging the Imperial government to undertake the road from Halifax to Quebec. Financiers gave no encouragement to the first suggestion, and the British government had not replied to the second by the end of the session of 1848-49. Accordingly, in April 1849 Hincks brought down a new policy, based upon a suggestion of the directors of the St Lawrence & Atlantic. The proposal was, to guarantee the interest, not exceeding six percent, on half the bonds of any railway over seventy-five miles long, and whenever half the road had been constructed the province was to be protected by a first charge after the bondholders' lien.

Even with this aid construction did not proceed swiftly. It was still necessary for the companies to complete half the road before qualifying for government assistance. This the St Lawrence road effected slowly, in face of quarrels with contractors, repudiation of calls by shareholders, and hesitancy of banks to make advances. The Great Western did not get under way until 1851, when American financiers connected with the New York Central took shares and a place on the directorate. In the same year the Toronto, Simcoe & Huron, later known as the Northern, began construction.

Meanwhile suggestions from the Maritime Provinces had brought still more ambitious schemes within practical range. These led Hincks to take the second step in his policy of aid to railways.

In the Maritime Provinces, from 1835 to 1850, many railways had been projected, but, with the exception of a small coal tramway in Nova Scotia, built in 1839 from the Albion coal mines to tidewater, not a mile was built before 1847. In 1835 a railway association was formed in St Andrews, an exploratory survey was made and the interest of lower Canada was enlisted. In the following year New Brunswick gave a charter to the St Andrews & Quebec Railroad, and the Imperial government agreed to bear the cost of a survey, but it was speedily halted because of protests from Maine. In 1842 the Ashburton Treaty assigned to the United States a great part of the territory through which the line was projected, and the promoters gave up. In 1845 the railway mania in England brought a revival of all colonial schemes. Sir Richard Broun took up the plan for a line from Halifax to Quebec. This discussion revived the flagging hopes of St Andrews, and a beginning was made by a railway from St Andrews to Woodstock, the New Brunswick & Canada, for which ground was broken in November 1847.

The provincial legislature early concluded that it would be impossible to induce private interests to build an intercolonial road unaided. They were unanimous also, not yet having emerged from colonial dependence, in wanting to throw the greater burden of such aid on the British government. In the absence of a colonial federation the United Kingdom was the main connecting link between the colonies in British North America and was presumably most interested in matters affecting more than a single colony. The British government, however, had by this time decided that the old policy of treating the colonies as an estate or plantation of the mother country, protecting or developing them in return for the monopoly of their trade, did not pay. It had reluctantly conceded them political home rule; it was soon to thrust upon them freedom of trade; and it was not inclined to retain burdens when it had given up privileges. Mr Gladstone, secretary for the Colonies, agreed, however, in 1846, to have a survey made at the expense of the three colonies concerned.

This survey, the starting point for the controversies and the proposals of a generation, was completed in 1848, under Major Robinson and Lieutenant Henderson of the Royal Engineers. 'Major Robinson's Line,' as it came to be known, ran roughly in the direction eventually followed by the Intercolonial—from Halifax to Truro, and thence

A surrealistic 1916 view of the old and new Canadian Pacific Railway Station in Quebec City, Quebec. Automobiles had made their appearance, but the train was still the preferred mode of transport.

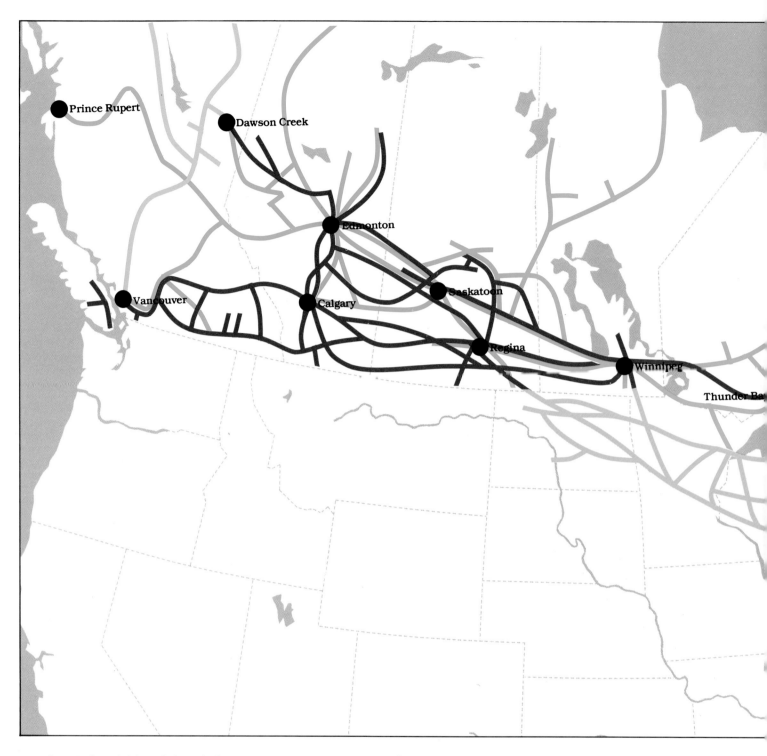

north to Miramichi and the Chaleur Bay, and up the Metapedia Valley to the St Lawrence.

After the plan of a northern route to Quebec was abandoned, interest shifted to the Portland connections. The building of the road from Montreal to Portland added further strength to the claims of this route. The name of the proposed road, the European & North American, expressed the hope that the road from Portland to Halifax would become the channel of communication between the United States and Europe, at least for passengers, mail and express traffic.

In July 1850 a great convention assembled in Portland, attended by delegates from New Brunswick and Nova Scotia as well as from Maine and other New England states. The delegates from the Maritime Provinces returned home full of enthusiasm, but increasingly uncertain about the securing of the necessary capital. At this stage Joseph Howe came to the front. He proposed to seek from

the Imperial government a guarantee of the necessary loan, in order that the province might borrow on lower terms. The Colonial Office, while expressing its approval of the Portland scheme, declined to give a guarantee more than a cash contribution. Not daunted, Howe sailed for England in November 1850 and in spite of Cabinet changes in London secured the pledge he desired.

Howe returned triumphant. The British government would guarantee a loan of $35 million which would build the roads to Portland and to Quebec and perhaps still farther west.

Then suddenly the bubble burst. The Colonial Office, late in 1851, declared that Howe had been mistaken in declaring that the guarantee was to extend to the European & North American project. The British government had no objection to this road being built, but would not aid it. The officials of the Colonial Office declared that they never meant to promise anything else. The whole plan thus fell to

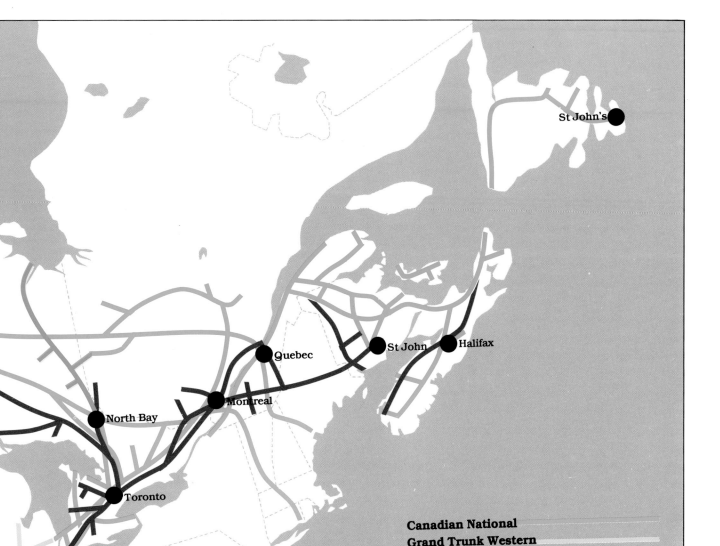

Canadian National
Grand Trunk Western
(Canadian National)
Canadian Pacific
Soo Line
(Canadian Pacific)
British Columbia Railway
Ontario Northland

The four largest Canadian railroad systems, CN, CP, BCR and ON operate on a total of almost 46,000 miles of track allowing cargo delivery throughout Canada and the US Midwest.

the ground. The consent of the three provinces was essential, and New Brunswick would not support the Halifax & Quebec project if the Portland road, running through the most populous and influential sections of the province, was to be postponed indefinitely. Finance Minister Hincks was determined to save the situation. Accompanied by John Young and E P Taché, he visited Fredericton and Halifax early in 1852, and hammered out a compromise. New Brunswick agreed to join in the Halifax to Quebec project on condition that the road should run from Halifax to St John and thence up the valley of the St John River; Nova Scotia agreed to this change, which made St John rather than Halifax the main ocean terminus, on condition that New Brunswick should bear five-twelfths as against its own three-twelfths of the cost. It remained to secure the consent of the Imperial government and Hincks, Chandler and Howe arranged to sail for England early in March. Upon a peremptory request from Hincks for a definite an-

swer within a fortnight, the British Cabinet, in spite of the previous promise to consider the route an open question, declined to aid any but a road following Major Robinson's line. The negotiations broke off, joint action between the provinces failed, and each province switched to its own separate track.

It was on 13 June 1854 that the first sod was turned for the construction of the Nova Scotia Railway—a beginning made at last. The road was to run from Halifax to Truro, with a branch to Windsor. Progress was slow, but by 1858 the 93 miles planned had been completed. Then came a halt, when reality succeeded the glowing visions of the prospectus, the service proved poor, and the returns low. Nine years later an extension from Truro to Pictou was constructed.

New Brunswick had a more variable experience. After the collapse of the Halifax & Quebec project, her efforts were confined to the road running north from St Andrews and to the European & North American.

By 1851 the St Lawrence, the Great Western and the Northern were under way, and more ambitious schemes proposed. The Guarantee Act of 1849, which was the first phase of Hincks' policy, assuring public aid for the second half of any road at least 75 miles in length, was proving inadequate, and the government was considering an extension of its policy.

In 1849 Hincks had argued against government ownership; now he argued for it. The new act, passed in April 1852, marked the second or Grand Trunk phase of his gradually shaping policy. The next move was to arrange terms with the other provinces and secure the promised Imperial guarantee.

It is clear, however, that the British government was unwilling to consider anything but the unacceptable Major Robinson line. Hincks was justified in looking elsewhere for capital, but he was not justified in binding himself to one firm of contractors, however eminent, which is what he had done.

Hincks returned to Canada in the summer of 1852 with a tentative contract in his pocket. To Canada, too, came Henry Jackson, a partner in the Brassey Company, the railway-building firm with whom Hincks had associated himself. The supposition of the government was that the English contractors would simply subscribe for the bulk of the stock in these companies, but the Canadian promoters were not willing to give up their rights so easily, and they subscribed for the full $3 million which was authorized. Hincks met this move by bringing down a bill to incorporate a new company, the Grand Trunk Railway Company of Canada, and the rights of the rival claimants' came before parliament for decision.

Hincks became alarmed at Montreal interests arrayed against him, and proposed as a compromise that the Grand Trunk should absorb the St Lawrence road and build the bridge at Montreal on the condition that the opposition to its westward plans should be abandoned. Upon this all parties agreed, and the English and Canadian promoters joined forces.

Negotiations were completed in England early in 1853. As yet the Grand Trunk Company was but a name. The real parties to the bargain were many. First came John Ross, a member of the Canadian Cabinet, but representing the future Grand Trunk, of which he was elected president. The Barings and Glyns, eminent banking houses, had a twofold part to play, as they were closely connected with the contractors and were also the London agents of the Canadian government. The contractors themselves, Peto, Brassey, Betts and Jackson, had spent a year studying the Canadian situation and put in anxious weeks hammering out the details of the agreement and the prospectus to follow it.

A glowing prospectus was drawn up. The amalgamated road would be the most comprehensive railway system in the world, comprising 1112 miles, stretching from Portland and eventually from Halifax (by both the northern and the southern route) to Lake Huron. The whole future traffic between west and east must therefore pass over the Grand Trunk, as both geographical conditions and legislative enactment prevented it from injurious competition.

It was backed by government guarantee and Canadian investment, and its execution was in the hands of the most eminent contractors. The total capital was fixed at $47.5 million.

A M Ross was appointed chief engineer, and S P Bidder general manager, both on the nomination of the English bankers and contractors. Plant was assembled in Canada, orders for rails and equipment were placed in England, and workers came out by the thousand. At one time 14,000 men were directly employed upon the railways in upper Canada alone. In July 1853 the last gaps in the St Lawrence & Atlantic had been filled up, though not permanently. In 1854 the Quebec and Richmond section was opened; in 1855, the road from Montreal to Brockville and from Lévis to St Thomas, Quebec; in 1856, the Brockville to Toronto and Toronto to Stratford sections. Not until 1858 was the western road completed as far as London. The year 1859 saw the completion of the Victoria Bridge, the extension from St Mary's to Sarnia, and a new road in Michigan, running from Port Huron to Detroit.

The Grand Trunk was complete from Lake Huron to the Atlantic in 1860. In the 10 years that followed, working expenses varied from 58 to 85 percent of the gross receipts, instead of the 40 percent which the prospectus had foreshadowed; not a cent of dividend was paid on ordinary shares.

The prophecy that operating expenses would not exceed 40 percent of earnings, based on English experience, failed partly because earnings were lower, but more because operating expenses were higher than anticipated. The company had more than its share of hard luck from commercial depression, and from loss on American paper money in the Civil War. Differences of gauge, lack of permanent connections at Chicago, lack of return freight, rate wars with the American roads which had been built west at the same time or later, the inferiority of Montreal to New York as of old in harbor facilities and ocean service, the failure of Portland to become a great commercial center—all meant hope and dividends deferred.

The Grand Trunk did Canada good service, however. In 1850 there were only 66 miles of road in all the provinces. In 1860 there were 2065. The Great Western and the Northern were pushed forward under the provisions of the earlier Guarantee Act; roads of more local interest were fostered by municipal rivalry. Their building brought new activity in every branch of commerce. The Great Western came nearest of any early road to being a financial success; alone of the guaranteed roads it repaid the government loan, nearly in full. The Northern Railway was opened as far as Allandale in 1853, and to Collingwood in 1855. It was scamped by the contractors, poorly built, and overloaded with debt. By 1859 the road was bankrupt. Most of the lesser roads constructed looked to the municipalities rather than to the provinces for aid.

## THE INTERCOLONIAL

The first 'age of iron—and of brass' came to an end before 1860. Between 1850 and 1860, the mileage of all the provinces grew from 66 to 2065. By 1867 it had increased only 213 miles. In two of the intervening years not a mile was built. A halt had come, for stock taking and heart searching.

The Canadian Pacific Railway Station at Ottawa, Ontario in 1899. Workers around the station were able to relax a bit in the slow times between trains.

The Grand Trunk, Great Western, and Northern roads owed the old province of Canada on 1 July 1967 $20 million for principal advanced and over $13 million for interest. Other roads were indebted to Canadian municipalities nearly $10 million for principal alone. There had been waste and mismanagement, but the railways had brought indirect gain that more than offset the direct loss. Farming districts were opened up rapidly, freights were reduced in many sections, intercourse was facilitated, and land values were raised.

In the first 30 years of Canadian railway development no question aroused more interest than that of the gauge to be adopted. The width of the carts used in English coal mines centuries ago determined the gauge of railway track and railway cars over nearly all the world. When the steam locomotive was invented, and used upon the coal-mine tramways, it was made of the same four-foot-eight-and-a-half-inch gauge. In England, in spite of the preferences for a seven-foot gauge, the narrower width soon triumphed, though the Great Western did not entirely abandon its wider track until 1892. In Canada the struggle was longer and more complicated.

It was a question on which engineers differed. Speed, steadiness, cost of track construction and cost of maintenance were all to be considered, and were all diversely estimated. In early years, before the need of standardizing equipment was felt, many experiments were made, especially in the United States. In the southern states five feet was the usual width, and the Erie was built on a gauge of six feet, to fit an engine bought at a bargain. But in the United States, as in England, the four-foot-eight-and-a-half-inch width was dominant, and would have been adopted in Canada without question except that local interests, appealing to patriotic prejudice, succeeded in clouding the issue.

Experience proved that it was impossible to maintain different gauges in countries so closely connected as Canada and the United States. As roads became consolidated into larger systems, the inconvenience of different gauges became more intolerable. The expedients of lifting cars bodily to other trucks, of making axles adjustable, and even of laying a third rail, proved unsatisfactory. Late in the 1860s and early in 1870s the Great Western and the Grand Trunk had to adopt the four-foot-eight-and-a-half-inch gauge only, and other lines gradually followed.

The Canada Southern was built in 1873, running between Fort Erie, opposite Buffalo, and Amherstburg on the Detroit River. It was controlled by the Vanderbilt interests and operated in close cooperation with their other roads, the Michigan Southern, Michigan Central, and New York Central. The Great Western met this attack upon its

The CP Railway Station at Vermillion Bay, Ontario at the turn of the century. With the tracks beckoning to far away places, it is easy to imagine the anticipation of these children as they await their train.

preserves by building in the same year the Canada Air Line, from Glencoe near St Thomas, to Fort Erie, giving more direct connection with Buffalo. Both roads made use of the magnificent International Bridge, built across the Niagara in 1873 under Grand Trunk control.

An interesting experiment, motivated by the same desire for cheap pioneer construction which in Ontario brought in the narrow gauge, was the wooden railway built in 1870 from Quebec to Gosford. The rails were simply strips of seasoned maple, $14' \times 7'' \times 4''$, notched into the sleepers and wedged in without the use of a single iron spike. The engine and wheels were made wide to fit the rail. In spite of its cheap construction the road did not pay, and the hope of extending it as far as Lake St John was deferred for a generation. A similar wooden railway was built from Drummondville to L'Avenir.

The outstanding achievement of the period after confederation, however, was the building of the Intercolonial. It had been projected largely in order to make closer union between the provinces possible, but, as it turned out, it was confederation that brought the Intercolonial, not the Intercolonial that brought confederation.

After the breakdown of the negotiations in London in 1852, each province had turned to its own tasks. Each in building its own roads provided possible links in the future Intercolonial chain. In Canada the Grand Trunk ran to a point 120 miles east of Quebec; in New Brunswick, St John was connected with both the east and west boundaries of the province; in Nova Scotia, a road ran north from Halifax as far as Truro. A gap of nearly 500 miles between Rivière du Loup and Truro remained. To bridge this wilderness seemed beyond the private or public resources of the divided provinces. Unanimous on one point only, they once more turned to the British government. In 1857 and 1858 dispatches and deputations sought aid, but sought it in vain. When the Civil War broke out in the United States, official British sympathy was given to the South. In 1861 the British sent 8000 troops to Canada in response to an incident in which Captain Wilks of the Union forces had seized two Confederate officers from aboard a ship named *The Trent. The Trent Affair,* as it came to be called, showed how near Britain and the North were to war, a war which would at once have exposed isolated Canada to American attack. The military argument for closer connection then took on new weight with the British government, and it proposed, to a joint delegation in 1861, to revert to its offer of 10 years earlier—to guarantee a colonial loan for a railway by an approved route. During the progress of the survey negotiations for the union of the provinces had begun, and when Confederation came about in 1867, the building of the Intercolonial at the common expense of the Dominion, with an imperial guarantee to the extent of $15 million, was one of the conditions of union.

The construction was entrusted in December 1868 to a commission of four, and six years later the minister of public works took over direct control. At last, on 1 July 1876, nine years after Confederation, the 500 miles between Truro and Rivière du Loup were opened for traffic throughout. In the meantime the Dominion had taken over the Nova Scotia, New Brunswick, and Prince Edward Island government roads. In 1876 there were in all 950 miles of railway under the control of the Dominion government, as against 4268 miles of private lines.

## THE BEGINNINGS OF THE CANADIAN PACIFIC

On 3 March 1841, Sir George Simpson, governor-in-chief of the Hudson's Bay Company's domains, left London for a journey round the world. All the resources of a powerful and well-organized corporation were at his disposal, and his own reputation for rapid traveling assured that on the actual journey not an hour would be lost.

His twelve-week crossing of Canada stood as the record for a generation. After the coming of the locomotive, however, it needed only imagination and a map to see all British North America clamped by an iron band. Engineers like Bonnycastle and Synge and Carmichael-Smyth wrote of the possibility in the 1840s. Promoters were not lacking. In 1851 Allan MacDonnell of Toronto sought a charter and a subsidy for a road to the Pacific, and the Canadian authorities, in declining, expressed their opinion that the scheme was not visionary and their hope that some day Great Britain and the United States might undertake it jointly. Seven years later the same promoter secured a charter for the Northwest Transportation, Navigation, & Railway Company, to operate between Lake Superior and the Fraser River, but could get no backing. In 1862, Sandford Fleming prepared an elaborate memorial on the subject. Edwin Watkin, of the Grand Trunk, negotiated with the Hudson's Bay Company for right of way and other facilities, but the project proved too vast for his resources.

Two things were needed before dreams on paper could become facts in steel—national unity and international rivalry. Years before Confederation, such far-seeing Canadians as William M'Dougall and George Brown had pressed for the annexation of the British territories beyond the Lakes. After Confederation, all speed was made to buy out the sovereign rights of the Hudson's Bay Company. Then came the first Riel Rebellion, to bring home the need of a western road, as the *Trent* affair had brought home the need of the Intercolonial. The decisive political factor came into play in 1870, when British Columbia entered the federation.

The other factor, international rivalry, exercised its influence about the same time. In the United States the railway had rapidly pushed westward, but had halted before the deserts and the mountains lying between the Mississippi and the Pacific. The rivalry of pro-slavery and anti-slavery parties in Congress had deadlocked all plans of public aid to either southern or northern route. Then the Civil War broke the deadlock: the need of binding the West to the side of the North created a strong public demand for a Pacific road, and Congress, so stimulated, gave loans and land grants. The Central Pacific, working from Sacramento, and the Union Pacific, starting from Omaha, met near Ogden in Utah in 1869. In 1871 the Southern Pacific and the Texas Pacific were fighting for subsidies, and Jay Cooke was promoting the Northern Pacific. The young Dominion of Canada was stirred by ambition to emulate its powerful neighbor.

These factors, then, brought the question of a railway to the Pacific on Canadian soil within the range of practical

Building the rail lines must have been a daunting experience for CP railway construction engineers. No structure on the original transcontinental railway compared with the size of the Mountain Creek Bridge of the eastern slope of the Selkirks. The tracks of this 1086 foot long bridge were 164 feet above the creek.

politics. Important questions remained to be settled. During the parliamentary session of 1871 the government of Sir John MacDonald decided that the road should be built by a company, not by the state, that it should be aided by liberal subsidies in cash and in land, and, to meet British Columbia's insistent terms, that it should be begun within two, and completed within ten, years. The opposition protested that this latter provision was uncalled for and would bankrupt the Dominion, but the government carried its point.

The first task was to survey the vast wilderness between the Ottawa Valley and the Pacific, and to find if possible a feasible route. Explorer and engineer Captain Palliser, had been appointed by the British government to report upon the country west of the Lakes. He had declared in 1863, after four years of careful labor in the field, that, thanks to the choice of the 49th parallel as Canada's boundary, there was no possibility of ever building a transcontinental railway exclusively through British territory. The man chosen for the task of achieving this impossibility was Sandford Fleming. Appointed engineer-in-chief in 1871, he was for nine years in charge of the surveys, though for half that time his duties on the Intercolonial absorbed much of his energy. Fleming possessed an unusual gift of literary style, and his reports upon the work of his staff gave the people of Canada a very clear idea of the difficulties to be encountered.

It had been decided, in order to hold the balance between Montreal and Toronto, to make the proposed Pacific road begin at some angle of Lake Nipissing. From that point nearly to the Red River stretched a thousand miles of woodland, rugged and rock-strewn, covered by a network of countless lakes and rivers, interspersed with seemingly bottomless swamps or muskegs—a wilderness which no white man had ever passed through from end to end. Then came the level prairie and a great rolling plain rising to the southwest in three successive steppes, and cut by deep watercourses. However, it was the third or mountain section which presented the most serious engineering difficulties. Four hundred miles from the Pacific coast ran the towering Rocky Mountains, some of whose peaks rose 15,000 feet. Beyond stretched a vast plateau, three or four thousand feet above sea-level, intersected by rivers which had cut deep chasms or, to the northward, wide sheltered valleys. Between this plateau and the coast the Cascades interposed, rivaling the Rockies in height.

Early in the survey a practical route was found throughout. Striking across the wilderness from Lake Nipissing to Lake Superior at the Pic River, the line might skirt the shore of the lake to Fort William, or it might run northerly through what is now known as the clay belt, with Fort William and the lake made accessible by a branch. Continuing westward to the Red River at Selkirk, with Winnipeg on a branch line to the south, the projected line crossed Lake Manitoba at the Narrows, and then struck out northwesterly, through what was then termed the 'Fertile Belt,' until the Yellowhead Pass was reached. Here the Rockies could be easily pierced; but once through Fleming was faced by the huge flanking range of the Caribou Mountains, in which repeated explorations failed to find a gap. At the

**Canadian Pacific Railroad's streamlined *Royal Hudson* H-1e steam locomotive No 2860 is used in excursion service on British Columbia Railways between North Vancouver and Squamish. The beautiful scenery and this grand old train combine to remind us of the 'good old days' of railroad history.**

foot of the towering barrier lay a remarkable deep-set valley 400 miles in length, in which northwestward ran the Fraser and southeastward the Canoe and the Columbia. By following the Fraser to its great southward bend, and then striking west, a terminus on Bute or Dean Inlet might be reached, while the valley of the Canoe and the Albreda would give access to the North Thompson as far as Kamloops, where the road might run down the Thompson and the lower Fraser to Burrard Inlet. The latter route, on the whole, was preferred.

Who was to build the road? It would be a tremendous task for either the government or the private enterprise of a nation of four million people. The United States had not begun its Pacific roads till it had over thirty million people and wealth and experience to correspond. It was estimated that the Canadian road would cost $100 million and it was certain that the engineering difficulties would be staggering. In Canada few roads had paid the shareholders, and though some had profited the contractors, the new enterprise meant such a plunge in the dark that contractors and promoters alike hesitated. In the United States, however, the Pacific roads had proved gold mines for their promoters.

In June 1880, Sir John MacDonald, speaking at Bath, made the announcement that a group of capitalists had offered to build the road, on terms which would ensure that in the end it would not cost Canada a single penny. Four months later a contract was signed in Ottawa by which the Canadian Pacific Syndicate undertook to build and operate the whole road. An entirely new turn had been given to the situation, and the most important chapter in Canada's railway annals, if not in her national life, had been begun.

## BUILDING THE CANADIAN PACIFIC

In the months and years that followed, no men were so much in the mind and speech of the Canadian public as the members of the new syndicate. The leading members were a remarkable group of men. Probably never in the history of a railway building, not even in the case of the 'Big Four' who built the Central Pacific—Huntington, Stanford, Crocker, and Hopkins—had the call of the railway brought together in a single enterprise men of such outstanding individuality, of such ability and persistence, and destined for success so notable.

The Canadian Pacific was not their first joint enterprise. It was the direct outcome of a daring venture in connection with a bankrupt Minnesota railway, which had brought them wealth beyond their wildest dreams, and had definitely turned their thoughts to railway work.

In St Paul, Minnesota in the early 1870s had lived two Canadians who saw the opportunity. The elder, Norman W Kittson, had been Hudson Bay agent and head of a transportation company on the Red River. The younger, James J Hill, an Ontario farmboy who had gone west while still in his teens, owned a coal and wood yard in St Paul and had a share in the transportation company. Neither had the capital or the financial connection required to take hold of the bankrupt company, but they kept on thinking of it. Soon a third man joined their ranks, Donald A Smith. A Highland lad who had come to Canada at age eighteen, Donald Smith had spent a generation in the service of the Hudson's Bay Company, mainly in the dreary wilds of Labrador and on the shores of Hudson Bay. When in 1871 he became chief commissioner of the organization he had served so long, it seemed to most men that he was definitely settled in his life work and probably near the height of his career. Donald Smith knew, however, that his

career was only beginning. Coming down from the north each year by the Red River to St Paul, on his way east, he talked over the railway situation with Hill and Kittson. The more they talked the greater grew their faith in the country and the railroad. It was a faith, however, that few in the moneyed East shared with them. It had been the smashing of the rival road, the Northern Pacific in 1873, that had given the signal for the brief panic and the long depression of the 1870s. The Minnesota road itself had twice become bankrupt.

In 1876 further needed allies came from the East. Thirty years earlier George Stephen, a younger cousin of Donald Smith, had left his Highland hills to seek his fortune in London, and after a short apprenticeship there had gone still farther afield, joining an uncle in Montreal. He rose rapidly to a foremost place in the wholesale trade of Montreal. Selling led him into manufacturing and manufacturing into financial activities, until in 1876 he became

CPR took over the Lakehead-Winnipeg section during the years 1881 to 1883. Included in the section was a wide assortment of rickety, poorly constructed, but later replaced, bridges such as Timber Trestle (*below*) near the Lake Of The Woods.

George Stephen (*facing page*) was the first president of CPR from 1881 through 1888. Donald A Smith (*right*) a cousin of Stephen and a former Hudson's Bay Company trader, envisioned CPR's role in the future commerce of Canada.

president of the Bank of Montreal. Associated with him in the same bank was still another shrewd financier, Richard B Angus, who had risen steadily in its service until appointed general manager in 1869.

A lawsuit in connection with the bank's affairs took both Stephen and Angus to Chicago in 1876. A week's adjournment left them with unaccustomed leisure. A toss of a coin sent them to St Paul rather than to St Louis to spend the week. Smith had already spoken of the project while in Montreal, but at that distance caution had prevailed. Now Stephen, who had never before seen the prairie, was immensely taken with the rich, deep soil he saw before him. He decided to join in the attempt to get control of the Minnesota road and its land grant, and the famous group was complete.

Once George Stephen had made up his mind, little time was ever lost. He sailed for Europe and interviewed the Amsterdam committee in charge of the bondholders' interests. The Dutch committee despaired of ever seeing their money back, and were weary of being assured by the receiver for funds to keep the road together. Stephen left Amsterdam with an option in his pocket, given for the sum of one guilder, agreeing to sell him the Dutch bonds for something like the amount of the unpaid interest, and further agreeing to wait until six months after reorganization for part of the payment. The next step was to provide the cash required for immediate necessities. About $300,000 was put up by the members of the group. Money was borrowed from the Bank of Montreal, $280,000 in the first advance, and under $700,000 in all, as Stephen stated to shareholders at the bank's annual meeting in 1880. Money was advanced to the receiver to complete the most necessary extensions, those required to save the land grant and that necessary to reach the Canadian border to join the government road being built south from Winnipeg. The threatened forfeiture of the land grant was thus averted for a time. Then the bonds were purchased for $6.7 million, the floating obligations and part of the stock were bought up, and the mortgage which secured the bonds was foreclosed. The assets were bought by the new company organized for the purpose, the St Paul, Minneapolis & Manitoba, of which George Stephen was president, R B Angus vice president, and James J Hill general manager. Thus in June 1879 the whole system, comprising 667 miles of railway, of which 565 were completed, and the land grant of 2.5 million acres came into their possession.

The road 10 years later expanded into the Great Northern. Recounting the harvest reaped from its construction by the adventurers would put the tales of El Dorado to shame. Settlers swarmed in, the railroad platforms were jammed with land seekers, and between the land buyers of today and the wheat shippers of tomorrow the owners of the once discredited railway saw their coffers fill to overflowing. In 1879 they divided among themselves the whole $15 million of stock issued, floating $16 million of bonds for extension and equipment. For three years they took no dividends, letting the profits go to further building. Aside entirely from interest and dividends, the stockholders of the Great Northern in the 17 years following 1889 were presented with over $300 million of interest-bearing securities. All the railway annals of the United States cannot present a duplicate of the startling success attained by these Canadians and their associates.

These were the men to whom the Canadian government turned when the minister of Railways, Sir Charles Tupper, urged them to unload upon a private company the burden of completing the road to the Pacific. 'Catch them before they invest their profits,' was the advice of Sir John's most intimate adviser, the shrewd Eastern Townships politician John Henry Pope. Probably they came halfway. They knew the West as well as any men, and with their road built to the Canadian boundary and with a traffic arrangement beyond to Winnipeg, they were already in the field. Of all the group Stephen was most reluctant to undertake the new enterprise, but he was assured by his associates that the burdens of management would be shared by all. The government had also approached Duncan M'Intyre, a Montreal financier who controlled the Canada Central, running from Brockville by way of Ottawa to Pembroke, and under construction from that point to Callender, the eastern end of the Canadian Pacific main line. He was more than willing to link up this railway with the larger project, and the group was formed.

They debated the question with the government early in 1880. It was felt, however, that negotiations could not be concluded in Canada. More capital would be needed than even these new millionaires could furnish, and nowhere

was capital so abundant as in London. In July, therefore, Sir John MacDonald, Sir Charles Tupper, and John Henry Pope sailed for London, accompanied by George Stephen and Duncan M'Intyre. London financiers did not bite as freely as anticipated. Barings and Rothschilds alike were cautious about the enterprise. Sir Henry Tyler, president of the Grand Trunk, was approached and agreed to build if the link north of Lake Superior were omitted in favor of a line through the United States, south of the lake, a condition which Sir John, strongly urged on by Tupper, would not accept.

The group returned to Ottawa on 21 October 1880, the contract was signed by Charles Tupper for the government and by George Stephen, Duncan M'Intyre, James J Hill, John S Kennedy, Morton, Rose & Company of London, and Cohen, Reinach & Company of Paris. Donald A Smith's name was not there. It was only two years since he and Sir John, on the floor of the House of Commons, had called each other 'liar' and 'coward' and it was to be a few years more before the two Highlander's could cover their private feud with a coating of elaborate cordiality. So, to preserve appearances, Smith's interest was kept a secret— but a very open one.

When Parliament met in December 1880 the contract was laid before it. For constructing some 1900 miles the syndicate would be given free the 710 miles already under construction by the government, $25 million in cash, and 25 million acres of selected land in the Fertile Belt. They were promised exemptions from import duties on construction materials, from taxes on land for 20 years after the patents were issued and on stock and other property forever, and exemption from regulation of rates until 10 percent per annum was earned on the capital. Assurance was given that for 20 years no competitive roads connecting with the western states would be chartered. Ten years were given to complete the task, and a million dollars were deposited as security. On a straight party vote the contract was ratified by Parliament and received the formal royal assent in February 1881.

The parties differed on the question of the Lake Superior link. The government urged the necessity of building at once an all-Canadian route, regardless of the added expense. The Opposition favored such a route eventually, but urged that it was better for the present to make use of a road running from Sault Ste Marie through northern Michigan and Minnesota. Such a road would bring to Montreal the traffic of the American as well as the Canadian West. Then, when the latter had been settled and traffic warranted, the task of cutting a road through the wilderness north of the lake could be faced, and meantime it would not be necessary to offer any company the extravagant terms necessary to induce it to assume this burden from the start. There was much weight in this argument, which Sir Charles Tupper himself had strongly urged only a few months before. Yet, on the whole, so necessary to national unity was an unbroken road, so hard a country was this to make into one, that it was best to err on the side of safety. The political interests at stake warranted some risk of money loss.

The road had to be operated as well as built, and few believed that for years to come there would be sufficient traf-

**Canadian Pacific Railway 'navvies', or construction workers, at their camp north of Lake Superior during construction.**

Canadian Pacific Railroad G-5 class 4-6-2 steam locomotive No 1201. Built in 1944, No 1201 was the last steam engine built by Canadian Pacific. This image of the engineer at the controls of 1201 is a classic in the sense that nearly every child has fantasized about being at the business end of a locomotive — ready to pull on the cord and blow the whistle announcing that 'my train is coming.'

fic to make ends meet. Its future depended on the future of the West, and it needed a robust optimism at times to believe that the West would overcome frost and drought and other plagues. The fact that in 1885 Canadian Pacific stock sold as low as 33¾ in London, and a shade lower on this side of the water, shows the estimate the world of finance put upon the bargain it had made. Nor was the road completed in 1886. It was then only begun. Grades had to be bettered, trestle-work filled up, extensions flung out, terminals secured, and a new road built every few years.

George Stephen was chosen president, and held the post until 1888. To him more than to any other man the ultimate success of the Canadian Pacific was due. Indomitable persistence, unquenchable faith and unyielding honor stamped his character. He was one of the greatest of empire builders. He never despaired in the tightest corner and never rested while a single expedient remained untried. Duncan M'Intyre became one of the two vice presidents and took an active part in the company's affairs until he dropped out in 1884. Richard B Angus came back from St Paul to become vice president and a member of the executive committee. His long banking experience and his shrewd, straightforward judgment proved a tower of strength in days of trial.

Donald A Smith, while after 1883 a director and a member of the executive committee, took little part in the railway's affairs, though at Stephen's urging he more than once joined in lending security when help was most needed. James J Hill left the directorate and unloaded his stock at the close of 1882 because the company refused to accept his advice to omit the Lake Superior section and because of the growing divergence of interests between the St Paul, Minneapolis & Manitoba and the Canadian Pacific. With him retired John S Kennedy. The Baron de Reinach also withdrew at an early stage. The English directors, representing Morton, Rose & Company of London, retired as soon as the road was completed, being replaced by representatives of Morton, Bliss & Company of New York. E B Osler came in with the Ontario & Quebec in 1884. The board became more and more distinctively Canadian.

One of the first steps taken by the directors was to open offices in Winnipeg, and put two men with United States experience in charge—A B Stickney, later president of the Chicago Great Western, as general superintendent, and General Rosser as chief engineer. The rate of progress was not satisfactory, and early in 1882 a fortunate change was made. William C Van Horne, at that time general superintendent of the Chicago, Milwaukee & St Paul and still under age forty, was appointed general manager with wide powers. Some years earlier, when he was president of the Southern Minnesota, the leading members of the St Paul syndicate had had an opportunity of learning his skill. He had been in railroading since he was fourteen, beginning as a telegraph operator on the Illinois Central, and had risen rapidly in the service of one Midwest road after another. His tireless driving force was precisely the asset the company now most needed.

The financial policy adopted by the Canadian Pacific was unique in the records of great railway enterprises on

Before the days of mechanization, tracks were laid by the sweat and muscle of construction gangs (*left*). CPR's passenger train *The Canadian* (*right*) along the Bow River between Lake Louise and Banff, Alberta in 1961.

from London, stormed it through caucus, and the loan was made.

The men behind the Canadian Pacific proved themselves possessed of courage and honorable determination. At more than one critical stage they staked their all to keep the work going even though the bulk of the resources used in the original building of the road were provided or advanced by the people of Canada. The Canadian Pacific is a monument of public as well as of private faith.

Meanwhile, the work of construction had been going ahead. Under William Van Horne's masterful methods the leisurely pace of government construction quickened into the most rapid achievement on record. A time schedule, carefully made out in advance, was adhered to with remarkably little variation.

Work was begun at the east end of the line, from the point of junction with the Canada Central, but at first energy was devoted chiefly to the portion crossing the plains. Important changes in route were made. The main line had already been deflected to pass through Winnipeg. Now a much more southerly line across the plains was adopted, making for Calgary rather than Edmonton. The new route was shorter by 100 miles, and more likely to prevent the construction of a rival road south of it later. For many years it had been assumed that the tillable lands of the West lay in a 'Fertile Belt' or rainbow, following roughly the Saskatchewan Valley and curving round a big wedge of the American desert projecting north. Certainly the short, withered, russet-colored grasslands of the border country looked forbidding beside the green herbage of the North Saskatchewan. But new investigations reported in 1879 showed that only a very small section was hopelessly arid. With this objection removed, the only drawback to the southern route was the difficulty of finding as good a route through the mountains as the northerly Yellowhead Pass route, but on this the company decided to take its chances.

Work on the plains was begun in May 1881, and by the end of the year 161 miles had been completed. This progress was counted too slow. Under Van Horne's management a contract was made in 1882 with Langdon and Shepard of St Paul to complete the line to Calgary. Later in the year a construction company was organized, the North American Railway Contracting Company, to build all the uncompleted sections of the main line for $32 million cash and $45 million common stock. This was really a financing rather than a construction expedient, and was abandoned within a year.

In this section the engineering difficulties were not serious, but the pace of construction which was demanded, and the fact that every stick of timber and every pound of food, as well as every rail and spike, had to be brought a great distance, required remarkable organization. Three hundred subcontractors were employed on the portion of the line crossing the plains. Bridge gangs and track layers followed close on the graders' heels. In 1882 over two-and-a-half miles of track a day were laid. In the following year, for weeks in succession, the average ran three-and-a-half miles a day, and in one record smashing three days 20 miles were covered. By the end of this year the track was within four miles of the summit of the Rockies.

this continent. It was simply to rely entirely on stock issues, to endeavor to build the road without incurring any bonded debt. Not until the last year of construction, 1885, were bonds based upon the security of the road itself issued for sale. It was doubtless desirable to avoid the methods by which so many American roads had been hopelessly waterlogged by excessive bond issues. The memory of the St Paul & Pacific's six-million share capital as against its $28 million bonded indebtedness was fresh in the minds of the members of the syndicate.

Stephen and Smith and M'Intyre pledged their St Paul or other stock for loans in New York and Montreal, but still the gap was unfilled. They turned to the government, requesting a loan of $22.5 million, to be secured by a first charge on the main line. In return, they agreed to complete the road by May 1886, five years earlier than the contract required. The request at first was scouted by Sir John MacDonald. Parliament would not consent, and if Parliament consented the country would revolt. Bankruptcy stared the company in the face when John Henry Pope came to the rescue. He soon convinced Sir John that if the Canadian Pacific smashed, the Conservative party would smash the day after, and the aid was promised. The Cabinet was won over, and Sir Charles Tupper, hastily summoned by cable

Workers take a break from their labor on a timber retaining wall in Rogers Pass. In the days before hard hats, workers wore head covering for protection from sunstroke.

The change of route across the plains had made it essential to pierce the Rockies by a more southerly pass than the Yellowhead. The Kicking Horse or Hector Pass, short but steep, was finally chosen, but here, as at the Yellowhead, to cross the first range did not mean victory. The towering Selkirk range faced the pass, as the Caribou Mountains flanked the Rockies farther north. Until the rails reached the hills the engineers had found no way through them, and had contemplated a long detour to the north, following the winding Columbia. Then Major Rogers, the engineer whom James J Hill had suggested to take charge of the location of the mountain section, found a route, steep but practicable, across the Selkirks, following the Beaver River Valley and Bear Creek, and then through Rogers Pass into the Valley of the Illecillewaet, and so through Eagle Pass to the settled location at Kamloops. Both in the Kicking Horse and in the Rogers Pass gradients of 116 feet to the mile were found necessary, but these difficult stretches were concentrated with one operating section of 120 miles and could easily be overcome by the use of additional engines. Unique provision was made against the mountain avalanches by erecting diverting timbers near the summits and building mile upon mile of snow sheds over which the avalanches passed harmless. As a result of these expedients and of raising the roadbed across the prairies unusually high, the Canadian Pacific lost less time through snow blockades than the great railways of the eastern United States.

It was not until 1884 that the wilderness north of Lake Superior was attacked in strong force. Nine thousand men were employed here alone. Rock and muskeg, hill and hollow, made this section more difficult to face than even the Fraser Canyon. In one muskeg area seven layers of Canadian Pacific rails are buried, one below the other. The stretch along the shore of the lake was particularly difficult. The Laurentian rocks were the oldest known to geologists and, more pertinent, the toughest known to engineers. A dynamite factory was built on the spot and a road blasted through. One mile cost $700,000 to build and several cost half a million. The time required and the total expenditure would have been prohibitive had not the management decided to make extensive use of trestle work. It would have cost over two dollars a cubic yard to cut through the hills and fill up the hollows by team haul; it cost only one-tenth of that to build timber trestles, carrying the line high, and to fill up later by train haul.

An unexpected test of the need of this section came before it was completed. Early in 1885 the government realized too late that serious trouble was brewing among Indians of the Northwest. Unless troops could be sent in before the grass grew, a long and bloody contest and a serious setback would be inevitable. The railway was far from complete, with 120 miles of gaps unfilled, and the government considered it impossible to get the troops there in time. Van Horne, who had had much experience in handling troops in the Civil War, astonished the authorities by offering to take men from Kingston or Quebec to Qu'Appelle in 10 days. Part of the gaps were bridged by temporary rails laid on ice and snow, only 90 miles being uncompleted by spring. In one stretch the men were

Diesel locomotive 5006, in 'action red' markings, and a yellow Canadian Pacific caboose idle in the snow near Smith Falls, Ontario on a crisp, chilly New Years Day in 1981. Incorporated in 1881, CPR's original charter was to build a transcontinental railroad through Canada. Today CPR is the rail division of Canadian Pacific Limited, which is also involved in trucking, shipping, air transportation and telecommunications. CP Rail currently operates in all Canadian provinces, except Newfoundland and Prince Edward Island, on 21,500 miles of track. The 'action red' color scheme was introduced in the mid-1970s to replace the former, understated, grey and maroon livery.

marched across the ice to save a long detour. Through the rest they were carried, covered with furs and straw, in contractors' sleighs from one camp to the next. Four days after leaving Kingston, the first troops landed at Winnipeg, and though the revolt was not prevented, it was speedily crushed. There was no longer any question about the value of the north shore link, and the opposition to the Canadian Pacific fell from that hour.

Meanwhile, the government section between Port Arthur (or Fort William) and Winnipeg had been taken over by the company in 1883, though not entirely completed. Two years later the thousands of Chinese laborers working on the difficult Kamloops-Port Moody section finished their task, and the government work was done. The only gap remaining lay in the Gold Range. There, in the Eagle Pass at Craigellachie, on 7 November 1885, the eastward and westward track layers met. It was only a year or so before that the Northern Pacific had celebrated the driving of the last golden spike by an excursion which cost the company a third of a million dollars and heralded the bankruptcy of the road. There was no banquet and no golden spike for the last rail in the Canadian Pacific. William Van Horne had announced that 'the last spike would be just as good an iron spike as any on the road,' and had it not been that Donald A Smith happened along in time to drive the spike home, it would have been hammered in by the worker on the job. Six months later the first passenger train went through from Montreal to Vancouver. The longest railway in the world was opened from coast to coast, five years before the time required by the original contract.

The CP Rail Station at Banff, Alberta (*above*) in the heart of the Canadian Rockies. CP built hotels to accommodate passengers who desired to linger and enjoy the spectacular scenery. Donald Smith (*below*) driving the last spike to allow the first transcontinental train to cross Canada. William C Van Horne (*right*) the then CPR General Manager who was the driving force behind the railroad's push across the continent.

To realize how great a work had been accomplished requires today some effort of the imagination. The Canada the present generation knows is a united Canada, an optimistic, self-confident Canada, with rapidly rounding-out industries and occupations which give scope for the most ambitious of her sons as well as for tens of thousands from overseas. It is a Canada whose provinces and whose railroads stretch from ocean to ocean. But the Canada of 1870 was much different. On the map it covered half a continent, but in reality it stopped at the Great Lakes. There was little national spirit, little diversity of commercial enterprise. Hundreds of thousands had been drawn by the greater attraction of United States.

It was the opening up of the West that changed the whole face of Canadian life, that gave a basis for industrial expansion, that quickened national sentiment and created business optimism. It was the building of the Canadian Pacific that opened up the West and bound it fast to the distant East. Certainly not least among the makers of Canada were the men who undertook that doubtful enterprise and carried it through every obstacle to success.

## THE CANADIAN NORTHERN

The discovery of gold in the Klondike in the 1880s afforded good advertising for Canada. In government, finance, industry and the railway were men who rose to the opportunity: no longer was Canada's light hid under a bushel of wheat. The most was made of the alluring gifts she had to offer. Men the world over who strove to better themselves began the flood of immigration.

The first result of the swarming of thousands to the West was a demand for new railways, to open up plain and prairie and mineral range, and to make connection between East and West. The building of the railways in its turn gave a stimulus to every industry. As in the early 1850s and early 1880s, this period of rapid railway expansion was an era of optimistic planning and feverish speculation.

First to seize the golden opportunities were the group of men who built the Canadian Northern. Railway history offers no more remarkable record than the achievement of these few men, who, beginning in 1895 with a charter for a railway 100 miles long in Manitoba leading nowhere in particular, succeeded in building in 20 years a road from ocean to ocean, and in keeping it in their own hands through all difficulties.

It was in 1895 that William Mackenzie and Donald Mann, along with two fellow contractors, James Ross and H S Holt—decided to buy some of the charters of projected western roads and to build on their own account. They secured the charter of the Lake Manitoba Railroad & Canal Company, carrying a Dominion subsidy of 6000 acres a mile for a line from Portage la Prairie to Lake Manitoba and Lake Winnipegosis. They induced the Manitoba government to add a valuable guarantee of bonds and exemption from taxes. In 1896 running rights were secured over the track of the Manitoba & Northwestern from Portage to Gladstone, and construction was pushed 100 miles northwest from Gladstone to Dauphin. The coming need of the West was an outlet from Winnipeg to Lake Superior, to supplement the Canadian Pacific. Accordingly in 1898, under powers given by Dominion, Ontario, and Minnesota charters, construction was begun both at Winnipeg and

Canadian Pacific Railway 4-8-4 steam locomotive No 6218 pulling passenger cars at Shawinigan, Quebec.

near Port Arthur. Three years later the line was completed. Meantime the earlier road had branched westerly at Sifton, and by 1900 had crossed the border into Saskatchewan at Erwood. In 1899, in amalgamation with the Winnipeg Great Northern, chartered and subsidized to Hudson Bay, the name of the combined roads was changed to the Canadian Northern.

Then came the coup which first made the public and rival railways realize the ambitious reach of the plans of the new railway. In 1888, when the ban upon competition southward with the Canadian Pacific had been lifted, the Northern Pacific had entered Manitoba. It had gradually built up a system of three hundred and twenty miles, but had not given the competition looked for, dividing traffic with the Canadian Pacific rather than cutting rates. Now the parent line was in the receiver's hands, and its straits gave the Manitoba government its opportunity. It leased for 999 years all the Manitoba lines of the Northern

Pacific, but decided it could not profitably operate them itself without connection with the lakes. The only question was whether to lease them again to the Canadian Pacific or to the Canadian Northern. After a lively contest the younger road secured the prize. At a stroke it thus obtained extensive terminals in Winnipeg, a line south to the American border, branches westward through fertile territory and a link which practically closed the gap between its eastern and western roads.

This coal-burning Canadian National 2-8-2 locomotive (*below*) is similar to the Baldwin Class Q 2-10-2. As Canadian National Railway matured, so has its logo. *Facing page*: CN was originally formed to control several failing railroads including Canadian Northern, Grand Trunk Railway and the Grand Trunk Pacific. Newfoundland Railway was added in 1949 when that province joined the Canadian federation and, slightly later, the Northern Alberta Railroad came under CN control. Today the CN Rail system extends from the Maritime Provinces to the Pacific and north to Hudson Bay. Entirely freight oriented, CN Rail operates on almost 23,000 miles of track.

Evolution of the Canadian National Logo

CN's history as defined by motive power (*above*). Included are examples of 19th century wood (*second from right*) and coal (*far right*) fueled locomotives. Three oil fueled models are present along with a vintage 1950s diesel (*far left*). A group of happy passengers are seen (*below*) enjoying the ride aboard a VIA Rail passenger train. Similar to the US AMTRAK service, VIA was established in 1977 for passenger service only. VIA operates over some 11,500 miles of track.

The Canadian Northern had now become the third largest system in Canada, stretching from Lake Superior to Saskatchewan, with nearly 1300 miles in operation in 1902. The feeders were extending through the rich farming lands of the West. The line to Port Arthur supplemented the Canadian Pacific, providing a second spout to the funnel. This merely local success, however, did not long content its promoters. They announced their intention to build from sea to sea. The Grand Trunk, the Trans-Canada and the Great Northern all planned extensive projects.

In 1902 and 1903 a junction of forces between the Grand Trunk and the Canadian Northern was proposed, and would have had much in its favor. The negotiators could not come to terms, however, and each road continued on its independent plan. Undaunted by the Canadian government's decision to recognize and aid the Grand Trunk, the Canadian Northern turned to a policy of piecemeal construction, seeking aid from the provinces as well as from the Canadian government. The Canadian Northern pressed forward extensions, flung out branches, filled in gaps on every side. The main line was pushed westward to Edmonton in 1905. In Ontario the gap north of Lake Superior was bridged by a line from Port Arthur to Sudbury, not completed until 1914. Toronto and Ottawa were linked with the western lines, and several feeders were acquired which gave connection with Kingston and Brockville.

The most difficult task still remained—building a third railway through the mountains to the Pacific. Surveys for a road from Yellowhead Pass to Vancouver by Sandford Fleming's old route were begun in 1908. By the aid of lavish guarantees and subsidies this last link in the transcontinental system was pushed to completion in 1915.

The men behind the Canadian Northern not only planned such a project, but carried it through, displaying at every stage of the undertaking a mastery of political diplomacy, an untiring persistence, and great financial resourcefulness.

Dominion and province vied in aid which took many forms. In 1894 Canada had abandoned its policy of giving land grants, but the original companies which combined to form the Canadian Northern had previously been promised and later received over four million acres. Up to 1914 about $18 million had been realized from the sale of parts of this land, and the grants unsold were worth millions more. In addition, Ontario gave two million acres and

Quebec one-third as much. The Liberal government of Sir Wilfrid Laurier voted cash to aid in building the link between Winnipeg and Lake Superior. It declined to recognize or aid the extension to the Pacific coast, but in 1912 the Conservative government of Sir Robert Borden gave over $6 million for this work, and in the following year $15 million more for the Ontario and western Alberta sections of the main line. The provinces were less lavish; Quebec, Ontario, and Manitoba offered a total of six million.

In 1896, the Canadian Northern was a railway 100 miles long, beginning and ending nowhere, and operated by thirteen men and a boy. In 1914, a great transcontinental system was practically completed, over ten thousand miles in length, and covering seven of Canada's nine provinces. The impossible had been achieved.

## THE EXPANSION OF THE GRAND TRUNK

The year 1883 saw the high-water mark of prosperity for the Grand Trunk. In that year dividends were paid not only on guaranteed but on first, second, and third preference stock.

In 1895 Sir Henry Tyler resigned from the presidency after 23 years of service. His place was taken by Sir Charles Rivers-Wilson, who had a record of efficient service on the borders of politics and finance. The new president and a committee of directors made a thorough investigation of the Grand Trunk and recommended some immediate improvements. Their chief contribution to its success, however, was the discovery of Charles M Hays.

The great rival of the Grand Trunk had pressed forward to prosperity under the driving power of an American general manager. The new administration decided that it, too, would look to the United States for a chief executive of the ruthless efficiency and modern methods which the crisis demanded. They found him in the man who had pulled the Wabash out of a similar predicament. Mr Hays was not quite forty when in 1895 he was appointed general manager. His presence was soon felt.

Equipment was overhauled, larger freight cars were ordered and new terminals acquired. The main bridges on the road—the Suspension at Niagara Falls, the International at Fort Erie, and the Victoria at Montreal—were all rebuilt on a larger scale between 1896 and 1901. The double tracking of the main line from Montreal westward was continued, and many of the sharp curves and heavy grades of the original construction were revised.

The rush to the Klondike in 1897 started a rate war between the Canadian Pacific and the Grand Trunk, with its American connections, which lasted nearly a year. In its course rates were cut in the East as well as in the West, and the Canadian Pacific sent its westbound freight from Toronto by Smith's Falls rather than the direct line of the Grand Trunk to North Bay. Peace was patched up, but the Canadian Pacific shortly afterwards set about building a road of its own from Toronto north to its main line, thus threatening the Grand Trunk with permanent loss of western business, and providing it with one incentive toward the great westward expansion it was soon to undertake.

In 1902 Mr Hays announced that the directors were considering building a line from North Bay, through New Ontario westward, to a terminus on the Pacific at Port

Simpson or Bute Inlet. It would be a line of the highest standards. Government aid, the announcement continued, would certainly be sought and expected. However, 1903 was not 1873, and Hays had learned on the Wabash and on the Grand Trunk how difficult it was for a second-class road to compete and how costly was the process of rebuilding with the line in operation.

The Grand Trunk Pacific was organized as a subsidiary company of the old Grand Trunk, which secured control of ownership of all but a nominal share of the $25 million common stock, given it in return for guaranteeing part of the Pacific bonds. Only $20 million preference capital stock was provided for, and this was not issued. The interest of the independent shareholder was thus negligible. The money required was secured by the issue of bonds and debenture loans guaranteed by the government or the Grand Trunk.

On the western section a good route through the prairies was decided upon, not without vigorous protest from the

The vistas from the *Continental Limited,* such as this view of Mount Robson in British Columbia, (*right*) are often spectacular. CN's electric double unit No 9000 (*below*) photographed in 1928, the year before entering service.

Canadian Pacific because of the close paralleling of its line. After repeated surveys of the Peace, Pine, Wapiti, and Yellowhead Passes, the last was chosen, and a line was settled upon down the Fraser and Skeena valleys, passing through two million acres of fertile land. Remarkably low grades were secured, as favorable as on the prairie section. Kaien Island, 550 miles north of Vancouver, was chosen as the terminus, rather than Port Simpson as originally designed, and soon on its magnficent harbor and most unpromising site of rock and muskeg the new and scientifically planned city of Prince Rupert began to rise.

As the main line ran far to the north of the St Lawrence lake and river system, the original plan provided for the construction of branch lines to Fort William, North Bay and Montreal. Of these only the first, aided by the Dominion and also by the Ontario government, was built. Later, in 1914, the Dominion government itself decided to build the Montreal branch.

The great Canadian railway companies are much more than railways. The Grand Trunk system, in its new expansion, branched into every neighboring field which could be made to increase the traffic.

## CANADA'S RAILWAYS ENTER THE TWENTIETH CENTURY

When the pace of construction slackened in 1914, Canada had achieved a remarkable position in the railway world. Only five other countries—the United States, Russia, Germany, India and France—possessed a greater mileage, and relative to population none came anywhere near her. Three great systems stretched from coast to coast. Need still existed for local extensions, but by great effort the main trunk lines had been built. Not only in mileage were the railways of Canada notable. In the degree to which the minor roads had been swallowed up by a few dominating systems, in the wide sweep of their outside operations, in their extension beyond the borders of Canada itself, and in the degree to which they had been built by public aid, they challenged attention.

While there were nearly 90 railway companies in Canada in 1914, the three transcontinental systems—the Canadian Northern, the Canadian Pacific and the Grand Trunk—controlled more than 80 percent of the total mileage and also owned a variety of subsidiary undertakings such as steamships, hotels, express service, irrigation and land development and grain elevators. The control by Canadian railways of seven or eight thousand miles of lines in the United States, with corresponding extensions into Canada by American lines, was an outcome of geographic conditions, intimate social and trade connections, and a civilized view of international relations which no other countries could match.

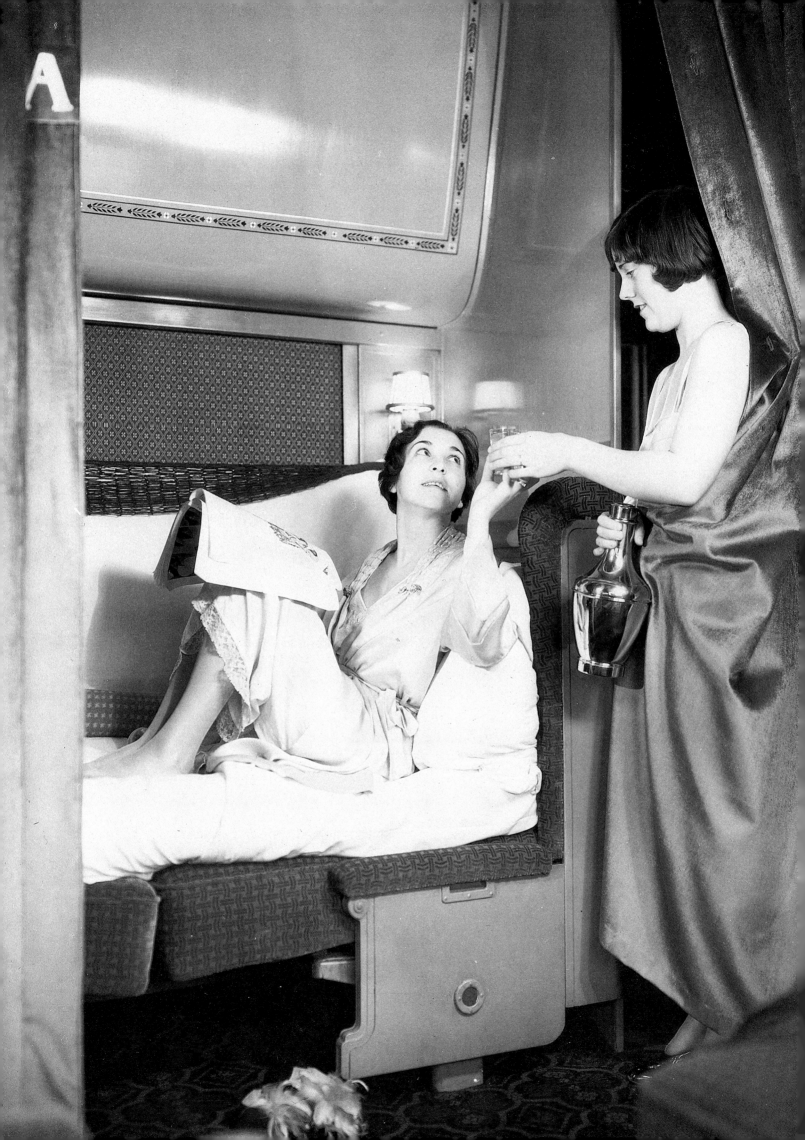

# CHAPTER 8

# THE AMERICAN RAILROADS ENTER THE TWENTIETH CENTURY

## William Cunningham

**I**n order to understand the railroad situation during and directly after America's participation in World War I, it is necessary to review the events which preceded the critical period from April 1917, when the United States declared war against Germany, to March 1920, when the railroads were restored to their owners after 26 months of operation by the federal government. That period of three years is marked by many fundamental changes in railroad administration. First came the voluntary unification of all railroads and the attempt on the part of the individual carriers to act together in the war emergency as one system under the direction of a Railroads' War Board invested by the carriers with power to suspend and disregard individual

**Passenger service reached its peak in the first half of the 20th century. This photograph (*left*), from about 1920, clearly shows the luxurious accommodations and suggests the smooth style of travelling by rail. The club car (*above*) of the Southern Pacific *Daylight* service.**

and competitive interests. This voluntary unification lasted from 11 April 1917 to 28 December 1917, or almost 9 months. The second change was the compulsory unification of all railroads under federal control, lasting 26 months until March 1920. The third came with the passage of the Transportation Act of 1920, which restored the railroads to private management and fundamentally modified the policy of public regulation.

Until a few years prior to the war, it had been the traditional policy of the typical American railroad to keep its equipment and facilities well ahead of the demands of growing traffic. The cost of additional or improved equipment, and of additional or enlarged terminals, trackage, and other physical facilities, was met either from current income or from the sale of new securities. As a result of this policy, the typical railroad was always equipped to handle its growing business economically. There was an ample factor of safety, so that the ever increasing volume of tonnage and passengers could be handled without congestion.

The ability to continue this policy depended upon net earnings sufficient to insure ample credit. So long as net earnings justified appropriations for improvements or were sufficient to assure the investor in new securities, there was no difficulty in keeping pace with expanding traffic.

This situation continued as long as net earnings were sufficient. But the gradual tendency of higher operating costs, coupled with a national and state policy of regulation which tended to reduce rather than to increase rates, soon had the effect of reducing net income. The turning point came in 1906, with the passage of the Hepburn amendment to the Interstate Commerce Act. This amendment, with its power to prescribe maximum charges, gave the Commission complete control over rates. The 1910 amendment went a step further in giving the Commission the power to suspend rates. The difficulty was aggravated by a conflict of regulating laws between the states themselves and between the states and the Interstate Commission.

Coupled with these adverse influences on net earnings came greater activity on the part of the railroad labor organizations in their demands for higher wages. Consequently it became difficult to appropriate money for improvements. Not only were the railroads as a whole unable to raise the funds necessary to equip themselves for prospective increases in traffic, but many were unable to maintain their solvency. The year 1915 marked the peak of railroad receiverships. In September of that year approximately 42,000 miles, or about one-sixth of the entire railroad mileage of the country was in the hands of the courts.

The bankrupt properties included the Atlanta, Birmingham & Atlantic, the Chicago & Eastern Illinois, the Cincinnati, Hamilton & Dayton, the Chicago, Rock Island & Pacific, the Colorado Midland, the International & Great Northern, the Missouri, Kansas & Texas, the Missouri Pacific, the Pere Marquette, the St Louis & San Francisco, the Toledo, St Louis & Western, the Wabash, the Western Pacific and the Wheeling & Lake Erie. Besides these 14 important railroads, 68 smaller properties were then in the hands of the courts.

Under such strained financial conditions it was but natural that railroad development should be halted. New construction practically ceased. The mileage of new railroad built in that year was less than in any year since the period of the Civil War. In 1906 there had been 5623 miles of new track constructed. In 1914 there were only 1532, and in 1915 just 933 miles were laid. Orders for new locomotives and cars dropped to an unprecedented low level, and drastic retrenchment and curtailment in service were in evidence.

No spokesman presented the railroad case with more vigor or with more vision than the late James J Hill. For several years before World War I he foresaw the ultimate

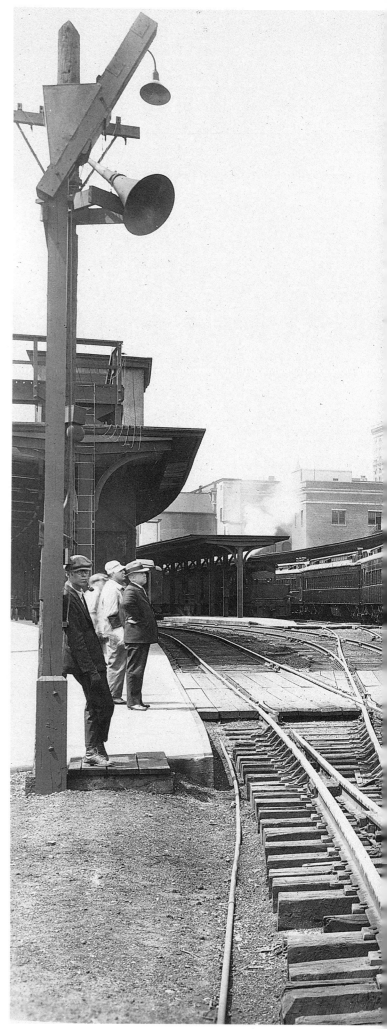

The Great Northern *Empire Builder* at the St Paul Union Depot on the day of its inaugural in June of 1929. The fleet of eight luxury trains cut five hours from previous schedules between Chicago and Seattle, making the run in 62 hours and 45 minutes. Great Northern continued the *Empire Builders* tradition into the 1950s adding new streamliners and dome cars to keep the feel of luxury travel. Since the 1970s, the *Empire Builder* has been operated by Amtrak, albeit with newer locomotives.

Railroad executive and financier James Hill (*right*). Born in Ontario in 1838, Hill's early education was interrupted to help support his family after the death of his father. He had shown such academic promise however, that the head of the Rockwood Academy, his former school, gave him help in the form of free tuition. Hill was an enthusiast of things Far Eastern and, at the age of 18, determined to make his way to the Orient. Not having sufficient funds for the passage from the East Coast, he made his way to St Paul where he hoped to join a band of trappers traveling to the West Coast. Forced to find employment while waiting for the trappers to organize, Hill worked for transportation companies and learned much about the problems of moving freight. He served as a clerk for a steamboat line and later became an independent freight agent and commodities broker. In 1867, Hill, who saw the future of coal as a desirable fuel for railroads, began supplying the St Paul and Pacific line. Before long he had expanded his business and became a partner with former competitors in the Northwestern Fuel Company. In 1878 Hill was able to purchase the nearly bankrupt St Paul and Pacific Railroad. He was able to return it to profitability, expand and, by 1880, his lines became the Great Northern Railway, a transcontinental railroad. When the competing Northern Pacific was on the verge of bankruptcy, Hill led efforts for its reorganization, and with the help of his associates was able to save the line. In conjunction with J P Morgan, Hill also acquired enough of Chicago, Burlington & Quincy stock to give the Great Northern and the Northern Pacific access to the cities of Chicago & St Louis. Hill was also closely associated with the beginnings of the Canadian Pacific Railway. Eventually, Hill initiated the Northern Securities Company, a kind of railroad trust company. However, the company was enjoined from operation under the Sherman Anti-Trust Act of 1890. By 1906 Hill controlled a group of profitable rail systems which operated on tracks extending from the Midwest to the Pacific (*below*). Hill died in 1916.

**The Hill Group**

Chicago, Burlington & Quincy Railroad
Burlington & Missouri River Railroad
Great Northern Railway
Northern Pacific Railway

effect of the slowing down of railroad development, and he sounded a note of warning, predicting that national embarrassment would come. He made the plea for a policy of regulation which would make it possible to invest one billion dollars annually in railroad facilities, particularly in terminals. But the plea was not heeded, and the railroads were able to spend but a fraction of the sum which he regarded as necessary. Consequently the natural increase in traffic (ton-miles had doubled about every 12 or 13 years) soon overtook and exceeded the capacity of the railroads to give satisfactory service. The point of traffic saturation was reached in 1915, when the flood of extra traffic incident to the great war broke upon the railroads.

They were not prepared for the overload, but met the emergency with resourcefulness. The year 1916 brought a further increase in traffic as the orders for war materials to be shipped abroad grew in volume. Then came the American declaration of war in April, 1917, and with it the mobilization of the Army and Navy, and the large scale production of ammunition and supplies of all kinds.

## THE FIRST WORLD WAR

Within five days after the declaration of war against Germany, the Railroads' War Board was organized under a resolution signed by the chief executive of practically every railroad in the United States. The resolution bound the railroads individually to voluntary coordination of their operations during the war within a continental railroad system, 'merging during such period all their merely individual and competitive activities in the effort to produce a maximum of transportation efficiency.'

The personnel of the Executive Committee of the War Board were Howard Elliott, chairman of the Northern Pacific Railway; Hale Holden, president of the Chicago, Burlington & Quincy Railroad; Julius Kruttschnitt, chairman of the Southern Pacific Company; Samuel Rea; president of the Pennsylvania Railroad and Fairfax Harrison, president of the Southern Railway, who served as chairman of the committee.

While the controlling motive was one of patriotic en-

Edward Harriman (*right*) an American railroad builder and financier was born in Hempstead, New York in 1848. By the time Harriman started to work on Wall Street as an office boy at the age of 21, he had already demonstrated that he had the skills and acumen to succeed in stock speculations. In 1883, he became affiliated with the Illinois Central, becoming President of the line in 1887. Ten years later he became a director of the Union Pacific, which was in receivership. By the turn of the century he had restored the road to a sound financial condition and he became president of the Union Pacific in 1903. When the UP board authorized the issue of $100 million of convertible bonds, Harriman was given control of the funds. He used much of the money to buy from C P Huntington's estate a 46 percent share of the Southern Pacific and ownership of the Central Pacific. Harriman next turned his attention to Chicago, a move that put him in direct conflict with James Hill in an attempt to control the Chicago, Burlington & Quincy. Outmaneuvered, Harriman then began to buy stock in the Northern Pacific, which had a half interest in the CB&Q. The intense battle between Harriman and Hill precipitated the panic of 1901. Subsequent court decisions on the distribution of the stock resulted in Hill control of the Northwestern Pacific and Chicago, Burlington & Quincy. No longer able to wield influence in these companies Harriman sold his stock. Harriman then began buying stock in roads all over the country, ostensibly to establish a Union Pacific community of interests. This buying spree led to an investigation by the Interstate Commerce Commission in 1906 and 1907. The report of the ICC stated that Harriman's use of the Union Pacific as a holding company for the stock of other companies was not in the public interest. Harriman had to be content with the combined route systems of the Union Pacific, Southern Pacific and other roads (*below*). Edward Harriman died in 1909.

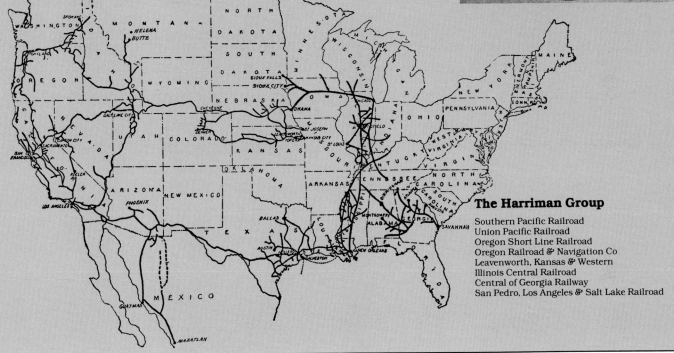

**The Harriman Group**

Southern Pacific Railroad
Union Pacific Railroad
Oregon Short Line Railroad
Oregon Railroad & Navigation Co
Leavenworth, Kansas & Western
Illinois Central Railroad
Central of Georgia Railway
San Pedro, Los Angeles & Salt Lake Railroad

deavor to make the railroads the greatest possible aid to the government in prosecuting the war, there was undoubtedly a desire on the part of many railroad executives to demonstrate to the public that American railroad men under private ownership and control of railroads could do their part in the emergency without formal government action such as that taken in England. The demonstration, if successful, would curb the activities of the growing number of people who then looked with favor upon government ownership of the railroads.

Each railroad individually was operated by its chief executive under instructions from the executive committee of the Board. Outside of freight car utilization and troop movements, an excess of centralized control of detail was avoided. While the first energies of the Railroads' Board were devoted to satisfying the demands of the Army and Navy, efforts were made to take care of the needs of other branches of the government, and to impose the minimum of hardship upon the civilian population. Considerable progress was made in bringing about the joint use of terminals and running tracks, in reducing the volume of traffic moving via circuitous routes, and in curtailing superfluous passenger trains established for competitive reasons. The statistical records of April to December 1917 show commendable improvements in the efficient utilization of locomotives and freight cars, and the inconvenience to the civilian travelers was much less than that which was imposed in England.

Yet the results as a whole were not satisfactory in the latter part of 1917. Freight congestions began to occur on the lines serving the Atlantic seaboard. Yards, sidings, and even running tracks were clogged with cars. The freight service as a whole on the lines between Chicago, Pittsburgh, and the Atlantic ports was badly demoralized. One reason for these congestions was the failure of the railroads to keep up their programs of enlargement and improvement and to maintain their usual scale of additions to the equipment of locomotives and freight cars that had in turn been the result of government over regulation in the early part of the century.

The failure to control the flow of export traffic was the second cause of the congestion. Freight for export was accepted without regard to the capacity of the available ships. Part of the war materials for the Allies was ordered from American manufacturers under contracts which provided that a large percentage of the invoice would be paid as soon as the materials were loaded on cars. There was, therefore, every inducement to load the materials into the cars at the earliest possible moment. The result was that the export tonnage on the rails very much exceeded the capacity of the ships, and the cars containing the excess were held for months at a time. If something like the permit system which was adopted later by the United States Railroad Administration had been put into effect, or if the Railroads' War Board had been able to curb the spirit of competition, the flow of this traffic might have been controlled at the source and the crisis might have been avoided. Freight cars held weeks and months under load were not released in time to be returned for new loads, and a car shortage resulted. Efforts to pick out certain cars from the accumulation added to the delay and confusion.

The original 1887 Act to Regulate Commerce provided that the railroads, in time of war, should give preference and precedence over all other traffic to the movement of troops and materials of war, and should adopt every means within their control to facilitate and expedite military traffic. Under this authority each branch of the government insisted upon priority in the movement of *its* freight, but there was no effective agency for coordinating these demands.

## COMPULSORY FEDERAL UNIFICATION

By December 1917 the railroad situation had become acute. The Interstate Commerce Commission, in a special message to Congress, recommended that complete unification of the railroads should be effected, either by the carriers themselves, with the assistance of the government, or by their operation by the president as a unit during the war.

Commissioner McChord, in a dissenting opinion, disagreed with the majority recommendation that the carriers be permitted to bring about complete unification themselves with aid from the government. Instead he argued that 'the supreme arm of governmental authority is essential,' either by the exercise of the president's authority to operate the roads or by the creation of a single government administration control. In his opinion unification of diversified governmental control was as vital as unification of the properties. On 26 December 1917, President Woodrow Wilson took possession of the railroads of the country as a war measure, and appointed William McAdoo, Secretary of the Treasury, as Director General of Railroads, to act for the president under the authority granted to the president by the Army Appropriations Act of August 29, 1916.

The tenseness of the labor situation was another ground for the federalization of railroads. The high wages paid in the shipbuilding yards, in munition plants, and in other work on war supplies, and the sharp advances in the cost

**Southern Pacific 4-8-2 oil fired steam locomotive No 4300 (*below*). The Los Angeles Union Pacific Terminal (*above*) in the late 1920s.**

The nerve centers of railroad terminals are the switch control rooms like this one from the 1920s. Although computers come into use much more today, there are still track maps to monitor the traffic.

of living, had caused much unrest among railroad workers. While the railroad executives were deliberating, there were threats of strikes. The situation during the latter part of 1917, just preceding federal control, was exceedingly acute.

The president's proclamation of 26 December 1917 directed Mr McAdoo, as Director General of Railroads, to take possession of, control and operate the railroads with the president of a railroad company acting as agent of the director general and at the same time as the chief executive of the corporation. This form of organization was continued until after the passage of the Federal Control Act, approved 21 March 1918. Immediately after the passage of the Control Act an attempt was made to draw a fairly sharp line between railroad activities which were purely corporate and those which were federal.

## STANDARDIZING THE DESIGN OF EQUIPMENT

During the period of federal control, much publicity was given to the administration's policy of standardizing the design of locomotives and freight cars. William McAdoo's statement in July 1918 that there were '2023 different styles of freight cars and almost as many different descriptions of locomotives,' appealed to the public imagination, as did also his announcement that a committee of experts of the Railroad Administration had agreed upon 12 standard types of freight car and six standard types of

freight locomotive of two weights each. Obviously the process of standardization would make the problems of new construction much easier and eventually would reduce the cost of maintenance. In 1918 McAdoo ordered 1430 locomotives and 100,000 freight cars of standard design.

Under the terms of the contract between McAdoo and the railroad companies he was required to secure the approval of the corporation before he could permanently assign any of the new standard equipment to that corporation. There was much opposition to the universal adoption of these standards and long drawn out controversies over the assignment of the new equipment to the individual companies.

An analysis of the conflicting views on the subject indicates, however, that the railroad companies had no quarrel with standardization as a principle. Many of the larger railroad systems, such as the Pennsylvania, the Union Pacific and the Southern Pacific, had been following the principles of standardization for years, and the Master Car Builders' Association and the American Railway Association had made substantial progress toward standardization in freight car design. There was a natural resentment against the upsetting of these programs by the enforced adoption of new standards which had been somewhat hurriedly adopted by the administration experts of no greater professional standing than the experts of the larger individual systems, who had a more intimate knowledge of the peculiar local needs.

Many flaws may be picked in the details of the government standards. It can easily be shown that the require-

(*Overleaf*) The construction of Southern Pacific's Mission Bay roundhouse in San Francisco during 1941. Southern Pacific's 4-8-4 locomotive No 4405 (*above*). The immensity of this Baldwin-built articulated 2-6-6-2 locomotive of the Baltimore & Ohio Line (*below*) is clear when compared to the Vauclain family standing in front of the huge wheels. Samuel Vauclain was an American inventor and locomotive manufacturer. In his early years he worked with his father on the Pennsylvania Railroad first in the machine shops and then as an inspector. He moved to Baldwin Locomotive where in 1889 he designed and built the first articulated locomotive which was delivered to the Baltimore and Ohio Railroad. This compound design greatly improved economy and fuel efficiency and was very successful. Vauclain rose through the ranks and, in 1929, was selected to the position of Chairman of the Board at Baldwin.

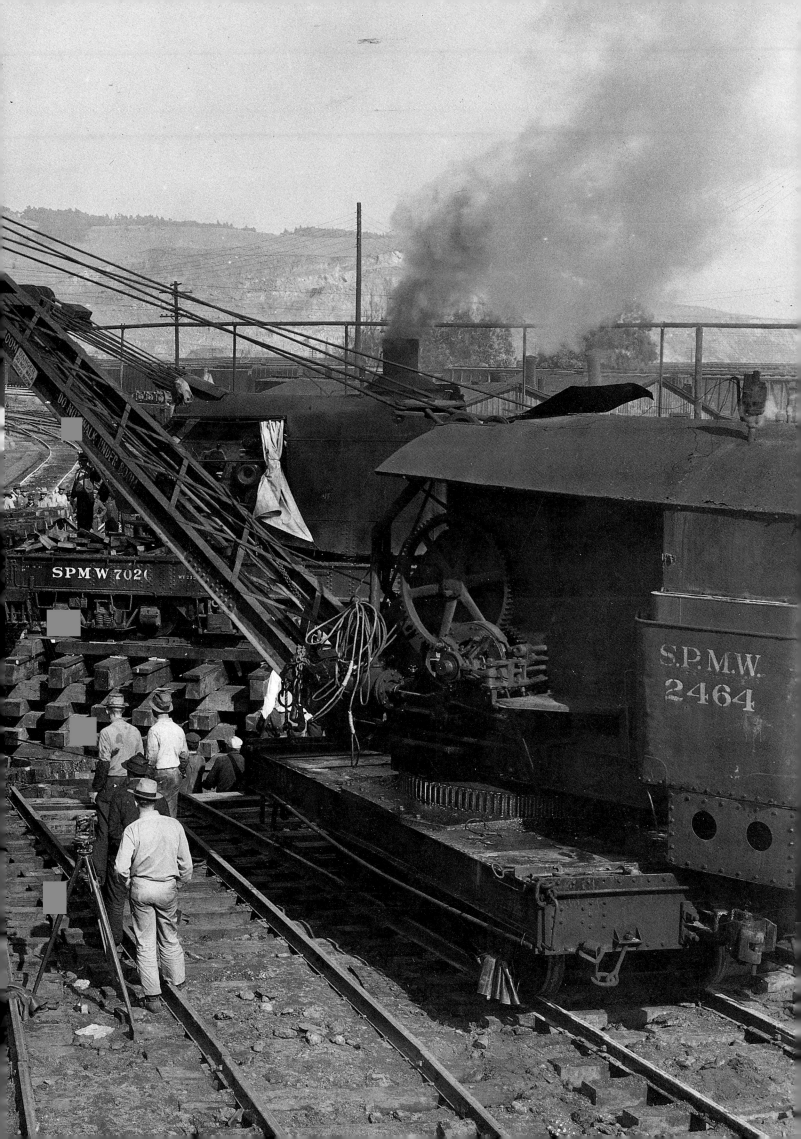

THROUGH

ments of an individual road could not be efficiently met by any one of the twelve standard types of locomotive. On one road, for example, the lighter type of locomotive designed for slow freight service was not quite powerful enough to haul the train which the locomotive of local design could haul. The heavier type of standard locomotive, on the other hand, exceeded the capacity of the bridges. That road had to choose between a loss in train-loading efficiency with the lighter type of locomotive, or undertaking an expensive program of bridge strengthening or rebuilding at a time when both labor and materials were scarce. If it accepted the second alternative it faced the fact that the additional capital expenditures for bridges would earn returns only on the heavier trains hauled by the relatively few new locomotives and could not avail itself fully of the additional capacity of its line until all of its own standard locomotives were displaced by the heavier standard of the United States Railroad Administration.

The case for the standardization of the freight car was stronger. Locomotives ordinarily were confined in service to the rails of the owning company. Freight cars then, as today, were used in common under car service rules and the *per diem* rules agreement. They are repaired (with certain exceptions) on the road where the need of the repairs develops. The average freight car of an individual road then, as now, was at home less than one-half of the time. Obviously if there were a common standard for the types of car used for the great bulk of the interchanged traffic, each road would be required to carry a much smaller stock of repair parts, and there would be a reduction in repair time.

Yet here, as in the case of locomotives, local traffic characteristics had an important bearing. Some roads had

The SP ticket office (*facing page*) in the Palace Hotel, San Francisco, California during the early 1900s. *Above:* Pennsylvania Railroad electric passenger service on a triple tracked main line. Service was name of the business in railroading as passengers (*below*) were able to have their bags waiting as they stepped off the train. *Overleaf:* Southern Pacific's Houston Station waiting area was typical of the spacious, art deco styling of the 1930s era station.

found it advisable to design their box cars with a special view to the requirements of grain traffic, while others found it necessary to consider the special requirements of automobile shipments. One type of box car could not be ideal for all classes of traffic. The standards of the Railroad Administration differed materially from those, for example, of the Southern Pacific who had been a leader in the movement toward standardization. Their freight car standards were the results of a very careful study of experts over a series of years. The officers of that company, therefore, quite naturally objected to the permanent acceptance of other standards prepared under wartime pressure by engineers whose qualifications were no greater than those of their own engineers and consultants.

The objections of the Southern Pacific are mentioned specifically because Chairman Kruttschnitt made the point that the excess weight in the Railroad Administration standard box car over the Southern Pacific standard was not justified by traffic or engineering requirements, and that its excess weight meant a needless expense, not only in first cost, but also in train operating expenses because of the increased dead weight.

## THE TRANSPORTATION ACT OF 1920

Federal control of railroads terminated at 12:01 am on 1 March 1920. The return of the roads to private management was accomplished under the terms of the Transportation Act, the final result of more than one year's active consideration by Congress of the whole railroad situation. The hearings before the appropriate committees began early in 1919, but the Act was not approved by the president until 28 February 1920, a day before it became effective. Many plans were proposed for adoption by Congress, and the discussion before the committees and on the floors of Congress attracted wide public attention.

The Act amended in some respects nearly every section of the existing Act to Regulate Commerce. It gave the Interstate Commerce Commission greater control over rates and service, routing of freight, extensions, abandonments and consolidations of lines, and joint use of terminals and equipment. It also vested the Commission with greater powers in determining the divisions of through rates on interline traffic between the carriers participating in the haul.

During the 26 months of federal control there were serious dislocations in the normal flow of traffic and much disturbance in operating and financial features from the viewpoint of the individual companies. Serious doubts were entertained whether many carriers could successfully stand the shock of the change, and there were fears that general financial embarrassment might follow the cessation of payment of the government rentals which the companies had received during federal control. To avoid disaster of that kind the Act provided for a six-month transition period in which the properties would be operated by the companies with their individual organizations, assured of net railway operating income equal to the rentals paid by the government during the World War I period of federal control.

A fair return, for the first two years, or until 1 March 1922, was set at 5½ percent. The rates must be uniform for all competitive traffic. Under any uniform scale of rates there would be wide differences in the earning power of the weak and the strong roads.

The problem of the weak road has always been a difficult one in rate regulation. Recognizing the fact that the new rate-making rule could not operate successfully so long as there were substantial differences in the earning power of the two groups of carriers, the strong and the weak, Congress in framing the Transportation Act laid down the principle that disparity in earning power shall be removed by a process of merging the weak with the strong. The law's aim was the ultimate merging of the railroads, so that instead of a large number of separately owned and operated properties varying widely in mileage and in earning power, there would emerge a small number of systems of fairly equal size and financial strength. As it turned out, this intention of the Transportation Act of 1920 would be the most far-reaching. It set the scene for the consolidations and mergers that marked the history of American railroading for the rest of the twentieth century (see chart on pages 14–15).

*Below:* **A streamlined locomotive by Baldwin, once the builder of most of the steam locomotives in the United States.**

*Overleaf:* **Playing grown-up was easy in the dining car. This photograph promoted a children's menu designed to accommodate the appetites of younger passengers.**

*Below:* A 5000 hp General Electric locomotive used by Great Northern for the 7.79-mile run through the Cascade tunnel in western Washington. Electrics, rather than diesels, were used because the tunnel was not ventilated. *Right:* The pantograph on top of one of the cars of the Interurban electric railway that connected San Francisco to the East Bay in the 1930s.

## ELECTRIC RAILWAYS

At the turn of the century, it was correctly predicted that the future development of the passenger service would be influenced very greatly by the use of electricity instead of steam for motor power. In 1887 there were 13 short lines, using altogether about 100 cars; twenty years later there were 2233 miles in Massachusetts alone, which had as many miles of street railways as of trunk-line railroads. In the beginning these electric lines were laid only in city streets, but they soon became suburban and interurban roads.

The electric railway had certain technical advantages over the steam railroad (and over the later diesel railroads as well), especially for passenger service. The power was supplied by central plants and could be used in small units to run a single car or in large units to propel a train; moreover, the power taken from the current could be applied to as many axles of the car or train as desired. The steam engine, in order to avoid a waste of power, had to haul several coaches, and the result was a very incomplete use of the capacity of the vehicle. The electric cars on the other hand could be run singly, at short intervals, and the number of cars could be closely adjusted to the requirements of the traffic. When compared with steam, or even diesel, the electric train was clean, safe, quiet and unquestionably economical for local service in the light freight, express, and passenger service. In the suburban and to a large extent in the interurban traffic, the electric cars were either run over the lines of the connecting street railways or with close connections that enabled passengers to travel directly without delay between their homes and places of business.

Electric roads were cheaper to build and operate, and their fares were less. Although they were in the hearts of urban areas, rights of way had usually cost little up to 1900, and the equipment had been relatively inexpensive. The electric lines handled local traffic at much lower fares than the steam roads, and the rate of profits in the electric railway business had exceeded the steam-railroad companies.

At the turn of the century, it was correctly predicted that electricity would take the place of steam as the motor power for short-distance urban traffic, as it had already begun to do in the steam roads entering such cities as New York.

# CHAPTER 9
# DECADES OF THE DIESEL: A NEW ERA COMES TO NORTH AMERICA'S RAILROADS

## Prepared by the Electro-Motive Division of General Motors

On 26 May 1934, a three-car, articulated streamlined train sped from Denver, Colorado, to Chicago, Illinois in 14 hours in a dawn-to-dusk, nonstop run that was to open officially the second year of Chicago's great 'Century of Progress Exposition.' The famous trip culminated on the stage of the 'Wings of a Century' pageant on Chicago's lakefront where the plaudits of World's Fair goers added to the acclaim the unique little train received at every village along the Burlington's right-of-way. The train, later known as the 'Pioneer Zephyr,' served its original purpose and accomplished far more than that—it ushered in a new era in rail transportation.

In the brief 14 hours of its spectacular run it had: dramatized application of the internal combustion engine in mainline railroad service, indicated practicability of the two-cycle diesel engine in rail service, and convinced railroad people and General Motors executives that the diesel engine could have an important future in railroad power.

Behind the story of that dawn-to-dusk run lies an account of inventive genius, teamwork and dedicated determination.

The successful trip of the 'Pioneer Zephyr' resulted from three streams of action which occurred almost simultaneously. One was the success of the Electro-Motive Company (founded in 1922 and a subsidiary of General

The gleaming *City of San Francisco* (*opposite*) that ran from Chicago to San Francisco was operated jointly by Union Pacific, Chicago & North Western and Southern Pacific. A Great Northern diesel (*above*) stops for gas in northern Montana.

Motors since 1930) in developing the gasoline-electric rail-car for branch line service on United States railroads. Harold L Hamilton, founder of Electro-Motive, and Richard M Dilworth, his chief engineer, were key figures in this activity in which Electro-Motive developed the variable voltage generator and for the first time evolved an electric transmission that could harness the mechanical energy of a gasoline engine successfully in rail service with a control system operated by a single throttle.

Second, was the desire of progressive railroad men to apply the inherent advantages of the internal combustion engine to mainline railroad service. The late Ralph Budd, then president of the Chicago, Burlington & Quincy Railroad, was one of these men.

Last, was the successful development of a lightweight, two-cycle diesel engine by the late Charles F Kettering and his associates in the General Motors research laboratories. This development was of singular importance in the evolution of the diesel locomotive as we know it today for it provided a new kind of diesel engine—one that was built, as Kettering said, 'the way it wanted to be built, not the way engineers thought it should be built.'

Electro-Motive would be the single most important factor in the evolution of diesel locomotive in North America. More than 80 percent of those which would take to the rails over the next half century would be built by Electro-Motive.

The first prototype Electro-Motive diesel engines were used in 1933 to provide power for the Chevrolet assembly line at the Chicago 'Century of Progress.' Although they were at the time strictly experimental and difficult to keep running, they attracted the attention of Ralph Budd, who at that time was contracting with the Budd Company in Philadelphia to build the small, three-car, Zephyr train. He needed a prime mover for the revolutionary new train and, through Hamilton, came in contact with Kettering.

Budd finally persuaded Kettering to make one of the new engines available for the train. He remarked later that while Kettering expressed qualms about the feasibility of using such an experimental prime mover before it had been thoroughly proven in the laboratory, he and his Burlington associates had no fears because once Kettering had committed himself he'd have to stand behind it. The subsequent events proved him right and sowed the seeds for tremendous locomotive power development which in two decades would see the end of steam power that had dominated the scene for more than 100 years of US railroad service.

With the success of the 'Pioneer Zephyr' came another famous train, the Union Pacific's M-10001, another articulated streamliner powered by a General Motors two-cycle diesel engine that set a new transcontinental record of 56 hours 55 minutes in running from Los Angeles to New York City in October 1934.

Soon came pressures from other railroads, notably the Baltimore & Ohio and the Santa Fe, for separately contained diesel power units that could haul standard passenger equipment. The decision was made to provide Electro-Motive with a manufacturing facility, and a site was selected at La Grange, Illinois, a suburb of Chicago.

*Right:* **The Burlington Route's** *Pioneer Zephyr* **was America's first diesel-powered streamlined train. It began operation on 9 April 1934 with an engine designed by Electro-Motive, the company that would provide more than 80 percent of the diesels used on the rails.**

The site provided access to all major railroads serving Chicago, was close to a skilled labor supply and had the necessary solid rock foundation to support the heavy lifting cranes needed.

Ground was broken at La Grange on 27 March 1935. Meanwhile, orders came from the Baltimore & Ohio for an 1800-horsepower diesel locomotive with two 12-cylinder engines. The Santa Fe ordered two such units for a 3600-horsepower locomotive to power the new 'Super Chief,' and work began on the prototype. Thus, while ground was being broken for its own plant, Electro-Motive was farming out contracts for the construction of five locomotive units. Its own demonstrator units, *No 511* and *512,* and the 1800-horsepower unit for the Baltimore & Ohio, which later became the Baltimore & Ohio *No 50,* were ordered constructed by the Erie locomotive shops of General Electric. The two units for the Santa Fe were placed with the St Louis Car Company.

The demonstrators were completed in June 1935, and went out on test runs over various railroads from coast to coast. The Baltimore & Ohio took delivery of *No 50* in August of that year and immediately put it to work on the new high-speed 'Royal Blue' between Jersey City and Washington. On its inaugural run, with many Washington and New York dignitaries aboard, the train came to an ignominious stop west of Elizabeth, New Jersey. Someone had failed to completely fill the fuel tanks in Washington and the train had to be hauled to its terminus in Jersey City by a steam engine. The incident served to keep Electro-Motive humble but dedicated to the tremendous task that

lay ahead—development of the diesel locomotive to its present state of efficiency.

In the winter of 1935–36, machinery was rolled into place at the La Grange plant which then boasted 200,000 square feet of manufacturing space and about 400 employees. The first locomotive to be built at the new plant came off the assembly lines on 20 May 1936. It was a 600-horsepower switching locomotive for the Santa Fe. This unit later was rebuilt and upgraded to a 900-horsepower locomotive.

Within two years another momentous decision was made at La Grange—to develop and build all major components of the locomotive, both electrical and mechanical. From this decision came the successful development of a V-type diesel engine, the General Motors 567 series engine that replaced the in-line 201-A engine which had powered the 'Pioneer Zephyr.' The first Electro-Motive designed and built generators and traction motors also began coming off the assembly line. Providing matched components designed to work harmoniously together in the locomotive and providing one manufacturing responsibility for the customer became the foundation for a rigid policy of standardization that required all improvements to be applicable to earlier models.

It was in this pioneering environment that the greatest single locomotive of the twentieth century (according to *Trains* Magazine) the General Motors *No 103,* was born in 1939. This four-unit 5400-horsepower diesel freight locomotive—the first mainline diesel-powered freight locomotive in the United States—left La Grange on 25 Novem-

Southern Pacific diesel locomotives: In 1946 Southern Pacific placed orders with the Electro-Motive division of General Motors for 20 diesel locomotives destined to be the first of a large fleet for freight service. These 4000 hp 4(B-B) class locomotives had a cab on each end so they could be operated in either direction without having to be turned. The following year the first of these mainline diesel freight locomotives began replacing the steam locomotives that had been well used during the war years. The diesels were much more efficient on steep grades, on curves and over long distances. These locomotives were numbered from 6240 through 6295. A second unit of locomotives was ordered in 1949 and was numbered in the 8000s. Each of the later locomotives (classed F-7 by the manufacturer) has identical specifications: the total weight was 923,900 lb on 16 pairs of 40-inch drivers; the starting tactive effort was 234,600 lb; and the continuous tractive effort at 9 miles per hour (the speed at which maximum pulling efficiency is achieved) was 209,600 lb. Each locomotive contained four 1500-hp 16-cylinder diesel engines of 8½-inch bore and 10-inch stroke. The overall length of each locomotive was 201 feet and 6¼ inches.

ber 1939, to begin a grueling 83,000 mile demonstration on 20 major railroads. By the time it completed its exhausting assignment under every conceivable operating condition, it had proven that it could do twice the work of a steam locomotive at half the cost. With this four-to-one economic leverage, the fate of the steam locomotive was sealed, once and for all.

Interestingly, no press releases were issued at that time to tell the story of the 'diesel that did it,' and none of the railroad trade publications carried as much as one line about the experiment.

However, ensuing events showed that this locomotive didn't require any fanfare. It wrote its own story, and with it carved a new niche in locomotive history. Later sold to the Southern Railway in May 1941, the lead unit of the famous train is now on permanent exhibition in the National Museum of Transport in St Louis.

## DIESELS REPLACE STEAM

**D**evelopment of the first diesel-powered freight locomotives coincided with World War II, and the railroad industry pressed every bit of equipment into the herculean task of transporting men and materials. Electro-Motive supplied the Navy with 567 engines for Tank Landing Ships and also built a vertical crankcase diesel for Navy submarine chasers. The company quit making locomotives for several months in 1942, but pressure from the railroads

*Opposite:* **Working on a diesel at the Baldwin plant. Baldwin had long been the leading builder of steam locomotives and expected to glide easily into the lead with diesels, but the venture failed and the company collapsed. Santa Fe Railroad's** *San Diegan* **(***above***) southbound along the southern California coast. In addition to the** *San Diegan* **Santa Fe RR operated several well known passenger lines including** *El Capitan,* **the** *Chief* **and the** *Super Chief.*

eventually brought allocations of sufficient critical materials to permit construction of one 1350-horsepower *Model FT* diesel freight locomotive per working day.

At the end of the war in 1945, most of the nation's railroads embarked upon sweeping dieselization programs to reap the economic benefits of the new power. The La Grange plant was doubled, then quadrupled, and finally reached over 3.5 million square feet of manufacturing space.

Additional manufacturing facilities were established in Chicago, for fabrication of major sub-assemblies to be included in final manufacture at La Grange and at Cleveland, Ohio where a second assembly plant was acquired for production of switching locomotives and general-purpose units.

At the same time, renewed emphasis was placed on research and development, resulting in 1946 with the 1500-horsepower model *F-3* locomotive. In 1949 came the *F-7* and the first of the general purpose series, the *GP-7.* With development work going on at an accelerated pace, the 567-C engine was introduced on 1 January 1954, and the so-called '9' series developed. Horsepower in the *GP-9* and *F-9* was increased to 1750 per unit. As the diesel power

A historical Santa Fe Hi-Level train streaking through the agricultural countryside in California's fertile San Joaquin Valley. This F-7 class train could cruise at 55 miles per hour.

fleets expanded on American railroads, a network of factory branches was established to provide component repair services and conveniently located parts-distribution centers.

The replacement of over 50,000 steam locomotives by about half that number of diesel locomotives in hardly more than two decades remains one of the most dramatic industrial developments of all time. However, from a purely economic standpoint, the replacement of older diesel locomotives by latest models of diesel power offers an equally thrilling chapter in the annals of railroad history.

With the substantial increases in horsepower that have occurred since 1958, when the 567 series engine was turbocharged, have come new and bigger opportunities for exploitation of locomotive power in winning back substantial volumes of freight traffic to the railroads. From the 1350-horsepower original *FT* locomotive, has come the 2000-horsepower *GP-20,* the 2250-horsepower *GP-30,* and the 2500-horsepower, four-motor *GP-35.* When purchased on a replacement basis (with the railroad customer turning in older locomotives on the purchase) these units can offer a return on net cash outlay equaling or surpassing that offered when the first diesels replaced steam power.

Diesels throughout North America. Canadian National Railways (*top left*) was the very first railroad to try a diesel locomotive. The Illinois Central (*bottom left*) served Florida and the southeast with its diesel locomotives. A westbound Great Northern freight train (*below*) hugs the Little Spokane River west of Milan, Washington in 1966.

Today's developments are dramatic when compared with the earliest beginnings of diesel power, but represent progress dictated by a dynamic society moving in an era of change.

## THE INTRODUCTION OF THE DASH 2

In 1972, the introduction of a new line of road freight locomotives, aimed at high reliability with simplified maintenance, along with new plant facilities to boost production for them, was announced by Electro-Motive. The new line, comprising five diesel-electric locomotives ranging in size from 2000 to 3600 horsepower, incorporates major changes in all principal components, including modular electrical controls. Included in the new series designated 'Dash 2' were two 2000-horsepower units, the 4-axle, 4-motor GP/38-2 and the 6-axle, 6-motor SD/38-2; two 3000-horsepower units, the 4-axle, 4-motor GP/40-2 and the 6-axle, 6-motor SD/40-2; and one 3600-horsepower, 6-axle, 6-motor unit, the SD/45-2.

'The Dash 2 units bring together a series of engineering advancements to improve significantly locomotive performance,' said B B Brownell, vice president of General Motors and general manager of Electro-Motive on 1 February 1972. At the same time, Brownell released details of a three-year plant expansion, rehabilitation and retooling program which increased Electro-Motive's locomotive production to the highest rate since the Korean War (1953), the peak year of the railroads' replacement of steam locomotives with diesels.

'With our improved production facilities, we will be able to increase our locomotive production rate over the present high level, and also improve supplies of replacement parts to our customers,' Brownell said. The new model line represented three years of intensive research and development, and the plant improvement program demonstrated Electro-Motive's confidence in the future growth of the American railroads. 'Of the present 30,000 diesel locomotives in service on the American railroads, almost half—or 12,600—are over 15 years of age, economically obsolete, and prime candidates for replacement, Brownell continued. 'Obviously, the rate of locomotive purchases has not been sufficient to keep the fleet modern. Even if the railroads were caught up on locomotive obsolescence, they would require some 1500 to 1600 new units each year to replace the number of units that annually become economically obsolete.'

Turning to the growth in railroad freight traffic, Brownell cited the 32 percent increase in intercity ton-miles hauled by the US railroads in the 12-year period after 1960. In 1960, the American railroads hauled 579 billion ton-miles of intercity freight. By 1970, this figure had increased to 765 billion, averaging about 3.5 percent a year. By 1975 it had actually decreased to 754 billion, but by 1980 it was up to 919 billion, representing a 20 percent increase over 1970 and a 59 percent increase over 1960.

'In order to handle this additional work load, the railroads have had to increase locomotive fleet horsepower a corresponding amount. During the past five years, the equivalent of 470 additional 3000-horsepower locomotive units would have been required just to attain the needed increase in horsepower.

The Electro-Motive Division (EMD) of General Motors Corporation built most of North America's diesels from 1945. This is one of the 'Dash 2' series dating from 1961.

The Electro-Motive Division of General Motors continues to build modern diesel locomotives. This SD-60 model, first introduced in 1984, is a 390,000 lb, 6-axle locomotive intended for heavy drag operation or medium-speed freight trains in domestic mainline service.

'By retiring low horsepower, obsolete locomotives, however, and replacing them with modern, high horse-power units, the total fleet has remained constant at about 30,000 diesel units.

'With the projected future growth in intercity ton-miles hauled by railroads estimated at four percent annually, there will be a corresponding increase necessary in total fleet horsepower, which will put additional emphasis on locomotive fleet modernization.'

Brownell also pointed out that the Dash 2 series had undergone the most intensive and exhaustive field testing of any locomotive line in the history of Electro-Motive. Principal components of the new high reliability series were incorporated in experimental locomotives placed in operation on several railroads, beginning in 1969. Locomotives in this program included a series of 8-axle, 8-motor, 6600-horsepower units and a series of 6-axle, 6-motor, 4200-horsepower units which had accumulated well over 15 million miles in heavy duty-freight service.

The 38/40/45 Dash 2 series was followed by the 50 Series, which was in turn followed by the 60 Series diesel locomotives in 1980.

## A NEW ENGINE, A NEW ERA

Electro-Motive's 60 Series locomotives introduced in 1984 featured a new diesel engine, the 710G. This engine represented the culmination of an extensive, four-year, $60 million development effort and a $78 million tooling investment. Standard on every 60 Series locomotive, the 710G was a giant stride forward in increased reliability, fuel efficiency and power for diesel engines. The keys to the 710G's impressive performance capabilities are its greater displacement and advanced turbocharger. Compared to its immediate predecessor, the 645F, the new 710G featured a piston stroke increased from 10 inches to 11 inches. This increased displacement by 10 percent— from 645 to 710 cubic inches per cylinder. The 16-cylinder, 710G is rated conservatively at 3950 brake horsepower at 900 rpm and has a compression ratio of 16:1.

The 60 Series consists of four mainline models, patterned after the SD50 and GP50, which were introduced in 1980. They are: the SD60—a 390,000 lb, 6-axle locomotive intended for heavy-duty drag operation or medium-speed freight trains in domestic type mainline service; the SD59 —a 6-axle, lower horsepower locomotive for intermediate service; the GP60—a 260,000 lb, 4-axle locomotive for intermediate and high-speed service; and the GP59—a 4-axle, lower horsepower locomotive for intermediate service.

Even though the 60 Series locomotive is conspicuously more powerful than any of its ancestors, it is also the most economical to operate. A major contributor to this exciting achievement is the 710G's advanced Model G turbocharger. The result of progressive engineering, the Model G turbocharger provides a 15 percent addition over the older model in air flow, thus reducing thermal loading of critical engine components.

By combining support system improvements with the new 710G diesel engine and the increased control abilities of the onboard microprocessors, the Electro-Motive 60 Series locomotives were capable of reaching new levels of fuel economy and power while requiring less maintenance than any other locomotive in the history of the industry.

# ALL THE ROADS THAT LED TO CONRAIL: THE FALL AND RISE OF AMERICA'S GREAT EASTERN RAILROADS

In 1986 the Consolidated Rail Corporation (Conrail) celebrated its 10th birthday as a healthy and profitable rail giant. This largest freight railroad in the Northeast quadrant of the nation operates in 15 states, the District of Columbia and Canada. Conrail is more, however, than just a 10-year-old railroad success story. As the inheritor of much of the history of America's eastern railroads, Conrail is an amalgam of other successes and some disastrous failures.

Conrail commenced operations on 1 April 1976, created by Congress to take over most of the freight operations of six bankrupt railroads serving the Northeast and Midwest: Penn Central (itself the result of the merger of the New York Central and the Pennsylvania, two of the most historically important and at one time among the largest railroads in North America), Central of New Jersey, Erie Lackawanna, Lehigh & Hudson River, Lehigh Valley and Reading. The Conrail components form a virtual who's who of eastern American railroad history.

The story began on 7 October 1826, when Conrail's oldest segment, Granite Railway Company was built to carry granite blocks for the Bunker Hill Monument from a quarry in West Quincy, Massachusetts. Through successive mergers Granite became part of New York, New Haven & Hartford Railroad. The Schuylkill Valley Navigation and Railroad Company, the oldest segment of Reading Company, was founded on 6 June 1829. The Mohawk & Hudson Railroad, the oldest portion of New York Central Railroad, began operations on 9 August 1831. The Camden & Amboy Railroad and Transportation Company, the earliest segment of Pennsylvania Railroad, followed in October 1832. Elizabethtown & Somerville Railroad Company, the oldest line of Central Railroad Company of New Jersey, was started on 1 January 1842.

The Erie Lackawanna component of Conrail had its roots in the Erie Railroad and in the Delaware, Lackawanna & Western. These two important railroads were themselves the product of mergers. Erie's predecessor the New York & Erie was founded on 14 May 1851, while the original Lackawanna & Western was founded on 15 October of the same year.

The earliest line of the Lehigh Valley Railroad Company, the Delaware, Lehigh, Schuylkill & Susquehanna Railroad, was founded on 11 June 1855.

Between the 1880s and the 1920s, railroads provided America's primary means of transportation, and as a whole they prospered. The Pennsylvania Railroad became the world's largest and referred to itself as the world's 'standard' railroad. By the 1960s, however, competitive modes, supported in part (directly and indirectly) by enormous government financial resources, severely cut into railroads' profitability and traffic. The railroads' capital

*Left:* **A Conrail locomotive pulls its load of coal through hill country. Conrail begins to pull a great load of history behind it in 1976 when it took over the freight operations of six bankrupt railroads that included some of North America's oldest and most colorful railroad lines.**

resources declined (especially in the northeast quadrant of America) and maintenance expenditures were deferred. On 17 October 1960, the Erie Lackawanna Railroad Company was formed by the merger of the Erie Railroad and the Delaware, Lackawanna & Western Railroad.

By the late 1960s, other railroads were beginning to feel pressure. On 22 March 1967, the Central Railroad of New Jersey entered bankruptcy. Even the big New York Central and the Pennsylvania were in trouble; they pooled their resources on 1 February 1968 and formed the Penn Central Transportation Company. On 31 December 1968, the New York, New Haven & Hartford Railroad also joined the Penn Central.

The next few years were bleak ones for the eastern railroads. On 21 June 1970, Penn Central entered bankruptcy. This was followed by the bankruptcies of the Lehigh Valley Railroad Company on 24 July 1970, the Reading Company on 23 November 1971, the Lehigh & Hudson River Railway Company on 18 April 1972 and the Erie Lackawanna Railway Company on 26 June 1972. On 8 February 1973, a one-day labor strike shut down Penn Central. The US government intervened to end the strike, setting in motion the process of government participation aimed at resolving the dilemma of rail bankruptcies in the Northeast.

On 21 December 1973, Congress passed the Regional Rail Reorganization Act (RRRA), paving the way for a new government-controlled rail corporation to take over the assets of the bankrupt northeast roads and keep them running. The first step in the plan came on 2 May 1974, when Penn Central, Reading, Central Railroad of New Jersey and Lehigh Valley were ruled unreorganizable by their respective bankruptcy courts. On 26 February 1975, the United States Railway Association (USRA) issued a Preliminary System Plan for restructuring the bankrupt lines. The Plan called for a 15,000 route-mile system including 3400 miles of light density lines, and for an expanded Norfolk & Western and Chessie System to provide competition for the new government-run rail system. On 16 April 1975, a Special Appeals Court in Washington upheld the decision of Erie Lackawanna's reorganization court to allow late inclusion of Erie Lackawanna in the Conrail system.

On 9 November 1975, the United States Railway Association Final System Plan for Conrail, which had been submitted on 28 July, was accepted by Congress. On 28 July 1976, the Railroad Revitalization and Regulatory Reform Act (RRRR, or Quad R) was passed by Congress amending the RRRA, and on 5 February, it was signed into law by President Gerald Ford. On 12 March, a Financing Agreement was concluded between USRA and Conrail giving the latter access to government investment funds of up to $2.026 billion with which to launch operations. On 1 April 1976, the rail properties of the component railroad companies were conveyed to Conrail and operations began on the new road with the bright blue locomotives.

*—Bill Yenne*

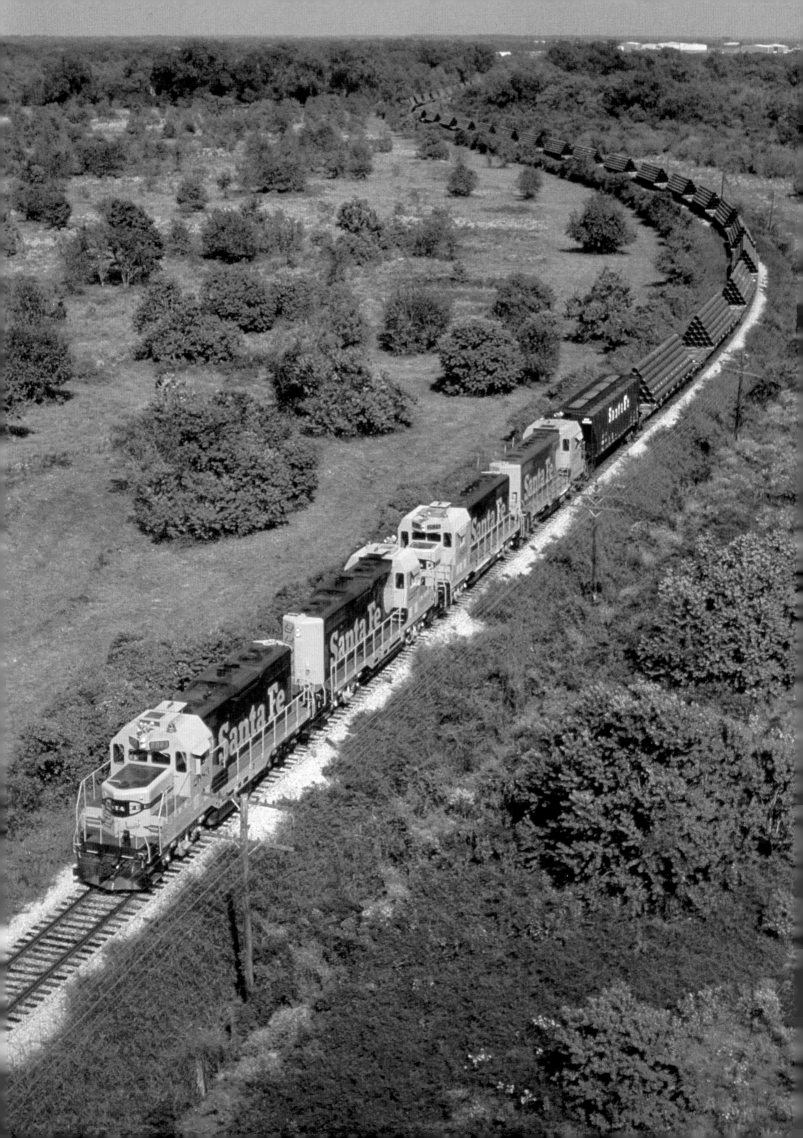

# CHAPTER 10

# THE RENAISSANCE ON THE RAILS: AMERICAN RAILROADING ENTERS THE 1980s

## Edited by Bill Yenne

### with data compiled and supplied by the Economics and Finance Department of the Association of American Railroads

Despite a fourth quarter affected deeply by a coal strike and spreading recession, America's railroad industry in 1974 posted its third consecutive all-time traffic record—and increased its share of intercity freight traffic for the second consecutive year. However, recession-induced traffic declines and continuing inflation combined to produce the lowest earnings since the depression of the 1930s for the railroad industry in 1975. Nevertheless, 1975 also was a year in which the most comprehensive railroad legislation of this century took shape, amid indications that national policy toward the rail segment of the transportation industry had reached a turning point. Passage of

the Railroad Revitalization and Regulatory Reform Act of 1976, coupled with a business revival, provided optimism early in 1976 that this would be a year of recovery.

The first half of 1975 was marked by steady declines in freight traffic and revenues and the first net deficit from operations in history. Ordinary net income after fixed charges reflected a loss of $244 million compared to a net profit of $307 million during the first half of 1974—a

A Santa Fe RR freight train (*facing page*) carrying pipe and a Chessie System Freight (*above*) pulling coal. Since 1980 the various rail systems carry only freight. All passenger service in the United States is conducted by Amtrak — the National Railroad Passenger Corporation.

record $550 million difference. Railroads no longer had to cope with car supply problems and, instead, reported more than 100,000 cars temporarily in storage because of a lack of business.

In recognition of continuing severe cost inflation, the Interstate Commerce Commission in April 1975 granted the first in a series of three freight rate increases that ultimately amounted to 13 percent of the average shipment. The first approval came three months after the ICC had initially postponed decision on the requested increase at a cost of some $250 million in lost revenue. Nevertheless, the first two increases helped to produce a narrow third-quarter profit of about $115 million in ordinary net income, less than half the third quarter profit of the previous year.

In 1974, there were 1.72 million freight cars on America's railways and 99,034 on order with a shift in emphasis from grain-carrying covered hoppers to open-top hoppers primarily used for coal. During 1974, a total of 67,605 new and rebuilt cars were installed, compared to 59,242 during the same period in 1973. Total installations would have been higher but for chronic shortages in materials and parts. Significant surpluses of boxcars and flatcars persisted after the first four months of the year. As a result of an increase of seven percent in the covered-hopper fleet, improved car utilization, and a decline in the general level of grain shipments, the grain crop was handled with no major or prolonged supply problem. The only continuing car supply problems after the early months of 1974 came in coal cars and gondolas for hauling various steel products, scrap and aggregates. Delays in receiving new cars from builders led some railroads to expand their own car building facilities for such cars.

The total railroad freight car fleet was expanded for the second year in a row as new coal cars dominated equipment acquisitions in 1975. Total new car deliveries reached 72,367—the highest since 1967—and 30 percent of these were open-top hoppers. New car orders fell from the high levels of the previous two years to 33,684 with 40 percent of these being coal cars. In addition to new coal cars, boxcar deliveries in 1975 totaled 16,299—most since 1969 —and covered-hopper deliveries totaled 10,859 in a continued expansion of grain-hauling capacity. Nearly half of the boxcars installed in 1975 went into the new boxcar pool operated by Railbox, a subsidiary of the Trailer Train Corporation. The railroads' power fleet also continued to expand in 1975—for the fourth straight year. In the previous four years, fleet horsepower had increased more than 10 percent.

Large surpluses of most types of freight cars were experienced through most of the year, but efforts to improve car utilization continued to make significant progress.

TRAIN II, the industry's advanced freight car information system, was implemented at mid-year. The expanded data base provided by TRAIN II presents an instant picture of the national car fleet and is a tool for improved management of the fleet. The ability to identify regional concentrations of cars gives the Car Service Division of the AAR an opportunity to issue more specific car relocation directives.

**Union Pacific locomotive No 2419 (*right*) backed up by locomotives No's 2930, 2938, 2903 carrying coal eastbound near Perkins, Wyoming. These locomotives are rated at 3000 horsepower each.**

A Southern Pacific Railroad freight (*left*) passing through a mountain pass during the spring thaw. The health of the nation still depends upon the capability of its railroads. *Above:* A diesel electric of the Burlington Northern Railroad.

In 1976, the United States railroad industry managed to make a moderate financial recovery from a serious national recession and, at the same time, significantly increased equipment and plant maintenance activities. More importantly, 1976 was a year in which the industry was the recipient of Congressional action that made possible the startup of Conrail to restructure most of the bankrupt eastern lines and legislation that set in motion changes to put the nation's railroads back on a track of more secure profitability.

A significant turnabout in the government's approach to the nation's freight-hauling railroads, first manifested in the Regional Rail Reorganization Act of 1973, continued with enactment of the Railroad Revitalization and Regulatory Reform Act at the outset of 1976. Called the most important railroad legislation in modern history, the 4-R Act facilitated the restructuring by Conrail of the six bankrupt railroads in the Northeast and parts of the Midwest and made available $2.1 billion in repayable financing to help the new road with a 10-year, $6.2 billion rehabilitation program. The 4-R Act also called for modernization of passenger service in the Washington-New York-Boston corridor at a cost of $1.75 billion over the next five years and authorized Amtrak to purchase, upgrade and operate trackage in the corridor. In addition, $1.6 billion in loans and loan guarantees was mandated to assist other qualifying railroads.

One of the key indicators of freight car utilization—net ton-miles per serviceable car day—rose to 1645 in 1976, equaling the record level of 1974. This represents an 8.9 percent improvement over the 1975 average of 1510. Most of the other measurements of utilization efficiencies also showed significant gains in 1976. Increased productivity also was achieved in terminal operations—notably with a pilot project at the Missouri Pacific terminal in St Louis, which was developed over a three-year period by a joint labor-management-government task force.

Severe winter weather, strikes by coal and ore miners and inflation were terms that echoed throughout the railroad industry in 1977, as the railroads saw earnings decline despite modest revenue gains and record levels of piggyback traffic. Nevertheless, modernization and rehabilitation programs continued to accelerate with capital and maintenance expenditures reaching record levels.

For the second year in a row, harsh weather conditions struck large segments of the nation late in the year and continued into the new year causing major problems for the railroads in the form of reduced operations, damaged equipment and repair difficulties.

Complicating matters were a series of prolonged strikes. Ore miners walked out in August and remained out until late in the year. The longest United Mine Workers' strike in history began in early December and eclipsed almost all of 1978's first quarter. Net railway operating income of $347 million for the year was the lowest since 1932.

Key operating figures that reached new highs in 1977 were net ton-miles per car-day, car-miles per car-day and net ton-miles per train-mile. Net ton-miles per car-day rose to 1750 in 1977, an increase of 6.2 percent over the previous year, while car-miles per car-day rose 2.5 to 58. Net ton-miles per train-mile, or average load per train, continued a seven-year growth trend by climbing 3.9 percent higher than in 1976 to 2030.

Officials of the Milwaukee Road, 13th largest in the nation, said in December 1977 they decided to file for bankruptcy because 'present operating results and financial projections indicate that the railroad won't be able to continue to meet all of its obligations as they become due during the next few months.'

In 1978, the Chessie System and Seaboard Coast Line announced a '50-50' merger proposal under which the two railroads would become a unified Virginia-based corporation. In addition, the Southern Pacific and the St Louis Southwestern proposed in December a purchase of nearly 1000 miles of line that had been operated by the Chicago, Rock Island & Pacific between New Mexico and St Louis.

The year 1978 was, for the railroad industry, one of records, growing progress on the legislative scene but continued inadequate earnings. Among the highlights of the year were record traffic levels, record capital outlays and the most freight cars ordered since 1955. The earnings picture, however, remained bleak. Despite the growth in traffic and revenues, the industry continued to be plagued by another crippling winter, extended strikes and escalating inflation.

A second straight bout with severe winter weather conditions slowed railroad operations throughout many parts of the country, not only curtailing service, but damaging equipment and making routine maintenance difficult at best. An extended United Mine Workers' strike in the coal fields that continued into March 1978 was the major factor contributing to a 6.3 percent drop in coal traffic for the year. Coal continued, however, to be the largest single commodity carried by the railroads.

Even though there were dark sides of the railroad picture in 1978, there were also bright spots. Traffic in 1978 advanced to 858 billion ton-miles, a record. That figure was 3.9 percent above the 1977 total. Piggyback traffic on Class I railroads set a record for the second year in a row, with carloadings up 9 percent over 1977 and the number of trailers and/or containers carried ahead 11.5 percent. Freight revenues of Class I railroads also topped the 1977 record level by climbing to $20.3 billion, compared with $18.9 billion the previous year, a gain of 7.6 percent.

Record traffic levels and increased earnings were among the highlights of the American railroad industry in 1979. Many of the traffic gains emanated from increases in coal, grain and piggyback traffic. Coal loadings were up 18.7 percent—a gain of almost 827,000 cars over 1978, which had seen a prolonged United Mine Workers' strike. Grain loadings were up 6.6 percent, a gain of some 88,000 cars. Piggyback continued its upward trend, setting records for the third straight year, and remaining second only to coal as a source of railroad traffic. At the same time, overall freight traffic grew to 914 billion ton-miles, a 6.5 percent increase over the previous record set in 1978. Freight carloadings also increased in 1979, reaching the highest level in five years.

Traffic statistics also reflected new performance levels in 1979. The industry's capability for meeting heavy traffic demands was illustrated by the movement of a record 914 billion ton-miles of freight. As a result of this performance, the rail share of the intercity freight traffic market

Two Seaboard System locomotives pass beneath a man-made 'hump' in Rice Yard at Waycross, Georgia. Rice is one of the busiest classification yards in the United States.

Two Santa Fe Railway locomotives. Notice the low-cut nose on these diesels allowing for good forward visibility.

advanced to 36.6 percent in 1979, up from 35.8 percent in 1978. The average serviceable freight car on Class 1 railroads in 1979 performed transportation service equivalent to moving one ton of freight 1869 miles each day, topping the record set a year earlier by 4.1 percent. Average ton-miles per loaded car also increased in 1979, going from 36,741 ton-miles in 1978 to 38,267. This figure had risen by some 41 percent in the previous decade, largely due to the replacement of smaller cars with larger ones and a longer average haul. The average weight of a carload of freight also set a new high in 1979, rising 3.6 percent to 64.0 tons—also due in a large part to higher-capacity cars. Average daily freight car mileage, which reached a record 59.2 miles per serviceable car on line in 1978, remained at the same level in 1979.

## AMERICAN RAILROADS ON THE REBOUND

The year 1980 can be considered a landmark in the long history of American railroads. In this year, many of the federal economic regulations affecting railroads were eliminated or altered in order to obtain a more open market environment. Concurrently, the financial posture of the railroad industry continued to improve in 1980 due largely to substantial increases in coal and grain traffic, and capital investment reached record levels in spite of a heavy reliance on outside financing. Finally, in view of the relaxed regulatory climate, additional efficiencies emanating from sound business practices and railroad consolidations, and a revived entrepreneurial spirit among management, the railroad industry faces an uncertain future with a positive and self-assuring spirit.

Said William H Dempsey, the president of the Association of American Railroads, 'Deregulation lays the foundation for a new era of railroad growth and prosperity by granting railroads greater opportunity to respond to the disciplines and opportunities of the marketplace.'

The Staggers Rail Act of 1980 (Public Law 96–448) was signed into law by President Carter on 14 October 1980. The new law, while short of total deregulation, nevertheless substantially eased the regulatory burden experienced by railroads since 1887. The most extensive changes provided by the Act were in provisions on ratemaking. While protection for shippers was retained, the Congress clearly intended that the railroads should be given substantially more freedom to compete in the marketplace. Thus, the majority of all railroad rates would be freed from regulatory review (the ICC would retain jurisdiction only where the railroads have 'market dominance') and in the remaining instances, railroads would have more flexibility to price their services in accordance with free market interplay.

Near record loadings of coal and grain pushed revenue ton-miles of Class I railroads to a new high of nearly 919 billion in 1980. Ton-miles of *all* railroads rose to 932 billion, accounting for 37.3 percent of total intercity freight traffic, up from 35.7 percent of the total in 1979. However, overall carloadings of the Class I roads were down 5.4 percent from 1979; all but three of the 21 major commodity groups declined from the previous year, with

Two Baltimore & Ohio locomotives (*right*) carrying merchandise freight over the Thomas Viaduct in Relay, Maryland. Though prominently marked as members of the Chessie System, these locomotives still carry a 'B&O'.

Santa Fe Railroad current model electric diesel locomotives No 7906 (*right*), a GE model rated at 2800 horsepower and four EMD models rated at 3000 horsepower. This lineup of modern motive power is an interesting contrast to a similar lineup of steam locomotives nearly half a century earlier (*see page 112*). *Overleaf:* Santa Fe Railroad on a run. Times may change and equipment may be updated but the romance of the railroad is still the serenity of the open countryside and the never ending variation of clouds and lights in the sky.

motor vehicles and equipment showing the biggest loss, down 24 percent. Coal, the number one commodity, was up 8.6 percent in carloadings and 10.3 percent in tons originated, with tonnage topping 500 million for the first time since 1948. Grain carloadings, which were up 10.1 percent over 1979, reached the highest level since 1973. In addition to the sharp decline in shipments of new automobiles and parts, nine other major commodities were off by more than nine percent. Piggyback traffic suffered its first year-to-year decline since 1975, but remained second only to coal as a source of traffic.

The average number of employees in 1980 declined five percent from 1979, partially due to the liquidation of the Rock Island Railroad and partially due to lower traffic levels in the East. But while employment was down, total compensation rose 3.8 percent as average annual earnings per employee increased to $24,659, up 9.2 percent over the previous year.

The Burlington Northern and St Louis-San Francisco merger plan, filed with the Interstate Commerce Commission in late December 1977, was approved by the ICC in July 1980.

Two large mergers were consummated in 1980 and applications were pending before the ICC to create two additional 'mega-systems.' In 1980, the Burlington Northern and Frisco merged to form a 27,300-mile system and the Chessie and Family Lines joined as a 26,600-mile system under control of the newly created CSX Corporation (see chart on pages 14–15). No fewer than six Class I railroads, with 1980 revenues totaling $4.4 billion, were included in the Chessie-Family Line consolidation.

Also in 1980, sizable segments of the bankrupt Milwaukee and Rock Island railroads were sold off to other railroads, to shipper groups and to state agencies. In some instances, where states and local municipalities had acquired abandoned branch lines, new short line railroads had been created to operate the lines.

While 1981 was not a banner year for the nation's railroads, it was a year of progress under difficult economic conditions. Despite a dismal fourth quarter, the industry continued to improve its financial posture. Rail traffic, measured in ton-miles, dipped only slightly below the record level of a year earlier, while the industry's share of the total intercity freight market inched upward. In fact, the railroad industry moved record volumes of coal in 1981. Additional gains in efficiency continued to emanate from sound business practices and, in some cases, from

consolidations. In view of the railroads' performance during a national recession, it appears that the market freedom gained through passage of the Staggers Rail Act of 1980 is having a positive impact on the industry.

The state purpose of the Staggers Act was 'to provide for the restoration, maintenance, and improvement of the physical qualities and financial stability of the rail system of the United States.' Although the act was only partially implemented and legal interpretations were required before the final implementation of some provisions, Staggers appeared to be fulfilling general expectations.

In 1981 the industry continued to establish new productivity gains over 1980. Average route miles operated in freight service were up to 5151 from 5133 (+0.4 percent); carloadings were up to 42,191 from 40,628 (+3.8 percent) and freight car-miles were up to 32.6 per car from 31.4 (+3.8 percent). These improvements were attributable to efficiency gains and the introduction of innovative equipment and operating procedures.

Another area of significant improvement in 1981 was the sharp decline in the number of loss and damage claims filed by shippers and consignees. The number of claims was the lowest since 1921 and the ratio of claim payments to freight revenues was the lowest since 1943. Compared with 1980, the number of claims filed dropped 23.7 percent and the claim/revenue ratio was 31.6 percent lower.

On the merger front, a 17,642-mile system was created on 1 June 1982, when the Norfolk Western and the Southern Railway merged and became the Norfolk Southern Corporation. In other merger action, Guilford Transportation Industries acquired the Maine Central Railroad, and its application to purchase the bankrupt Boston & Maine Corporation went before the court overseeing the Boston & Maine's reorganization. The commission also approved an application by Guilford to purchase the Delaware & Hudson Railway.

In March 1982, the Commission ruled that merged railroads will no longer be required to honor conditions previously imposed to protect other railroads from adverse effects of mergers. These protective conditions were now considered by the Commission to be anticompetitive and contrary to the public interest.

In 1982 the railroads continued to move steadily forward in the area of productivity. Carloadings were up to 43,005 over 42,113 in 1981 and freight car-miles were up to 33.4 from 32.5 in 1981. In another area, the loss and damage bill for freight railroads in the United States and Canada was down 9.3 percent from 1981, while new claims fell nearly 27 percent.

The Family Lines Rail System became the Seaboard System Railroad Inc, on 1 January 1983, while later in the year the expected consolidation of the Union Pacific, the Missouri Pacific and the Western Pacific railroads took place. In June 1983, Guilford Transportation Industries (GTI) received permission from the Interstate Commerce Commission to acquire the Boston & Maine and the Delaware & Hudson railroads. Earlier, GTI had purchased the Maine Central Railroad. Common ownership of the three adjacent railroads formed a 4000-mile system stretching from

Loading 'piggyback' trailers (*left*) aboard Santa Fe ten-pack train in Los Angeles. *Overleaf:* A Southern Pacific freight train moving through the snowy wonderland of the Sierra Nevada. When the merger of Santa Fe Industries and the Southern Pacific Transportaion Company takes effect, the new railroad will be the West's largest.

New England to Buffalo, New York, with legs running north to Montreal and south to the New York port area, Philadelphia, and Washington, DC.

During 1983, the railroad industry emerged from one of the deepest recessions since the Great Depression. Piggyback traffic reached record levels for the second consecutive year. The railroad share of agricultural product movements increased for the first time in many years. Loss and damage claims dropped substantially, continuing steady progress.

In 1983, 56.5 percent of total freight car-miles on Class I railroads were made by loaded cars—up slightly from 56.2 percent in 1982. The average freight train in 1983 consisted of 70.4 cars, up 1.4 percent from 1982. Average tonnage per train increased by 3.7 percent. In 1984, 57.0 percent of total freight car-miles on Class I railroads were made by loaded cars. The average freight train in 1984 consisted of 71.5 cars, up 1.6 percent from 1983. Average tonnage per train increased by 4.6 percent.

Over the next two years, railroad productivity continued to increase, but at a slower rate. Revenue ton-miles per car-load increased to 44,057 in 1983 and to 45,510 in 1984 for annual gains of 2.4 percent and 3.4 percent respectively. Average revenue freight car-miles increased to 34 in 1983 and 35 in 1984 from the 1982 level of 33.3. The average freight train weight set new records in 1983 and 1984. The average train carried 2543 tons of freight in 1984 compared to 2432 tons in 1983 and 2345 tons in 1982.

Record traffic levels in 1984 and a sharp rise in earnings for the year led US railroads into 1985 on an optimistic note. The railroads carried a record 921.5 billion ton-miles of freight in 1984, toppling the previous record of 918.6 billion ton-miles set in 1980. At the same time, piggyback traffic soared to record highs in terms of both the number of cars loaded and the number of loaded trailers and containers carried.

*Below:* **Santa Fe and Southern Pacific diesels together at the Tehatchapi Loop in California. The two roads merged in 1983, subject to ICC approval in 1986.**

*Right:* **A Burlington Northern 'big green' Dash-2 class diesel. Burlington Northern is an amalgam of the old Jim Hill roads which today dominate the nation's northern tier from Seattle to Chicago.**

# AMTRAK: AMERICA'S PASSENGER RAILROADS

## The Creation of Amtrak

In 1929, the nation's railroads, operating some 20,000 passenger trains, carried 77 percent of intercity passenger traffic by public mode in the United States. Buses carried 15 percent, and the airlines served an immeasureably small number. By 1950, more than half the passenger trains had disappeared, and the railroads' share of the intercity passenger traffic had declined to 46 percent. In the meantime, traffic on buses increased to 38 percent and the airlines' share had grown to 14 percent.

Twenty years later, in 1970, railroad passenger traffic dropped to 7 percent of the commercial share and the number of trains still operating was less than 450. Of these, about 100 were in the process of being discontinued and many were operating with only one or two passenger cars. Airlines dominated the public carrier market with 73 percent, while buses, still in second place, held on to barely 16 percent. There was a substantial growth in automobile traffic throughout this period. By this time, it was increasingly recognized that the country's excessive reliance during the past four decades on the private automobile and the airplane for intercity travel had left the nation with a serious imbalance in its transportation network.

The formation of Amtrak was proposed as it became more evident that the United States could not rely solely upon further massive construction of highways and airports to meet its transportation needs. It was argued that the strangulation of our central cities and such environmental problems as air and noise pollution, excessive land use and dislocation of people make unrestricted expansion of these facilities impractical and hazardous.

Creation of a national rail passenger system was viewed as a method to save an alternate form of transportation that possessed a priceless asset—existing tracks and rights-of-way into the major population centers of the nation. These rail facilities could be upgraded quite economically when compared to the costs for construction of new highways and airports.

The country's growing population and increasing mobility was also offered as evidence that an efficient rail passenger service was needed, in corridors with high population densities. In some corridors rail was the most feasible mode to be developed given environmental and public funding constraints. Furthermore, in 1970, about 20 percent of United States households did not own an automobile. Further, fear of traveling by air is a phobia that touches the lives of an estimated 25 million Americans. Adequate public transportation was deemed essential to insure mobility for these and other groups and, it was stressed, rail passenger service must be retained as an important part of the transportation system.

Little was said during the debate to create Amtrak about the vital role railroad passenger service would play during a future energy crisis. It was not until the fuel shortage of 1974 that railroad passenger transportation was seen as potentially the most energy efficient form of people movement.

An Amtrak diesel plows through a Cascade snowpack on a crisp winter day. This passenger route, the *Coast Starlight*, was originally established by Southern Pacific, but was taken over by Amtrak when the National Rail Passenger Corporation took over most American passenger routes.

The Rail Passenger Service Act, enacted on 30 October 1970, created Amtrak and specified that a Board of Incorporators consisting of eight presidential appointees would be formed to organize the corporation. The incorporators were faced with enormous tasks when they began work on 1 January 1971, just four months before the obligation to operate rail passenger service would be transferred to Amtrak. They had to begin organizing what was comparable to a $200 million public service corporation; to decide what specific routes should connect the 21 pairs of cities designated by the secretary of transportation; and decide what trains, frequencies and type of service to be operated effective 1 May.

The incorporators sought out full-time professional help. A management consulting firm was hired to develop the organizational structure as well as provide interim staff support until the corporation could hire its own personnel. Two executive search firms were put to work to find management prospects. Lawyers began drafting articles of incorporation and numerous contracts needed for train operations. Engineering experts inspected and surveyed available passenger terminals, cars and locomotives. A major airline was asked to study and make recommendations on a nationwide ticketing and reservations system. A national public relations agency, along with an advertising agency, was retained to help promote increased passenger traffic.

Up until this time, the corporation had been commonly known as 'Railpax.' A leading design firm was retained to develop a new name, and Railpax became 'Amtrack,' for America, travel and track.

## Objectives of the New Corporation

The underlying thrust of Amtrak's first efforts was gradually to revitalize public confidence in rail passenger service through improvements in service and comfort to induce the traveling public to return to train travel.

The corporation began with some specific goals: to improve employee courtesy and service to the public; to offer reliable performance and better-maintained equipment; and to issue accurate information to travelers. Most of all, Amtrak developed positive programs to entice an increasing share of the travel market to train travel. The principal target: those travelers who relied principally on the private automobile for intercity trips, which at that time represented 87 percent of the intercity travel market.

## Amtrak's First Days

Beginning 1 May 1971, Amtrak assumed responsibility for managing intercity passenger train service over 23,000 route miles, an extensive system by railroad standards. Actual train operations continued to be performed by the railroads under contract with Amtrak. On Amtrak's first day of operation, it inherited an antiquated business. With passenger losses steadily increasing, the railroads had little or no incentive to maintain or modernize equipment or facilities. Not one railroad operated a modern computerized reservations system and many of the passenger cars were old and in disrepair. Too many of the stations and

*Above:* One of Amtrak's Turboliners, the Empire State Express, glides across the Mohawk River at Rotterdam Junction on a daily run between New York City and Niagara Falls.

*Below:* Four Amfleet cars, pulled by one of Amtrak's latest AEM-7 electric locomotives, stop at the newly-opened Baltimore Washington International (BWI) Airport station.

maintenance facilities had become unsightly after years of neglect and were inefficient to operate.

When Amtrak first offered service, it did not own any railroad tracks, stations, terminals, yards, repair facilities, locomotives, passenger cars or other railroad assets. At that time, there was not one manufacturer in the United States with an open production line for intercity rail passenger equipment because no such equipment had been purchased for years.

For the first two years, Amtrak was almost totally dependent on the private railroads, leasing equipment from them and using their facilities. An Amtrak customer could make a reservation, buy a ticket and complete his journey without ever coming into contact with an Amtrak employee. Congress had given Amtrak only a two-year experimental period of life, and planning future improvements was excruciatingly difficult.

Meanwhile, even Amtrak supporters were in disagreement about what Amtrak should become. Some wanted 150-mph short-distance corridor 'trains of the future' while others called for restoration of great long-distance 'name trains' of the past. There was agreement, however, that Amtrak was not to be a commuter railroad. Although some short-distance trains in densely populated corridors might be used by business travelers, Amtrak was by definition an intercity carrier. Today, after several legislative changes, Amtrak is authorized to operate commuter services for local commuter agencies as long as the corporation is fully compensated for the cost of providing the service. Amtrak also operates some limited commuter services as part of its basic system where those services meet the same ridership and financial performance criteria applied to all short-distance trains.

In its initial route structure, Amtrak trains began operating over the tracks of 13 railroads. In return for being relieved of the responsibility for operating passenger trains, each of the 13 railroads agreed to pay Amtrak 50 percent of its passenger service loss for the year ending 31 December 1969. The railroads had the option of paying cash or contributing equipment or services of the same value. The railroads could also elect to receive common stock for the value of these payments rather than taking a tax writeoff. Four railroads—Burlington Northern, Milwaukee Road, Grand Trunk Western and Penn Central—accepted the stock option and were permitted three representatives on Amtrak's first Board of Directors.

Three railroads—the Denver & Rio Grande Western, the Rock Island and the Southern—continued to operate their own passenger trains and did not immediately join the Amtrak system. After 1 January 1975, these companies were free to petition appropriate regulatory bodies to discontinue service, and today all three are out of the passenger business. The Rock Island went out of the passenger business in 1979. Amtrak assumed the operation of Southern Railway's popular Southern Crescent in 1979, and D&RGW's scenic Zephyr route through the Colorado Rockies in July 1983. Today Amtrak is the only intercity rail passenger carrier in the United States and is the United State's sixth largest public carrier in numbers of passengers carried.

*—National Rail Passenger Corporation*

# CHAPTER 11

# AMERICAN RAILROADS TODAY

## Prepared by the American Association of Railroads

For all its past glamor, America's multibillion dollar railroad industry is no historical relic. It is today a vital component of the national transportation system, providing more than 37 percent of intercity freight service, or almost as much as the total provided by trucks and barge lines together.

Coal, grain, forest products, chemicals, metallic ores and many other essential commodities move by rail each day from mine and farm to factory and processing plant and, ultimately, as finished products to the consumer. If you can eat it, wear it, build with it or use it as fuel, chances are it either rode the rails itself or was put together with something that did.

The rail industry is modern, as contemporary as today's technology and constantly seeking innovations in equipment, in services and in operating procedures. For example, railroads were among the earliest business to employ computers and are today one of the largest and most diversified users. Computers keep tabs on nearly two million freight cars moving over some 300,000 miles of track; they help take apart and assemble trains in automated classification yards; and they permit long-distance push-button control of traffic over much of the national system.

## THE HUMAN SIDE OF RAILROADING

At the heart of the American rail system are the men and women who run the railroads, a work force of almost half a million dispersed through every state of the union except Hawaii, and equipped with a wide range of skills and educational backgrounds. This diversity is reflected in the 128 categories under which the Interstate

Linda Timmons (*above*), a Southern Pacific locomotive engineer out of Tucson, Arizona, personifies the modernization of American railroads as women take their place behind the throttle. Santa Fe diesels (*left*) carrying freight.

Commerce Commission classifies railroad occupations and positions.

These are filled by the people who operate the locomotives and who work on the trains; the track maintenance crews and the communications technicians; the car repairers, machinists and electricians responsible for keeping equipment in operating condition; the marketing analysts, computer scientists and industrial engineers less visible but no less important than the frontline workers; and many others whose functions are an integral part of a complex but smoothly working transportation network.

Despite the growth of automation, with innovations that improve the efficiency of personnel and equipment, and an increasing number of mergers within the industry, attrition and normal turnover indicate the need for about 50,000 new employees each year.

More than 70 percent of railroad employees are engaged in three main areas of rail operations—train and engine service, the maintenance of equipment and supplies and the maintenance of track and structures. Managing or supporting these people are the other 30 percent—the executive and supervisory staff, personnel in professional positions, clerical workers and those whose duties are performed in yards or terminals.

Training for railroad operations is generally provided by the railroad. On most railroads, new employees receive a

**Locomotive engineers are among the most skilled operating workers on a railroad. They must know how to run every type of locomotive in service on their railroad, accelerating and braking according to the special characteristics of each train. Engineers have primary responsibility for the smooth and safe operation of the train.**

Louise Munyan was one of Southern Pacific's first woman locomotive engineers (*above*). No longer is the world of Casey Jones still the exclusive domain of men. A Southern Pacific diesel (*right*) pulling out of the yards.

week or more of orientation and equipment and safety instruction—covering such areas as how to get on and off moving freight cars and locomotives, throw switches, set hand brakes on cars and signal other crew members. They may then be assigned to work with an experienced crew where they will receive more on-the-job training.

New employees, especially those in operational jobs, such as assembling cars and dispatching or running trains, start on the extra board. This is a roster of workers without regular assignments who are called in to substitute for full-time employees who are on vacation, ill or absent for other reasons, or to meet the need for extra personnel when there are temporary surges in traffic.

Extra board workers can be asked to come in at short notice and must be available at any hour of the day or night, weekends and holidays included. With experience they gain seniority and become eligible for regular assignments, but there is no way to determine when these might be available. The time spent on the *extra* board varies with the job and the number of openings. Some workers do not receive regular assignments for several years.

Seniority is very important in the industry. The seniority system, to which management and labor adhere by common agreement, governs the advancement and working conditions of all unionized employees. About 90 percent of those who work for the railroads are represented by one of 13 major rail labor organizations. Employees with the longest service get the first choice of job assignments for which they are qualified, whether they are moving off the extra board or competing for higher-paying positions.

The largest group of railroad workers are those in operating jobs. They include switchmen, brakemen, conductors, engineer's helpers, engineers, yardmasters and train dispatchers.

Switchmen, or switch operators, work in terminals or yards, where they operate the switches that allow cars to be moved from track to track as trains are taken apart or assembled. They couple and uncouple cars, set the hand brakes to keep cars from accidentally moving away from where they have been placed, and communicate with the engineer through hand signals or two-way radio. In the newer, automated classification yards, where cars are routed electronically, switchmen are needed mainly to couple cars and switch them in blocks to departure tracks and generally assure a continual smooth operation.

Brakemen, occasionally called brake operators, although they do much more than set hand brakes, are a part of the crew of road freight trains. Sometimes employees transfer from switchman to brakeman. Many, but not all, freight trains, have two brakemen—a head-end brakeman who rides in the cab with the engineer, and a rear brakeman, often called a flagman, who rides in the caboose. Before a train starts on a trip, brakemen make sure all couplers and air hoses are secured, hand brakes are released and air brakes are functioning. During runs, they look for smoke, sparks and other indications of faulty equipment, and may make minor repairs to couplers and air hoses. If the train makes an unscheduled stop, they may be required to set out signals to protect both ends of the train from approaching traffic. Brakemen work under the

A westbound Atchison Topeka & Santa Fe Railway freight train descends the grade of the Cajon Pass in Southern California. The Atchison Topeka & Santa Fe is the major component of Santa Fe Industries, which has recently merged with Southern Pacific.

supervision of conductors, with whom they share responsibility for running the train according to the railroad's operating and safety regulations.

Conductors are the 'commanders' of their trains, in charge of the complete train crew, including the locomotive engineer. Conductors take responsibility for the safety of passengers and freight, conferring with others in the crew before departure to make sure train orders are clearly understood. On freight trains, they see to it that cars are dropped off and picked up at the right points; on Amtrak or commuter trains, they collect tickets and provide answers to passengers seeking information. During a trip they make periodic checks of equipment and, if they find defective cars, arrange for repairs or for the defective cars to be left at the nearest siding. Yard conductors, or yard foremen, supervise switching crews in yards and terminals. In automated yards, they operate the consoles that control track switches. Openings for conductors' positions are filled by qualified brakemen who have sufficient seniority and have passed examinations in signals, timetables, brake systems and operating rules.

Engineer's helpers, once called firemen because they stoked the fires in the steam engines, are the workers generally hired as prospective locomotive engineers. They are given on-the-job training in railroad rules and procedures and are then assigned to ride with the locomotive engineer—watching for signals and track obstructions, monitoring gauges, and looking out for signs of defective equipment. Some railroads hire engineer trainees direct; others promote and train qualified brakemen.

Wherever they come from, aspirants for locomotive engineers' positions usually undergo extensive training on simulators. They must then take tests covering locomotive equipment, air brake systems, train handling techniques, and operating rules and procedures.

Locomotive engineers are among the most skilled operating workers on a railroad. In addition to knowing how to run every type of locomotive in service on their railroad, they must be thoroughly familiar with signal systems, speed regulations, and the yards and terminals along the routes they travel. They must be able to make rapid adjustments to changes in weather conditions, and be able to correctly handle acceleration and braking according to the particular makeup of each train. Misjudgment could lead to injuries, damaged cargo or even derailment. Locomotive engineers, who are primarily responsible for the smooth and safe operation of the train, can never take chances; they constantly monitor performance by watching dials, meters and alarm systems that relay warnings of potential trouble. They are always alert to the track and signals ahead.

Positions for locomotive engineers are filled from the extra board, on which qualified engineer's helpers, brakemen or engineer trainees have been placed.

Yardmasters are responsible for directing operations in a switching yard or terminal. They must be able to survey the activities going on, determine what needs to be done, and assign appropriate tasks to switching and road crews. Yardmasters generally rise from the ranks of switchmen or clerical workers.

Train dispatchers supervise the enroute movement of trains, and it is on their decisions that the safe and smooth movement of traffic depends. They must have a thorough knowledge of operating rules and of the layout of that

A new SD-50 locomotive of the Chesapeake & Ohio, a member of the Chessie System. Southern Pacific switch engines (*above*) at work at a Beaumont, Texas chemical plant.

part of the system under their control. Dispatchers can be selected from almost any discipline, but usually have operating department experience. Most railroads require that dispatchers update their knowledge regularly through periodic tours over their part of the railroad.

After those in operations, the second largest group of railroad workers comprises employees in the shop trades. Every railroad has its own skilled technicians who maintain, repair and rebuild locomotives, cars and other equipment. They work in yards, terminals and engine houses, as well as in car and locomotive repair facilities. Shop work is strenuous, much of it done outdoors in all kinds of weather or in surroundings that are constantly noisy.

Railroads generally hire apprentices, favoring applicants who have had some shop experience in high school or vocational school, but they also upgrade laborers and helpers for training in shop skills. Apprenticeships last from three to four years, depending on the previous work experience the apprentice has had.

The six principal shop trades are car repairers, machinists, electricians, boilermakers, blacksmiths and sheet-metal workers.

Car repairers keep freight and passenger cars and some sections of locomotives in running order. They inspect such parts as wheels, brake assemblies and couplers, looking for defects that might cause accidents or delays. They also rebuild old or badly damaged cars and modify standard cars for specialized purposes. Machinists are responsible for the mechanical overhaul of diesel engines; they examine and test all components for needed repair or replacement. When major overhauls are undertaken, machinists are called upon to strip the engine completely. Electricians maintain and repair all wiring as well as the

Santa Fe Railway's westbound ten-pack 'Fuel Foiler' train (*left*) crosses the Colorado River near Needles, California. Technology has improved the railroad business, trains are faster and bridges are stronger. There are still rivers to cross, bridges to build and tracks to lay and there will always be a need for 'steel driving men' (*facing page*) to keep trains rolling.

generators and traction motors for locomotives, the cooling units in refrigerated freight cars, and the air-conditioning in passenger cars. Sometimes they are responsible for maintaining the wiring in railroad buildings as well. Boiler-makers and blacksmiths are entrusted with the repair and fabrication of locomotive frames and other heavy structural parts of locomotives and freight cars. Sheet-metal workers, sometimes classified as pipe-fitters, repair the sheet-metal sections of locomotives and are responsible for the orderly working of the pipes and tubes of the engine's lubricating, cooling and air systems.

The third largest group of railroad workers comprises those engaged in the maintenance of track and structures. The trend towards mechanization has steadily reduced the number of conventional track workers using hand tools or small power tools and increased the number of operators of portable power equipment. Jobs formerly done with picks, shovels and spike mauls are now completed more speedily with machines. Signal installation and maintenance are also among the functions of this group of railroad workers.

Track workers are trained on the job, receiving instruction from experienced crew members. They can advance from laborers to portable equipment operators as they acquire the skills to operate track-maintenance machines. Further advancement, as opportunities occur, would be to track supervisor. Management positions include road-master, division engineer and chief of engineering.

Signal workers install and maintain train control, communication and signaling systems. They are also responsible for automatic grade crossing protection devices. New employees, usually assigned as helpers to installation crews, are high school or vocational school graduates, preferably with some knowledge of electricity, electronics and blueprint reading. They can advance to signal installers or signal maintainers.

These are some of the frontline jobs of the industry performed by the men and women who make up the bulk of the labor force.

Less visible but no less important to the efficient operation of a railroad are the professionals, the people with college degrees or other advanced training in computer science, engineering, marketing, transportation and a host of other skills. They are needed to staff management, research and supervisory positions.

Opportunities for professionals vary with the size of the railroad and the extent of its operations, but these are a few typical positions.

The transportation department, responsible for the safe movement of freight and passenger trains, depends not only on train crews but on managerial personnel who back them up. The trainmaster maintains smooth operating schedules and must work closely with train crews, mechanical and maintenance-of-way personnel, the sales staff, and shippers. The trainmaster has a job with 24-hour responsibilities, requiring a broad understanding of operating procedures, labor contracts and customer service. But in return for long hours of hard work, the position offers a variety of challenging situations. A degree in transportation is the usual requirement for entrants. The trainmaster position is often the first stepping stone for advancement and promotion in the executive ranks.

The traffic, or sales, department seeks to attract more business for the railroad, going after new customers and inducing industries to locate their plants in the railroad's territory. Applicants with degrees in economics, business administration, marketing or transportation are trained in sales or in the highly complex field of freight rates. There are opportunities for advancement to such positions as district sales manager or industrial development analyst.

The marketing department identifies the special requirements of customers and strives to meet them. Market research, planning and innovative pricing are the elements that may enter into this service. Entrants with degrees in economics, transportation and business administration are trained for such positions as marketing analyst or planning analyst and may move up as marketing manager.

Railroads need degreed engineers of every specialization: civil, mechanical, electrical, chemical, industrial, environmental. Engineers supervise the maintenance of rights-of-way. They design new track layouts, rolling stock and electronic equipment for automated classification yards. They find ways to improve the productivity of personnel and equipment, and undertake operations and applied research.

Computerization of numerous functions is steadily increasing in the industry. With this expansion, there is a growing demand for programmers, systems analysts, communications specialists and others skilled in the application of computers to railroad operations. A recent study indicated that by the middle of this decade there would be more than 500 minicomputers in use by railroads, mainly in the control of operations.

The Santa Fe Railway diesel servicing yard at Barstow, California.

# A CHRONOLOGY OF AMERICAN RAIL HISTORY

Prepared by the Association of American Railroads

**1807** —Silas Whitney operated a gravity and horse-drawn wooden tramway on Beacon Hill in Boston; it was a form of railroading, the first in this country.

**1809** —Thomas Leiper built a wooden tramway, powered by horses, to connect quarries in Delaware County, Pennsylvania, with tidewater.

**1815 (6 February)**—John Stevens of Hoboken, New Jersey, granted first railroad charter in America, by the New Jersey Legislature, but did not undertake construction between Delaware and Raritan rivers.

**1825 (February)**—First locomotive to run on rails in America, built by John Stevens, operated experimentally on a half-mile circular track in Hoboken.

**1826 (7 October)**—Gridley Bryant's three-mile-long Granite Railway opened at Quincy, Mass., to transport granite used in building Bunker Hill Monument, horses supplying power; later operated as a steam railroad; line still in use.

**1827 (28 February)**—Maryland charter granted to Baltimore & Ohio, making it the oldest American railroad in continuous existence; first stone was laid for construction on 4 July 1828.

**1829 (8 August)**—Locomotive *Stourbridge Lion,* imported from England, put on track at Honesdale, Pennsylvania, as first steam engine to run on commercial railroad tracks in this country; it operated three miles with Horatio Allen as engineer.

**1829 (21 December)**—Carrollton Viaduct, first large railroad bridge in the United States, opened near Baltimore; still in use.

**1830 (25 August)**—Trial trip made by Peter Cooper's locomotive *Tom Thumb* from Baltimore to Ellicott's Mills, Maryland, and return.

**1830 (25 December)**—First scheduled steam passenger service inaugurated at Charleston, South Carolina using American-built locomotive *Best Friend of Charleston;* marked the first use in America of steam power for regular service.

**1830** —Robert L Stevens designed forerunner of T-rail used today; first iron rails of American design rolled in 1844; Bessemer steel rails first rolled at North Chicago Rolling Mills on 25 May 1865.

**1831 (9 August)**—First steam train in New York State ran from Albany to Schenectady, pulled by locomotive *DeWitt Clinton.*

**1831 (12 November)**—Locomotive *John Bull* placed in service at Bordentown, New Jersey, inaugurating rail-water link between New York City and Philadelphia.

**1831 (November)**—US mail carried for first time by rail—in South Carolina.

**1831** —A pine-knot fire on open platform car in South Carolina served as first locomotive headlight; 1830s to 1850s, candles and whale oil were used in reflector lamps; 1859, kerosene lamps, followed by gas; 1881, electricity; 1936, figure-8 oscillating headlight; 1944, oscillating headlight that flashes white or red, for safety purposes; 1946, sealed-beam headlight.

**1832 (23 November)**—*Old Ironsides,* Matthias Baldwin's first locomotive, made initial run from Philadelphia toward Germantown.

**1833 (6 June)**—Andrew Jackson became first president of the United States to ride on a railroad train—between Ellicott's Mills, Maryland, and Baltimore.

**1835 (4 July)**—Thomas Viaduct opened at Relay, Maryland—the oldest multiple-arch railroad bridge in use in the United States.

**1835 (25 August)**—First railroad to Washington DC opened from Baltimore.

**1836 (5 February)**—Henry R Campbell, of Philadelphia, patented an eight-wheeled engine (4-4-0) subsequently termed American type; engine was completed 8 May 1837; with numerous modifications, it remained popular type until 1895.

**1836 (18 April)**—First known railroad merger united the Maryland & Delaware and the Wilmington & Susquehanna; retained latter name.

**1836 (April)**—First rail car ferry, the 'Susquehanna,' placed in service on the Susquehanna River, between Havre de Grace and Perryville, Maryland.

**1836 (13 July)**—John Ruggles, US Senator from Maine and 'Father of the US Patent Office,' issued Patent No 1 for device to increase power of railway locomotives and to prevent wheels from sliding.

**1836** —First two American locomotives known to have been equipped with whistles built at Lowell, Massachusetts, under supervision of George Washington Whistler; the *Hicksville* put in service in Jamaica, Long Island and was reported to make 'a shrill, wild unearthly sound'; the *Susquehanna* tried out in

A silhouette drawing of the 'DeWitt Clinton' (*above*). The first excursion with passengers was made from Albany to Schenectady in August of 1831.

Wilmington, Delaware, traveling at '35 or 40 miles an hour,' and was said to 'give awful notice of its approach.'

**1837** —World's first sleeping car operated between Harrisburg and Chambersburg, Pennsylvania—a remodeled day coach, crudely built.

**1838 (January)**— New York (South Amboy) and Washington, DC linked by a chain of railroads, with ferry service across major rivers and omnibus service through principal cities.

**1838 (7 July)**—Act of Congress making every railroad a mail route signed by President Martin Van Buren.

**1839 (4 March)**—America's first long-distance railway express service started by William F Harnden, former railroad conductor, between Boston and New York.

**1842 (1 January)**—First major railway consolidation completed by merger of four railway companies in New Hampshire, Massachusetts and Maine to form the present Boston & Maine Railroad Co.

**1848 (24 October)**—Chicago's first locomotive, the *Pioneer,* placed on tracks; first run made following day.

**1848 (29 December)**—First direct rail route between Boston and New York completed.

**1850 (20 September)**—President Millard Fillmore signed first federal railroad land grant act; last grant to aid in pioneer railroad development made in 1871; in return, railroads provided reduced rates on government traffic and mail until 1 October 1946, resulting in savings to federal government of more than $1 billion from time of first grants.

**1850** —Oil lamps introduced on trains for interior lighting; followed by gas light in 1860; Pintsch gas in 1883, electricity in 1885, fluorescent lights in 1938.

**1851 (1 July)**—First refrigerator-type car known to have been built in this country began service when eight tons of butter were transported to Boston from Ogdensburg, New York.

**1851 (16 August)**—First international railway link on North American continent opened between Laprairie, Quebec and Rouses Point, New York; by international agreement, first of its kind in the world, rolling stock of foreign ownership was permitted free entry into Canada and United States—ruling still in effect.

**1851 (22 September)**—First recorded use of telegraph for train dispatching took place at Turner (now Harriman), New York.

**1852 (21 May)**—First passenger train from the East (Detroit) entered Chicago.

**1852 (9 December)**—First train to operate west of Mississippi River made its initial run from St Louis to Cheltenham, a distance of five miles, and returned; powered by locomotive, *The Pacific.*

**1852 (10 December)**—Philadelphia linked by rail with Ohio River at Pittsburgh; 10 incline planes used.

**1852 (24 December)**—Railroad from Baltimore completed to Ohio River at Wheeling, West Virginia.

**1853 (24 January)**—All-rail route completed between eastern cities and Chicago; several changes of cars were necessary.

**1853 (June)**—Passenger train equipped for first time with flexible connections providing enclosed passageways (vestibules) between cars.

**1854 (22 February)**—Railroad completed from Chicago to Rock Island, Illinois, opening first rail route to Mississippi River from Eastern Seaboard.

**1854** —Adjustable, reclining-seat coaches placed in service between Philadelphia and Baltimore.

**1855 (February)**—Susan Morningstar, of Baltimore, Maryland, recorded as first woman railroad employee.

**1855 (March)**—Niagara Suspension Bridge completed, opening another rail route between East and West.

**1856 (21 April)**—First railroad bridge to span Mississippi River opened between Davenport, Iowa, and Rock Island, Illinois; partially burned on 6 May 1856 following collision by steamer *Effie Afton;* rebuilt and reopened on 8 September 1856.

**1856 (2 December)**—First sleeping car patents issued to T T Woodruff.

**1857 (1 April)**—First Southern rail route between Atlantic Seaboard and Mississippi River completed—Charleston to Memphis.

**1859 (1 September)**—First Pullman sleeping car left Bloomington, Illinois, on overnight trip to Chicago: first Pullman conductor was Jonathan L Barnes.

**1860** —Chicago, with 11 railroads, had become America's leading railway center.

**1862 (1 July)**—President Lincoln signed act authorizing construction of a line of railroads from Missouri River to Pacific Coast.

**1862 (28 July)**—Experimental post office car for sorting mail en route placed in service between Hannibal and St Joseph, Missouri.

**1863 (3 March)**—President Lincoln signed act to establish the gauge of the Pacific Railroad at 4 ft 8½ in; gauge was virtually standardized by 1886 when 13,000 miles of track in the South were changed from 5 ft to 4 ft 9 in; American Railway Association (a predecessor of the Association of American Railroads) officially fixed gauge of 4 ft 8½ in as standard for the United States in 1897 and in 1907 as standard for the North American continent.

**1863** —Block-signal system, devised by Ashbel Welch, installed between New Brunswick, New Jersey and Philadelphia.

**1863** —Dining cars introduced; ran between Philadelphia and Baltimore.

**1864 (28 August )**—First permanent Railway Post Office car for picking up, sorting, and distributing mail en route placed in operation on run from Chicago to Clinton, Iowa.

**1865 (1 November)**—Tank car especially built for transporting oil took on initial load at Titusville, Pennsylvania.

**1866 (20 April)**—First code of rules to govern interchange of freight cars adopted at meeting of fast freight lines held in Buffalo.

**1868 (21 April)**—Eli H Janney obtained patent for automatic coupler; second patent issued 29 April 1873, for basic car coupler design generally in use today; standard interchangeable, automatic car couplers introduced in 1887 following extensive experiments; further advance improvements made and standardized in subsequent years.

**1868** —First Pullman-built dining car, the 'Delmonico' placed in service.

**1869 (10 May)**—Golden Spike ceremony at Promontory, Utah, signaled completion of first transcontinental rail route; Union Pacific had built from East, Central Pacific (now part of Southern Pacific) from West.

**1869 (4 July)**—First bridge to span Missouri River opened in Kansas City, thus establishing through route from Chicago.

**1873 (24 December)**—First through passenger train ran between Chicago and New Orleans, using ferry across Ohio River; car trucks changed at Cairo on account of difference in gauge.

**1876 (1 July)**—Great Hoosac Tunnel, in Western Massachusetts, officially opened for traffic.

**1877 (21 May)**—Telephone communication for railroad purposes first tested in Altoona, Pennsylvania.

**1881** —Railway mileage in United States exceeded 100,000 route miles for first time.

**1881** —Steam heating system first installed in passenger

trains, replacing stoves and hot water heaters.

**1883 (12 January)**—Direct rail route complete from California to New Orleans.

**1883 (8 September)**—Entrance of first rail route from Great Lakes into Washington Territory celebrated; many American and foreign notables attended spike-driving ceremony; extended to Puget Sound via Cascade Mountains, 1 July 1887.

**1883 (18 November)**—Trains began operating on railroad-conceived 'standard time,' which was generally adopted by the rest of the country and which was ultimately made official by Congress with passage of the Standard Time Act on 19 March 1918.

**1884 (25 November)**—Middle transcontinental route from Chicago to Pacific Northwest joined at Huntington, Oregon; through traffic commenced 1 December 1884.

**1887 (4 February)**—Interstate Commerce Act, creating Interstate Commerce Commission, signed by President Grover Cleveland.

**1887 (14 April)**—General Time Convention, a predecessor of Association of American Railroads, adopted first standard code of train rules.

**1887 (April)**—First train with solidly built vestibules connecting passenger cars placed in service, between New York and Chicago.

A Union Pacific 'camel' locomotive built by Rogers of Patterson, New Jersey in 1887. The 'camel' type was first built by Ross Winans in 1848. It was named for its having the cab between its two boilers.

**1887 (17–18 June)**—Successful test runs made by passenger train hauled by oil-burning locomotive, Altoona to Pittsburgh and return.

**1887 (December)**—Completion of direct rail route linked Seattle and Portland with San Francisco, Los Angeles and San Diego.

**1887**—Extensive air-brake tests conducted during 1886–87 on 50-car freight trains at Burlington, Iowa, led to adoption of automatic, quick-action, triple-valve brake for freight service.

**1887**—First passenger trains fully equipped with electric lights placed in service.

**1888**—Number of freight cars on US railroads reached one million for first time; rose to peak of 2.7 million with average capacity of 45.1 tons in 1926; by 1979, fleet stood at 1.7 million with an offsetting increase in average capacity to 78.8 tons.

**1893 (10 May)**—Locomotive *No 999* made world's first 100-mile-an-hour run.

**1895**—First electrification of sections of steam railroads in United States completed—in Massachusetts, New Jersey and Maryland.

**1898**—First railroad in Alaska opened from Skagway to White Pass City, British Columbia; line opened through to Whitehorse 15 August 1900.

**1900**—Total investment in railroad properties exceeded $10 billion for first time; figure stood at almost $39 billion by end of 1979.

**1901**—Mechanical coal stokers for locomotives introduced.

**1902**—Railroad route mileage in United States passed 200,000-mile mark and reached a peak of 254,037 by 1916; gradually reduced thereafter to about 185,000 by the end of 1979.

**1904**—All-steel passenger cars placed in service.

**1907**—Number of line-haul operating railroads reached peak of 1564; consolidations and mergers reduced number to 337 by the end of 1979.

**1914**—Tests begun looking to use radio in railroad communications.

**1917 (28 December)**—Federal government took control of railroads as wartime emergency measure; fiscal control became effective 1 January 1918; returned to owners by federal government 1 March 1920.

**1920 (26 August)**—Motion pictures shown on trains between Atlanta, Georgia, and Montgomery, Alabama, with musical accompaniment furnished by Edison phonograph; showings continued for several months.

**1925 (20 October)**—First diesel-electric locomotive (a switcher) installed in railroad service.

**1927 (25 July)**—System of centralized traffic control, installed on 40-mile route near Berwick, Ohio, was placed in operation; by 1980 'CTC' had been installed on over 53,000 miles of track.

**1928 (26 February)**—In formal opening, first train passed through the 6.2-mile Moffat Tunnel, west of Denver, then the longest in the US.

**1928 (7 December)**—Railway Express Agency (later REA Express) organized to handle nationwide express business.

**1919 (12 January)**—Cascade Tunnel, 7.79 miles in length, now longest in Western Hemisphere handling normal railroad operations, opened in Washington State.

**1929 (9 September)**—First air-conditioned Pullman car operated between Chicago and Los Angeles.

**1931 (24 May)**—World's first completely air-conditioned passenger train placed in service between Washington and New York.

**1932 (21 November)**—Recreation car, 'Miami Biltmore,' placed in service between New York and Miami, providing entertainment and recreation facilities supervised by hostess.

**1934 (26 May)**—First diesel-electric powered streamlined train ran non-stop 1,015 miles, Denver to Chicago, at average speed of 77.6 miles per hour, breaking existing speed and distance records; later became first streamlined passenger train placed in regular service (11 November 1934, between Lincoln, Nebraska, and Kansas City, Missouri).

**1934 (12 October)**—Association of American Railroads formed by consolidation of American Railway Association and other organizations, some of which dated to 1867.

**1937 (March)**—Two-way train telephone communications system inaugurated in mainline railroad operation, between Albion, Pennsylvania, and Pittsburgh.

**1937 (1 July)**—Federal Railroad Retirement Act went into effect for all railroad employees, replacing voluntary retirement and disability benefits on some 80 major railroads.

**1938 (1 March)**—Anti-telescoping tightlock couplers adopted as alternate standard for passenger-train cars; became standard in 1946 after years of service tests.

**1941**—First diesel-electric road freight locomotives placed in regular service.

**1944**—Passenger travel reached peak of 95.6 billion passenger-miles; under pressure of airline and automobile competition, rail travel declined to a low of 8.6 billion passenger-miles in 1972; energy crisis helped reverse trend to 10-year high of 11.3 billion passenger-miles in 1979.

**1945 (17 May)**—Federal Communications Commission allocated radio channels for exclusive railroad use; first construction permit granted by FCC on 27 February 1946.

**1945 (23 July)**—First modern domed observation car introduced, operating between Chicago and Minneapolis.

**1945 (2 September)**—V-J Day ended World War II; during 45 months of war, railroads moved 90 percent of all Army and Navy freight and more than 97 percent

A Baltimore & Ohio Railroad merchandise freight train thunders through the mountains of West Virginia. The B&O is an affiliate of the Chessie System, which in turn became part of CSX Corporation in 1980.

of all military personnel in organized groups within the United States; included operation of 113,891 special troop trains.

**1948** (**15 November**)—Track tests begun on first gas-turbine-electric locomotive to be built and operated in the United States; first unit went into regular pool service 1 January 1952.

**1949** —First long-distance railroad microwave communications system installed between Goodland and Norton, Kansas, 106 miles; by 1980, there were 19 railroads operating systems over 41,500 path miles.

**1952** (**May**)—Diesel ownership, as expressed in power units, exceeded ownership of steam locomotives for first time—19,082 diesel-electric units to 18,489 steam locomotives; by 1980, there were 28,483 diesel-electrics and only 12 steam locomotives.

**1955** (**November**)—First electronic computer installed in the railroad industry; by mid-1980, there were some 725 computers in use by 60 railroads and allied organizations throughout the nation, performing not only bookkeeping functions but also making possible automated classification in yards and car location systems as well as other advanced applications.

**1960** (**21 January**)—Unit train operations inaugurated in daily coal-mine-to-power-plant runs in Alabama.

**1962** (**26 October**)—Railroad train information first transmitted instantaneously from St Louis, Missouri, to Dallas, Texas, via Telstar.

**1965** (**30 September**)—President Johnson signed legislation authorizing joint railroad-government high-speed program in Northeast Corridor; high-speed Metroliner rail service inaugurated between Washington and New York and Turbo Train service between New York and Boston in 1969.

**1967** (**5 July**)—Railroads announced plans for TeleRail Automated Information Network (TRAIN), a nationwide computerized information system to keep track of the country's fleet of freight cars; became operational in 1970.

**1970** (**30 October**)—President Nixon signed bill creating National Railroad Passenger Corporation (AMTRAK), which took over most US intercity passenger trains beginning 1 May 1971.

**1973** (**30 May**)—TRAIN II, computerized expansion of TRAIN, approved by AAR Board of Directors; became fully operational in 1975, with capability not only of further improving car utilization but also of forecasting future demands to minimize car shortages.

**1976** (**5 February**)—Enactment of Railroad Revitalization and Regulatory Reform Act provided for government aid in restructuring Northeast railroads and for modernization of rail regulation.

**1976** (**1 April**)—Consolidated Rail Corporation (Conrail) began operations. Considered the largest corporate reorganization in history, Conrail took over the properties of six bankrupt railroads in the Northeast and Midwest as part of a restructuring mandated by Congress.

**1979** —ICC made first use of 4-R Act exemption provision to eliminate regulation over rail movements of most fresh fruits and vegetables. Rail market share —which had dropped from more than 40 percent to less than 10 percent in less than a decade—began to increase immediately.

**1980** (**14 October**)—Staggers Rail Act of 1980 signed by President Carter, substantially loosening economic regulations governing railroads.

**1980** —Freight traffic on Class I railroads in United States reached an all-time high of 918 billion revenue ton-miles.

**1982** —Railroad industry assumed management and financial responsibilities for the US Department of Transportation's Transportation Test Center in Pueblo, Colorado. Generally regarded as the most advanced rail research facility in the world, the Center began operations in 1971.

**1983** —For the second consecutive year, railroad piggyback volume sets a record. Revenue car loadings total 2,338,527, up 21.8 percent from 1982. A total of 4,078,454 loaded trailers and containers were moved in piggyback service, up 20.1 percent from the prior year.

**1984** —Railroad industry announced plans to develop a new type of freight train. This so-called High Productivity Integral Train could reduce operating costs as much as 50 percent on intermodal movements and as much as 35 percent on bulk movements.

# APPENDIX 2

# STATISTICAL TABLES FOR AMERICAN RAILROADS 1929–1984

Source: The American Association of Railroads

## Railroad Mileage

| Year | Miles of Class 1 Rail Line | Miles of Class 1 Track | Tons of New Rail Laid | Thousands of Cross Ties Laid |
|------|------|------|------|------|
| 1929 | 229,530 | 381,417 | 2,281,316 | 81,964 |
| 1939 | 220,915 | 364,174 | 991,896 | 46,410 |
| 1944 | 215,493 | 355,880 | 1,772,810 | 51,259 |
| 1947 | 214,486 | 355,227 | 1,639,746 | 40,206 |
| 1951 | 213,401 | 354,546 | 1,281,850 | 32,457 |
| 1955 | 211,459 | 350,217 | 963,350 | 27,173 |
| 1969 | 197,414 | 321,212 | 574,918 | 20,088 |
| 1970 | 196,479 | 319,092 | 548,505 | 19,611 |
| 1971 | 195,840 | 317,711 | 648,625 | 22,777 |
| 1972 | 194,421 | 315,211 | 648,625 | 22,251 |
| 1973 | 192,813 | 313,282 | 698,506 | 19,893 |
| 1974 | 192,991 | 313,006 | 708,362 | 21,175 |
| 1975 | 191,520 | 310,941 | 537,537 | 20,548 |
| 1976 | 185,395* | 304,100* | 802,441 | 27,002 |
| 1977 | 182,380* | 295,500* | 952,144 | 27,270 |
| 1978 | 175,912 | 283,573 | 838,714 | 27,228 |
| 1979 | 169,927 | 277,240 | 1,064,827 | 26,667 |
| 1980 | 164,822 | 270,623 | 881,783 | 25,984 |
| 1981 | 162,160 | 267,589 | 800,340 | 26,529 |
| 1982 | 159,123 | 263,330 | 502,718 | 20,726 |
| 1983 | 155,879 | 258,703 | 538,597 | 22,132 |
| 1984 | 151,998 | 255,748 | 642,998 | 23,581 |

*Partially estimated.

## Freight Cars in Service

| Year | Total | Class 1 Railroads | Other Railroads | Car Companies and Shippers |
|------|------|------|------|------|
| 1929 | 2,610,662 | 2,277,505 | 46,178 | 286,979 |
| 1939 | 1,961,705 | 1,650,031 | 30,488 | 281,186 |
| 1944 | 2,067,948 | 1,769,578 | 27,434 | 270,936 |
| 1947 | 2,025,008 | 1,734,239 | 25,519 | 265,250 |
| 1951 | 2,046,600 | 1,752,430 | 25,448 | 268,722 |
| 1955 | 1,996,443 | 1,698,814 | 24,933 | 272,696 |
| 1970 | 1,784,181 | 1,423,921 | 29,787 | 330,473 |
| 1971 | 1,762,135 | 1,422,411 | 27,291 | 312,433 |
| 1972 | 1,716,937 | 1,410,568 | 22,749 | 283,620 |
| 1973 | 1,710,659 | 1,395,105 | 23,114 | 292,440 |
| 1974 | 1,720,573 | 1,375,265 | 25,977 | 319,331 |
| 1975 | 1,723,605 | 1,359,459 | 29,407 | 334,739 |
| 1976 | 1,699,027 | 1,331,705 | 34,452 | 332,870 |
| 1977 | 1,666,533 | 1,287,315 | 40,378 | 338,840 |
| 1978 | 1,652,774 | 1,226,500 | 68,881 | 357,393 |
| 1979 | 1,700,310 | 1,217,079 | 91,427 | 391,804 |
| 1980 | 1,710,827 | 1,168,114 | 102,161 | 440,552 |
| 1981 | 1,672,565 | 1,111,115 | 101,091 | 460,359 |
| 1982 | 1,587,537 | 1,039,016 | 91,452 | 457,069 |
| 1983 | 1,542,278 | 1,007,165 | 91,395 | 443,718 |
| 1984 | 1,486,282 | 948,171 | 91,009 | 447,102 |

Source: Beginning in 1971, data for car companies and shippers from Transportation Division, AAR; earlier data from American Railway Car Institute and Official Railway Equipment Register.

## Passenger Cars in Service

| Year | Total | Pullman Company | National Rail Passenger Corporation (AMTRAK) |
|---|---|---|---|
| 1929 | 61,728 | 9,469 | — |
| 1939 | 45,479 | 7,052 | — |
| 1944 | 46,558 | 8,751 | — |
| 1947 | 44,841 | 6,071 | — |
| 1951 | 42,406 | 6,276 | — |
| 1955 | 36,871 | 4,776 | — |
| 1970 | 11,177 | — | — |
| 1971 | 8,713 | — | 1,165 |
| 1972 | 7,589 | — | 1,571 |
| 1973 | 7,189 | — | 1,777 |
| 1974 | 6,848 | — | 1,848 |
| 1975 | 6,741 | — | 1,913 |
| 1976 | 5,478 | — | 2,062 |
| 1977 | 5,512 | — | 2,154 |
| 1978 | 4,493 | — | 2,084 |
| 1979 | 4,241 | — | 2,026 |
| 1980 | 4,347 | — | 2,128 |
| 1981 | 3,945 | — | 1,830 |
| 1982 | 3,736 | — | 1,929 |
| 1983 | 2,610 | — | 1,880 |
| 1984 | 2,580 | — | 1,844 |

## Locomotives in Service on Class 1 Railroads

| Year | Total | Diesel Electric Units | Steam | Electric Units | Other |
|---|---|---|---|---|---|
| 1929 | 57,571 | 22 | 56,936 | 601 | 12 |
| 1939 | 45,511 | 510 | 41,117 | 843 | 41 |
| 1944 | 43,612 | 3,049 | 39,681 | 863 | 19 |
| 1947 | 41,719 | 5,772 | 35,108 | 821 | 18 |
| 1951 | 40,036 | 17,493 | 21,747 | 780 | 16 |
| 1955 | 31,429 | 24,786 | 5,982 | 627 | 34 |
| 1970 | 27,086 | 26,796 | 13 | 268 | 9 |
| 1971 | 27,189 | 26,897 | 13 | 250 | 29 |
| 1972 | 27,358 | 27,064 | 13 | 252 | 29 |
| 1973 | 27,790 | 27,540 | 12 | 238 | — |
| 1974 | 28,084 | 27,857 | 12 | 215 | — |
| 1975 | 28,210 | 27,985 | 12 | 213 | — |
| 1976 | 27,612 | 27,383 | 12 | 217 | — |
| 1977 | 27,667 | 27,450 | 12 | 205 | — |
| 1978 | 27,400 | 27,184 | 12 | 204 | — |
| 1979 | 28,097 | 27,922 | 12 | 163 | — |
| 1980 | 28,396 | 28,243 | 12 | 141 | — |
| 1981 | 27,808 | 27,732 | 2 | 74 | — |
| 1982 | 27,073 | 27,700 | 2 | 71 | — |
| 1983 | 25,838 | 25,775 | 2 | 61 | — |
| 1984 | 24,506 | 24,443 | 2 | 61 | — |

Note: Units not self-powered are omitted **after** 1972. (Formerly reported under 'Other.')

## Revenues and Expenses for Class 1 Railroads

| Year | Operating Revenues (in thousands) | Operating Expenses (in thousands) | Freight Revenues (in thousands) | Net Return on Investment (in thousands) |
|---|---|---|---|---|
| 1929 | $ 6,279,521 | $ 5,109,118 | $ 4,825,622 | $1,251,698 |
| 1939 | 3,995,004 | 3,511,310 | 3,251,096 | 588,829 |
| 1944 | 9,436,790 | 7,179,655 | 6,998,615 | 1,106,327 |
| 1947 | 8,684,918 | 7,725,423 | 7,041,185 | 780,694 |
| 1951 | 10,390,611 | 8,991,365 | 8,634,101 | 942,542 |
| 1955 | 10,106,330 | 8,621,255 | 8,538,286 | 1,127,997 |
| 1970 | 11,991,658 | 11,477,549 | 10,921,813 | 485,853 |
| 1971 | 12,689,017 | 11,947,362 | 11,786,064 | 595,171 |
| 1972 | 13,409,815 | 12,528,414 | 12,570,326 | 653,827 |
| 1973 | 14,770,082 | 13,844,765 | 13,770,734 | 649,828 |
| 1974 | 16,922,841 | 15,782,658 | 15,766,710 | 768,106 |
| 1975 | 16,401,860 | 15,935,542 | 15,389,809 | 350,682 |
| 1976 | 18,536,482 | 17,881,047 | 17,400,241 | 451,832 |
| 1977 | 20,090,482 | 19,533,970 | 18,892,437 | 343,093 |
| 1978 | 21,721,332 | 21,043,143 | 20,236,065 | 427,451 |
| 1979 | 25,219,115 | 23,994,154 | 23,447,418 | 837,232 |
| 1980 | 28,102,946 | 26,249,920 | 26,200,348 | 1,312,400 |
| 1981 | 30,898,610 | 28,586,890 | 28,925,436 | 1,360,611 |
| 1982 | 27,503,503 | 26,490,278 | 25,627,354 | 742,231 |
| 1983 | 26,729,392 | 24,106,254 | 25,835,519 | 1,837,854 |
| 1984 | 29,453,446 | 25,800,454 | 28,471,789 | 2,536,673 |

## Freight Service on Class 1 Railroads

| Year | Freight Train Miles (in thousands) | Freight Train Tonnage (in thousands) | Average Freight Train Load (in tons) | Average Freight Train Size (in number of cars) |
|---|---|---|---|---|
| 1929 | 613,444 | 1,339,091 | 804 | 47.6 |
| 1939 | 451,991 | 901,669 | 806 | 48.1 |
| 1944 | 698,761 | 1,491,491 | 1,124 | 52.3 |
| 1947 | 616,071 | 1,537,546 | 1,131 | 52.2 |
| 1951 | 528,573 | 1,477,402 | 1,283 | 59.0 |
| 1955 | 476,444 | 1,396,339 | 1,359 | 65.5 |
| 1970 | 427,065 | 1,484,919 | 1,820 | 70.0 |
| 1971 | 429,530 | 1,390,960 | 1,751 | 67.9 |
| 1972 | 451,032 | 1,447,864 | 1,774 | 67.1 |
| 1973 | 468,992 | 1,532,165 | 1,844 | 66.6 |
| 1974 | 469,268 | 1,530,686 | 1,875 | 65.5 |
| 1975 | 402,557 | 1,395,055 | 1,938 | 68.6 |
| 1976 | 424,571 | 1,406,732 | 1,954 | 67.1 |
| 1977 | 427,686 | 1,394,742 | 2,029 | 67.2 |
| 1978 | 432,944 | 1,390,175 | 2,029 | 67.2 |
| 1979 | 437,835 | 1,502,251 | 2,096 | 67.2 |
| 1980 | 428,488 | 1,492,414 | 2,175 | 68.3 |
| 1981 | 407,520 | 1,453,021 | 2,265 | 68.6 |
| 1982 | 344,936 | 1,268,645 | 2,345 | 69.4 |
| 1983 | 345,916 | 1,292,607 | 2,432 | 70.4 |
| 1984 | 369,403 | 1,429,388 | 2,543 | 71.5 |

The Denver & Rio Grande *Zephyr* eastbound between Thistle and Guilluly, Utah on a cold and snowy day in 1983. The Rio Grande was the last non-AMTRAK streamliner in service in the continental United States.

# INDEX

**Scenes from the golden age of North American rail history: California Governor Pardee and friends (*below*) on a Sierra fishing trip; and a recent photo (*overleaf*) of Southern Pacific's 1744 crossing Deer Creek Trestle in Utah.**